David Herbert has been obsessed with food since childhood. Growing up in a small seaside town, his spare time was spent fishing and thinking of new ways to cook his daily catch. David is the author of *The Perfect Cookbook*, *More Perfect Recipes*, *Picnics*, *Complete Perfect Recipes* and *The Really Useful Cookbook*. He writes for *The Weekend Australian Magazine*, is the food editor of *Easy Living* magazine in the UK, and is a regular contributor to numerous other magazines.

David is currently living and working in London, surrounded by his kitchen treasures, cookbooks and copper saucepans.

DAVID HERBERT'S

BEST-EVER

BAKING RECIPES

PHOTOGRAPHY BY NATO WELTON

LANTERN
an imprint of
PENGUIN BOOKS

FOR DIANA WILSON
IN CELEBRATION OF A LIFETIME OF
DRINKING TEA AND EATING CAKES TOGETHER

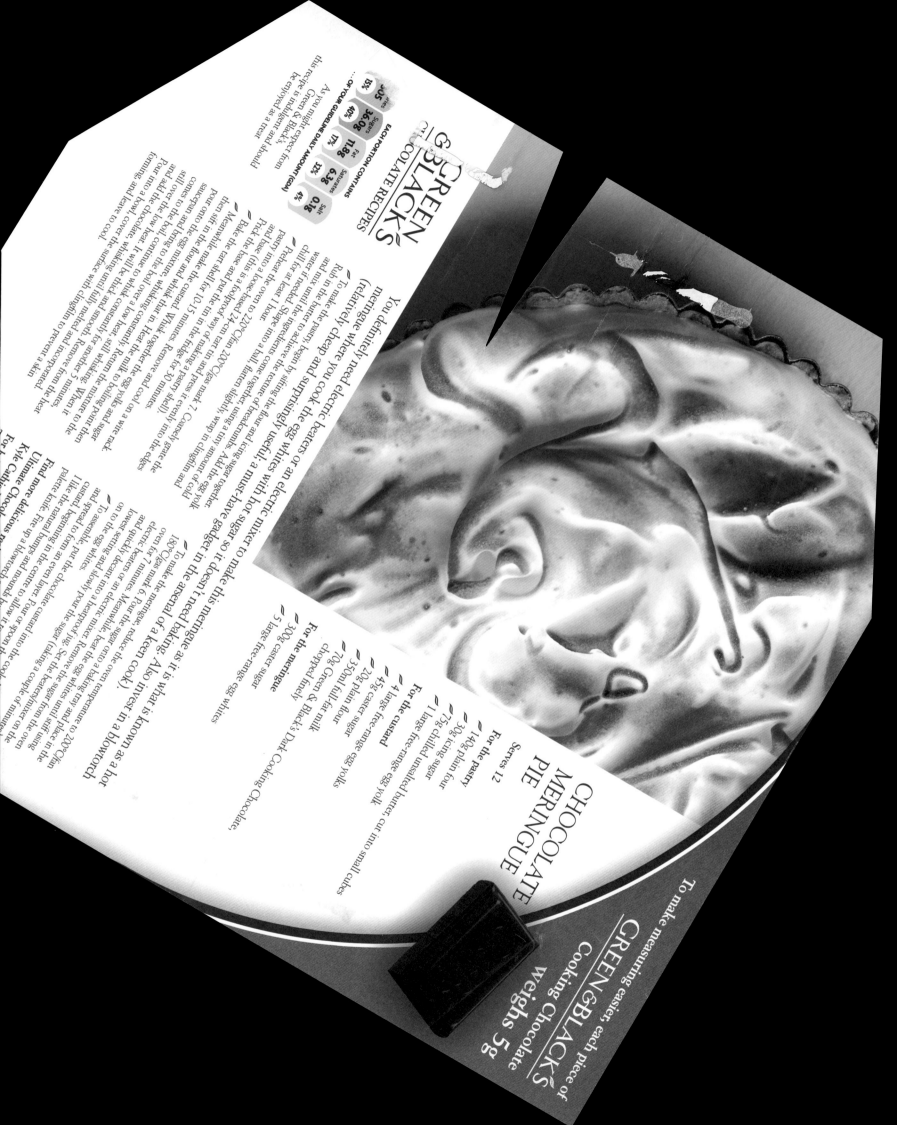

GREEN & BLACK'S
CHOCOLATE RECIPES

EACH PORTION CONTAINS

205 cals	Sugars 36.6g	Fat 32g	Saturates 6.5g	Salt 0.3g
5%	40%	17%	12%	4%

...% OF YOUR GUIDELINE DAILY AMOUNT

As you might expect from Green & Black's, this recipe is as indulgent as it should be – enjoyed as a treat.

CHOCOLATE MERINGUE PIE

Serves 12

For the pastry
30g icing sugar
140g plain four
1 large free-range egg yolk
75g chilled unsalted butter, cut into small cubes

For the custard
4 large free-range egg yolks
45g caster sugar
20g plain flour
350ml full-fat milk
70g Green & Black's Dark Cooking Chocolate, chopped finely

For the meringue
5 large free-range egg whites
300g caster sugar

You definitely need electric beaters or an electric mixer to make this meringue as it doesn't need the arsenal of a keen baking cook. Also invest in a blowtorch if you can (this is what is known as a hot meringue where you cook the egg whites with hot sugar so it doesn't need the arsenal of a keen baking cook).

To make the pastry, begin by sifting the flour and icing sugar together. Add the egg yolk and mix until the pastry begins to come together. Rub in the butter to achieve the texture of breadcrumbs, using a mixer or fingers. Add a mini amount of cold water if needed, then shape into a ball, flatten slightly, wrap in clingfilm and chill for at least 1 hour.

Preheat the oven to 200°C/fan 180°C/gas mark 7. Coarsely grate the pastry into the tin and press it evenly into the edges (this is a foolproof way to make the pastry case). Prick the base and put the tin in the fridge for 30 minutes.

Bake the tart shell for 10–15 minutes. Remove and cool on a wire rack.

Meanwhile make the custard. Whisk together the egg yolks, sugar and flour. Heat the milk to boiling point then pour onto the egg mixture, whisking all the while. Return the mixture to the pan and continue whisking over a low heat until it thickens and coats the back of a wooden spoon. Remove from the heat and add the chocolate. When it melts, incorporate and pour into a bowl, cover the surface with clingfilm to prevent a skin forming, and leave to cool.

Find more delicious recipes in:

Kyle Cathie's Ultimate Chocolate recipes

To make the meringue, put the sugar onto a baking tray and place it in an oven at 200°C/fan 180°C/gas mark 6. Meanwhile, put the egg whites into an electric mixer and beat until stiff. Remove the sugar from the oven and slowly add it to the egg whites while beating. Reduce the speed and beat for a further 5 minutes until the meringue is cool and glossy. Pour or spoon the meringue into the centre of the tart (taking care to form even layers and mounds) and use a palette knife to form a flowery peak. Finish by heating the natural-looking peaks and lower settings of the chocolate custard, and spread to form an even layer. Pour the custard into the pastry case and allow to set for a couple of minutes on the cool...

TASTING NOTES

Our Dark Cooking Chocolate is ideal for chocolate recipes because of its high content of cocoa solids - a combination of cocoa mass, which gives the chocolate its intense flavour, and cocoa butter, which gives it a smooth consistency for easier melting.

ORGANIC DARK COOKING CHOCOLATE

Ingredients: Cocoa mass #, raw cane sugar #, cocoa butter #, emulsifier (soya lecithin), vanilla extract #.

ORGANIC DARK CHOCOLATE: MINIMUM COCOA SOLIDS 70%
Cocoa, Sugar, Vanilla: traded in compliance with Fairtrade Standards, total 99%. Visit www.info.fairtrade.net

May contain nuts, milk. # = Certified Organic

5 011382 2390

Nutrition Information	Per 100g
Energy	2405 kJ
	580 kcal
Fat	25.0g
of which Saturates	36.5g
Carbohydrate	28.5g
of which Sugars	10.0g
Fibre	9.1g
Protein	0.13g
Salt	

Green & Black's, 3 Sanderson Road, Uxbridge, UB8 1DH, UK. www.greenandblacks.co.uk
Please address any UK consumer comments and enquiries to: FREEPOST, GREEN & BLACK'S CUSTOMER CARE' or call us on 0800 840 1000.
Soil Association Symbol Holder P1117.
Organic Certification PL-EKO-07
This product meets the Soil Associations standards for organic food and farming.

Best Before
20 05 2019
0WR0374653 22

STORE IN A COOL, DRY PLACE.

recycle

e150g

PL-EKO-07
Non-EU
Agriculture

SCAN FOR RECIPE IDEAS

SOIL ASSOCIATION ORGANIC

...ic Trinitario cocoa beans
...ced cooking chocolate
Cocoa
...e 5g pie...
Ch...te

Buy online at greenandblacksdirect.com

...ram, visit our website www.greenandblacks.co.uk

...Ltd; photography by Jenny Zarins. RRP £16.99.

...ecipes in the Green & Black's

...Recipes cookbook, published by

...and colour the meringue all over.

...it can be smoothed with a

...slightly flow to the edges.

...the meringue over the

...pastry case

CONTENTS

INTRODUCTION

Who doesn't love someone who bakes a cake? I'm the most popular guy in the office when I take in homemade cake or biscuits, or muffins left over from a photo shoot. There is no better feeling than sharing something you've made yourself and seeing the pleasure it gives.

I am the son of a woman who has won prizes for her sponge cakes, so you could say baking is in my blood. For me, it is something that comes from the heart; it connects you with family and friends, as well as traditions – whether handed down, learned or new. As a child, I spent a lot of time watching my mother, two grandmothers and an uncle in their kitchens. I'm sure these experiences have rubbed off as I have always approached baking with the knowledge of how to line a cake tin, whisk egg whites, and cream butter and sugar.

I decided to write a book on baking to communicate some of that knowledge, and to share my favourite recipes and tips acquired over many years. But I wanted it to be more than simply a compilation of recipes; it is also a collection of experiences – both mine and the many friends I have in this great world of cooking and recipe writing.

Over the years I have learnt to worry less and to bake more. Funnily enough, my favourite recipes are the simplest: the carrot cake, lemon cake, all-in-one coffee and walnut cake and cheese scones are the ones I make the most, and more than once I've taken a ginger cake to a job interview (with success). But as you browse through the chapters, I hope you will agree that there is something here for everyone.

The aim of this book was to produce an easy-to-use collection of delicious recipes to both inspire novices and challenge seasoned bakers. I have included as many tips as possible and also offer helpful ideas learned while writing and testing the recipes. All of the recipes have been tested at least twice.

Baking combines many pleasures: creative pride in the making, social satisfaction in the sharing and sensual delight in the eating. I hope you have a wonderful time with this book.

only a little flour. It is very sweet and light, and goes well with a cup of black coffee.

170g unblanched almonds
4 large eggs, separated
200g caster sugar
grated zest of 1 orange
3 drops of vanilla extract
250g carrots, finely grated
1 heaped tbsp self-raising flour
60g ground almonds
icing sugar, for dusting

1 Heat the oven to 180°C (160°C fan oven) gas mark 4. Line the base and sides of a deep 20cm cake tin with baking parchment.

2 Grind the unblanched almonds in a food processor, but leave them fairly chunky as this will give a nice texture to the cake. Put the egg yolks, sugar, orange zest and vanilla extract in a bowl and beat with an electric whisk for about 5 minutes

mixture into the prepared tin and bake for 40-45 minutes. Leave to cool in the tin, then turn out and dust with icing sugar.

RED FLORENCE ONION TATIN

Preparation 35 minutes, plus chilling Cooking 1 hour 5 minutes Serves 4

With their pink-crimson colour and pleasing shape, Red Florence onions are outstandingly beautiful.

8 Red Florence onions (or ordinary red onions)
75g butter
3 sprigs of thyme
2 dessertspoons raspberry vinegar
FOR THE CHEESE PASTRY
170g plain flour
a pinch of cayenne pepper
115g chilled butter, diced
115g cheese (half Cheddar, half Parmesan), grated
1 egg yolk
1 tbsp cold water

fingertips until the mixture resembles breadcrumbs. Stir in the grated cheese with a knife.

2 Mix the egg yolk and water together and add them to the dry ingredients, working with the knife to form a dough. Knead briefly until smooth, then wrap in clingfilm and chill for at least half an hour.

3 Peel the onions, cut in half or into quarters, depending on size, then trim the root so that the pieces remain intact. Melt the butter over a moderate heat in a 24cm Tatin tin (a 24cm oven-proof frying pan will do, provided it is at least 4cm deep). Arrange the onions cut-side down in the tin, packing them in tightly. Fry over a low heat so they soften rather than colour at first, then increase the heat a little until the onions are browned underneath – about 20 minutes.

the heat to build and the onions to cook thoroughly. Cook for about 20 minutes, until the onions are golden and caramelised, then remove the lid or foil and allow to cool a little.

5 Heat the oven to 190°C (170°C fan oven) gas mark 5. On a lightly floured worksurface, roll out the pastry to a circle about 8cm bigger than the diameter of your tin or frying pan. Cover the onions with the pastry, tucking it down the side of the tin. Bake for about 25 minutes, until the pastry is golden brown.

6 Remove from the oven and leave to settle for about 5 minutes. Run a knife around the edge of the Tatin to loosen it, then place a serving plate on top and turn them both over to turn out the Tatin. Serve hot or cold, with salad.

shop.countryliving.co.uk

BUTTER CAKES AND SPONGES

TIPS

1 First off, a word about the equipment you use. It's not easy to make a good cake without scales – I find that using cup measures is not as accurate as weighing the ingredients. Kitchen scales don't have to cost the earth and you will use them time and time again. Unless stated otherwise, spoon measurements should be level.

2 Use the correct tin size, otherwise you won't get the best results. For example, if you're making a Victoria sponge or an all-in-one layer cake and you bake it in a larger tin than specified, it will cook more quickly and won't rise as well. The resulting cake will be thinner and not as spongy. Only ever fill the tin two-thirds full.

3 The majority of cakes in this chapter are made by first beating together the butter and sugar (often called creaming) and then incorporating the eggs, flour and other ingredients. The butter should be nice and soft (take it out of the fridge at least 2 hours beforehand) and make sure you beat until the mixture is light and fluffy – this usually takes a good 5-7 minutes.

4 The expression 'folding in' has been known to cause confusion. What you are trying to do is fold in the ingredients (usually flour and other dry ingredients) without beating out any of the air, and for this you will need a large metal spoon. Think of it as cutting a figure of eight through the mixture in the bowl. Go halfway around the inside of the bowl, pulling the mixture down towards the middle and then cut through the middle. Then do the same around the other side of the bowl. Take your time and continue until everything is incorporated.

5 Before you put the batter in the oven, check the temperature by using an oven thermometer. If you put the batter in before the oven is correctly heated, the cake will not rise properly.

6 Don't open the oven door until at least three-quarters of the cooking time has passed. Too much sudden movement or cold air coming in can cause the cake to sink.

7 When ready, the cake will be golden and risen and should feel firm when lightly pressed in the middle. A skewer inserted in the centre of the cake should come out clean. I recommend testing it before the end of the stated cooking time as temperatures can vary so much between ovens. Test it again before removing it from the oven.

8 Once cool, most simple cakes should be stored in an airtight container or wrapped in plastic film. Generally, plain cakes will keep for about 5-7 days. Un-iced cakes can be frozen for up to 2 months. Thaw them at room temperature before icing and eating.

BASIC POUND CAKE

PREPARATION TIME: 20 MINUTES

COOKING TIME: 1 HOUR

SERVES 8

250 g unsalted butter, diced and softened at room temperature

250 g caster sugar

1 teaspoon vanilla extract

4 free-range eggs, lightly beaten

250 g plain flour, sifted

pinch of salt

3 tablespoons milk

A traditional pound cake (or butter cake) recipe uses equal weights of the four basic ingredients: butter, sugar, eggs and flour. Following the imperial system, one pound of each ingredient was used. The result of this simple equation is a lovely cake with a good even texture and a moist yellow crumb. It is delicious as is, or top with a simple buttercream icing (see page 313).

1 Preheat the oven to 180°C (Gas Mark 4). Grease a 20 cm round cake tin and line the base with baking paper.

2 Place the butter, sugar and vanilla in an electric mixer and mix on medium speed for 7-8 minutes or until pale and fluffy. Transfer the beaten egg to a jug. Reduce the speed of the mixer and, with the motor running, add the egg to the mixture, followed by an occasional spoonful of flour.

3 Add the remaining flour and salt and fold in by running a large metal spoon around the side and base of the bowl and then gently folding the mixture over onto itself. Rotate the bowl and repeat until combined, being careful not to knock out the air. Fold in the milk.

4 Spoon the batter into the tin and bake for 50-60 minutes or until firm to the touch. A skewer inserted in the centre should come out clean. Cool in the tin for about 10 minutes, then turn out onto a wire rack to cool completely. The cake will keep in an airtight container for up to 5 days.

QUICK VARIATIONS

To make a lemon or orange pound cake, add the finely grated zest of 1 lemon or 1 small orange when beating the butter and sugar.

To make a simple sponge, divide the mixture between two 18 cm sandwich tins and bake for about 25 minutes. When cool, sandwich the cakes together with lemon curd or strawberry jam and whipped cream and dust with icing sugar.

ORANGE AND CHOCOLATE CHIP POUND CAKE

PREPARATION TIME: 20 MINUTES

COOKING TIME: 1 HOUR

SERVES 8

250 g unsalted butter, diced and softened at room temperature

250 g caster sugar

finely grated zest of 1 orange

4 free-range eggs, lightly beaten

250 g plain flour, sifted

pinch of salt

3 tablespoons milk

125 g dark chocolate chips

A pound cake is infinitely variable. Here, I have added orange zest and chocolate chips to make a 'jaffa' cake. Although delicious served plain, this cake takes on another dimension when topped with a chocolate butter cream or dark chocolate ganache icing (see page 316).

1 Preheat the oven to 180°C (Gas Mark 4). Grease a 20 cm round cake tin and line the base with baking paper.

2 Place the butter, sugar and orange zest in an electric mixer and mix on medium speed for 7-8 minutes or until pale and fluffy. Transfer the beaten egg to a jug. Reduce the speed of the mixer and, with the motor running, add the egg to the mixture, followed by an occasional spoonful of flour.

3 Fold in the remaining flour and salt by running a large metal spoon around the side and base of the bowl and then gently folding the mixture over onto itself. Rotate the bowl and repeat until combined, being careful not to knock out the air. Fold in the milk and chocolate chips.

4 Spoon the batter into the tin and bake for 50-60 minutes or until firm to the touch. A skewer inserted in the centre should come out clean. Cool in the tin for about 10 minutes, then turn out onto a wire rack to cool completely. The cake will keep in an airtight container for up to 5 days.

CAPPUCCINO CAKE

PREPARATION TIME: 30 MINUTES

COOKING TIME: 40 MINUTES

SERVES 8

1 teaspoon instant coffee powder

2 tablespoons boiling water

3 free-range egg yolks, lightly beaten

125 ml double cream

1 teaspoon vanilla extract

225 g unsalted butter, softened
at room temperature

215 g plain flour

185 g caster sugar

1½ teaspoons baking powder

pinch of salt

drinking chocolate, for dusting

COFFEE ICING

100 g unsalted butter, softened
at room temperature

200 g icing sugar, sifted

2 teaspoons instant coffee powder

1 tablespoon boiling water

Coffee and chocolate are classic playmates, with each enhancing the other. The flavour and look of this cake is inspired by my morning cappuccino. If you have strong espresso coffee, use 2-3 tablespoons of this in the cake batter and the icing instead of the coffee powder and boiling water. Dust the top of the cake with a little drinking chocolate as a final flourish.

1 Preheat the oven to 180°C (Gas Mark 4). Grease a deep 20 cm round cake tin and line the base with baking paper.

2 Dissolve the coffee in the hot water in a medium jug. Add the egg yolks, cream and vanilla and whisk until combined.

3 Using hand-held electric beaters (or an electric mixer), beat the butter with half the coffee mixture until combined and fluffy. Gradually beat in the remaining coffee mixture. Sift the flour, sugar, baking powder and salt into the mixture and fold in with a large metal spoon.

4 Spoon the batter into the tin and bake for 35-40 minutes or until firm to the touch. A skewer inserted in the centre should come out clean. Cool in the tin for 10 minutes, then turn out onto a wire rack to cool completely.

5 To make the coffee icing, place the butter in an electric mixer and beat until soft and pale. Add the icing sugar and beat until smooth and creamy. Dissolve the coffee powder in the boiling water then mix it into the butter cream. When cool, spread over the top of the cake. Dust with a little drinking chocolate and serve. The cake will keep in an airtight container for up to 5 days.

RIVER COTTAGE GLUTEN-FREE
LEMON DRIZZLE CAKE

PREPARATION TIME: 20 MINUTES

COOKING TIME: 40 MINUTES

SERVES 10

185 g unsalted butter, diced and softened at room temperature

200 g caster sugar

4 free-range eggs

200 g ground almonds

2 teaspoons baking powder

pinch of salt

250 g plain, cold mashed potato

finely grated zest of 3 lemons

LEMON TOPPING

juice of 2 lemons

75 g caster sugar

ICING

300 g icing sugar

4 tablespoons lemon juice

The idea for this cake came from the River Cottage, food writer Hugh Fearnley-Whittingstall's well-known restaurant and cooking school in the UK. Believe it or not, it is made with cold mashed potato. For best results, mash or rice about 330 grams of cold whole potatoes – you can make it with leftover mash, but make sure it doesn't contain too much butter, milk or cream, or any seasonings such as salt, pepper or mustard.

1 Preheat the oven to 180°C (Gas Mark 4). Grease a 23 cm springform tin and line the base with baking paper.

2 Place the butter and sugar in an electric mixer and mix on medium speed for 5-6 minutes or until pale and fluffy. Beat in the eggs, one at a time, adding a spoonful of ground almonds with each addition to stop the mixture curdling. Stir the baking powder and salt into the remaining almonds, then fold them into the mixture, followed by the mashed potato and lemon zest.

3 Spoon the batter into the tin and bake for 30-40 minutes or until firm to the touch and a skewer inserted in the centre comes out with just a few moist crumbs clinging to it. Check the cake after 25 minutes to make sure it is not colouring too much, and cover with a sheet of foil if it is.

4 While the cake is still hot in its tin, pierce it all over with a skewer, going quite deep but not right through to the base. To make the topping, combine the lemon juice and sugar. Before the sugar has a chance to dissolve, pour the mixture slowly and evenly all over the cake. Leave to cool completely before icing.

5 To make the icing, sift the icing sugar into a bowl and mix in enough lemon juice to give a thick, spreadable consistency. Spread over the cooled cake, allowing some of the icing to run down the sides. The cake will keep in an airtight container for up to 5 days.

GENOISE SPONGE

PREPARATION TIME: 20 MINUTES

COOKING TIME: 30 MINUTES

SERVES 8

6 free-range eggs

165 g caster sugar

1 teaspoon vanilla extract

150 g plain flour, sifted

75 g self-raising flour, sifted

pinch of salt

75 g unsalted butter, melted and cooled

200 g strawberry, raspberry or blackberry jam

icing sugar, for dusting

A genoise sponge is lighter in texture than a pound cake or Victoria sponge. The air is incorporated into the mixture by beating the eggs and sugar until thick. Although often made without any butter or fat, I have added a little as it helps the cake to keep a little longer. It is important to fold in the flour and butter very gently – if you are too vigorous at this stage, you will lose a lot of volume in the egg mixture. Jam is the traditional filling but lemon curd makes a delicious alternative.

1 Preheat the oven to 180°C (Gas Mark 4). Grease two 22 cm round, shallow cake tins and line the bases with baking paper.

2 Combine the eggs, sugar and vanilla in a large heatproof bowl. Place the bowl over a saucepan of gently simmering water, making sure the base of the bowl doesn't touch the water. Beat with hand-held electric beaters for 6-7 minutes, or until pale, thick and doubled in bulk. Remove from the heat and continue to beat for 3 minutes. It will be quite thick by this stage.

3 Using a large metal spoon, gently fold in the sifted flours and salt, followed by the cooled melted butter. Fold until just combined and there is no trace of white flour.

4 Divide the batter evenly between the tins and bake for 25-30 minutes or until golden and firm to the touch. Cool in the tin for 5 minutes, then turn out onto a wire rack to cool completely.

5 Spread the jam evenly over one of the cakes. Top with the remaining cake and dust with icing sugar. The cake will keep in an airtight container for up to 2 days.

ALL-IN-ONE BUTTER CAKE

PREPARATION TIME: 10 MINUTES

COOKING TIME: 50 MINUTES

SERVES 8

185 g unsalted butter, diced and softened at room temperature

185 g caster sugar

3 free-range eggs, lightly beaten

1 teaspoon vanilla extract

185 g self-raising flour, sifted

pinch of salt

1 tablespoon ground almonds (optional)

The 'all-in-one' butter cake is one of the simplest cakes I know – everything goes in the bowl and then all you need to do is to mix it all together. The important thing is that the butter should be softened at room temperature before you start so it will be easier to incorporate. The ground almonds are optional but they do add moisture and texture to the cake. To make a simple lemon or orange version, add the finely grated zest of an orange or lemon to the mixture. Serve with a simple dusting of icing sugar or top with vanilla or lemon buttercream icing (see page 313).

1 Preheat the oven to 180°C (Gas Mark 4). Grease an 18 cm round cake tin and line the base with baking paper.

2 Put all the ingredients in a large bowl and beat with a wooden spoon or hand-held electric beaters until just combined. It's important not to beat the batter too much – just long enough to make it smooth.

3 Spoon the batter into the tin, smooth the top and bake for 45-50 minutes or until risen and golden. A skewer inserted in the centre should come out clean. Cool in the tin for 5 minutes, then turn out onto a wire rack to cool completely. The cake will keep in an airtight container for up to 5 days.

ALL-IN-ONE COFFEE AND WALNUT CAKE

PREPARATION TIME: 25 MINUTES

COOKING TIME: 25 MINUTES

SERVES 8

220 g unsalted butter, diced and softened at room temperature

220 g caster sugar

4 free-range eggs, lightly beaten

220 g self-raising flour, sifted

1 teaspoon baking powder

pinch of salt

1½ tablespoons instant coffee powder dissolved in 1 tablespoon boiling water

75 g walnuts, roughly chopped

COFFEE FROSTING

200 g unsalted butter, softened at room temperature

500 g icing sugar, sifted

1 tablespoon boiling water

2 teaspoons instant coffee powder

walnut halves, to decorate (optional)

As a child, I was allowed to have a slice of this wonderful cake once the adults had finished their portions (and only if I sat quietly). Years later, I found the recipe in my grandmother's tatty old handwritten cookbook. Her version used coffee or chicory essence, but I've found that instant coffee powder is the perfect substitute. My grandmother often decorated the top with walnut halves, but this is entirely optional.

1 Preheat the oven to 180°C (Gas Mark 4). Grease two 21 cm sandwich tins and line the bases with baking paper.

2 Put all the cake ingredients in a large bowl and beat with a wooden spoon or hand-held electric beaters until just combined. It's important not to beat the batter too much - just long enough to make it smooth.

3 Spoon the batter into the tins, smooth the top and bake for 20-25 minutes or until risen and golden. A skewer inserted in the centre should come out clean. Cool in the tins for 5 minutes, then turn out onto a large wire rack to cool completely.

4 To make the frosting, beat the butter with hand-held electric beaters until soft and pale. Add the icing sugar and beat until smooth and creamy. Stir the boiling water into the coffee powder, then mix it into the butter cream.

5 Place one of the cooled cakes upside-down on a plate and spread with about one third of the butter cream. Sandwich with the second cake and spread the remaining butter cream over the top. Decorate with walnut halves, if desired. The cake will keep in an airtight container for up to 5 days.

MARBLED RING CAKE

PREPARATION TIME: 20 MINUTES

COOKING TIME: 45 MINUTES

SERVES 8

2 tablespoons instant coffee powder

1 tablespoon boiling water

½ teaspoon vanilla extract

185 g unsalted butter, diced and softened at room temperature

185 g caster sugar

3 free-range eggs, lightly beaten

185 g self-raising flour, sifted

1 teaspoon baking powder

pinch of salt

finely grated zest of 1 small orange

2 tablespoons orange juice

melted dark or white chocolate (see page 91), for drizzling (optional)

I love the element of surprise in a marble cake. In this simple-to-make recipe, I've combined orange and coffee, but you can play around with other flavours and colours. This cake can also be made in deep loaf tin with a base measurement of 20 cm × 8.5 cm. Just increase the cooking time to 55-60 minutes.

1 Heat the oven to 180°C (Gas Mark 4). Grease a 22 cm ring tin.

2 Dissolve the instant coffee in the boiling water, then add the vanilla extract and transfer to a large bowl.

3 Place the butter, sugar, beaten egg, flour, baking powder and salt in a large bowl and beat with a wooden spoon or hand-held electric beaters until just combined. It's important not to beat the batter too much – just long enough to make it smooth.

4 Transfer half the batter to a separate bowl and carefully stir in the coffee and vanilla mixture. Add the orange zest and juice to the other bowl and stir through.

5 Spoon alternate heaped tablespoons of the two batters into the tin. Tap the tin on the bench to knock out any air bubbles and then gently swirl the batter with a skewer. Bake for 40-45 minutes or until risen and golden; the top should spring back when lightly touched with a fingertip. Cool in the tin for 5 minutes, then gently run a knife around the edge and turn the cake out onto a wire rack to cool completely.

6 Drizzle with melted chocolate (if using). The cake will keep in an airtight container for up to 5 days.

VICTORIA SPONGE (CLASSIC BUTTER SPONGE)

PREPARATION TIME: 25 MINUTES

COOKING TIME: 25 MINUTES

SERVES 8

175 g self-raising flour

pinch of salt

175 g unsalted butter, diced and softened at room temperature

175 g caster sugar

3 large free-range eggs, at room temperature

½ teaspoon vanilla extract

3–4 tablespoons fruit jam (such as raspberry, apricot or plum)

icing or caster sugar, for dusting

A Victoria sponge was the first cake I ever made – a lovely, easy-to-make cake that's perfect in its glorious simplicity, but can also be dressed up to suit any occasion. For that first-ever attempt I followed the recipe in Katie Stewart's *The Times Cookery Book*, a recipe I still use to this day.

1 Preheat the oven to 180°C (Gas Mark 4). Grease two 19 cm sandwich cake tins (4 cm deep) and line the bases with baking paper.

2 Sift the flour and salt onto a plate.

3 Place the butter and sugar in a bowl and mix with hand-held electric beaters for 5–7 minutes or until pale and fluffy. Whisk the eggs and vanilla with a fork, then gradually beat into the creamed butter (in about five batches). Beat well after each addition. Add a little of the sifted flour with the last of the egg if the mixture looks as if it might separate.

4 When all the egg has been beaten in, lightly fold in the remaining flour with a large metal spoon until combined. The mixture should drop from the spoon if given a slight shake.

5 Divide the batter evenly between the tins and smooth the surface, then bake in the centre of the oven for 20–25 minutes. Touch the centre of each cake with your fingertips – if they feel springy and no imprint remains, they're done. Cool in the tins for 5 minutes, then turn out onto a large wire rack to cool completely.

6 When cool, sandwich the layers together with the jam and dust the top of the cake with sugar. The cake will keep in an airtight container for up to 5 days.

LIME AND PASSIONFRUIT SPONGE

PREPARATION TIME: 20 MINUTES

COOKING TIME: 1 HOUR

SERVES 8

185 g self-raising flour

pinch of salt

185 g unsalted butter, diced and
softened at room temperature

185 g caster sugar

finely grated zest of 2 limes

3 free-range eggs, beaten

juice of 1 lime

icing sugar, for dusting

PASSIONFRUIT FILLING

250 g mascarpone

4 tablespoons icing sugar, sifted

2-3 ripe passionfruit

**One of the pitfalls of cooking with passionfruit is that
you can end up with too many seeds. To avoid this
I usually strain the seeds from the pulp, then only
return about one third of the seeds to the mixture.**

1 Preheat the oven to 170ºC (Gas Mark 3). Grease a 20 cm
× 8.5 cm loaf tin and line the base with baking paper.

2 Sift the flour and salt into a large bowl. Add the butter,
sugar, lime zest, beaten egg and lime juice. Beat with
a wooden spoon or hand-held electric beaters on low
speed for 2 minutes or until combined.

3 Spoon the batter into the tin and bake for 50-60 minutes
or until firm to the touch. A skewer inserted in the centre
should come out clean. Cool in the tin for 10 minutes, then
turn out onto a wire rack to cool completely.

4 To make the filling, combine the mascarpone, icing sugar
and some of the passionfruit pulp in a small bowl. Continue
adding the passionfruit pulp, stirring constantly, until the
mixture reaches a spreadable consistency.

5 Cut the cake in half horizontally and sandwich together
with the passionfruit filling. Dust with icing sugar and serve.
The cake will keep in an airtight container for up to 3 days.
Store in the fridge during the warmer months.

LEMON AND COCONUT SPONGE

PREPARATION TIME: 25 MINUTES

COOKING TIME: 25 MINUTES

SERVES 8

150 g plain flour

2 teaspoons baking powder

pinch of salt

175 g unsalted butter, diced and softened at room temperature

175 g caster sugar

finely grated zest of 1 lemon

3 large free-range eggs, lightly beaten

50 g desiccated coconut

2 tablespoons lemon juice

LEMON ICING

250 g icing sugar, sifted

30 g unsalted butter, softened at room temperature

finely grated zest of 1 lemon

2-3 tablespoons lemon juice

I have fond childhood memories of helping my mum make this cake and being allowed to lick the bowl – the taste of the coconut batter still transports me back to sixth grade. The cake can also be made using the all-in-one method; simply place all the ingredients into a large bowl and beat until just combined.

1 Preheat the oven to 180°C (Gas Mark 4). Grease two 19 cm sandwich cake tins (4 cm deep) and line the bases with baking paper.

2 Sift the flour, baking powder and salt onto a plate.

3 Place the butter, sugar and lemon zest in a bowl and mix with hand-held electric beaters for 5-7 minutes or until pale and fluffy. Whisk the eggs with a fork, then gradually beat into the creamed butter (in about five batches). Beat well after each addition. Add a little of the sifted flour with the last of the egg if the mixture looks as if it might separate.

4 When all the egg has been beaten in, lightly fold in the remaining flour and baking powder with a large metal spoon until combined. Fold in the coconut and lemon juice.

5 Spoon the batter evenly into the tins and spread level, then bake in the centre of the oven for 20-25 minutes. Touch the centre of each cake with your fingertips – if they feel springy and no imprint remains, they are done. Cool in the tins for 5 minutes, then turn out onto a large wire rack to cool completely.

6 To make the icing, place the icing sugar, butter, lemon zest and 2 tablespoons of lemon juice in a bowl and whisk until smooth. Add a little more juice if needed to make it spreadable.

7 Sandwich the cakes together with half the icing and spread the rest over the top. The cake will keep in an airtight container for up to 3 days.

LEMON CURD AND RASPBERRY SWISS ROLL

**PREPARATION TIME: 30 MINUTES,
PLUS REFRIGERATION TIME**

COOKING TIME: 12 MINUTES

SERVES 8

4 large free-range eggs

125 g caster sugar, plus extra for dusting

125 g self-raising flour

finely grated zest of ½ lemon

icing sugar, for dusting

LEMON CURD AND RASPBERRY FILLING

200 ml double cream

120 ml lemon curd

finely grated zest of ½ lemon

200 g raspberries, fresh or frozen

The trick to making a swiss roll is to roll it up in sugared baking paper while it is still warm, then let it cool while rolled up. Don't worry about any cracks in the cake – they are hard to avoid and perfection is not what we are aiming for here. A good dusting of icing sugar should cover any imperfections.

1 Preheat the oven to 190°C (Gas Mark 5). Grease and line a swiss roll tin, leaving the edges of the baking paper sticking up around the sides.

2 Place the eggs and sugar in a large bowl and whisk for 6–8 minutes or until the mixture is pale, creamy and tripled in volume. Sift the flour over the top in batches, carefully folding it in with a large metal spoon after each addition. Gently fold in the lemon zest. Pour the mixture into the tin, spread it evenly into the corners and smooth the surface. Bake for 10–12 minutes or until the cake is golden and feels slightly springy when pressed.

3 Cut a piece of baking paper slightly larger than the size of the tin and lay it flat on the work surface. Dust with caster sugar. Remove the tin from the oven and gently pull the paper to loosen the sponge from the sides. Invert the sponge onto the sugared paper and peel away the paper.

4 Roll up the cake and the paper from the narrow end to form a neat log, then leave the sponge to cool, rolled inside the paper.

5 While the cake is cooling, make the filling. Whip the cream until it forms soft peaks, then fold through the lemon curd and zest.

6 Carefully unroll the sponge and spread with the lemon curd mixture, leaving a 2 cm border all the way around the edges. Sprinkle the raspberries on top, then reroll the cake to form a neat log. Place seam-side down on a plate and chill for 30 minutes. Dust with a little icing sugar before serving. The cake will keep in the fridge for 3 days.

STRAWBERRY SWISS ROLL

**PREPARATION TIME: 30 MINUTES,
PLUS REFRIGERATION TIME**

COOKING TIME: 12 MINUTES

SERVES 8

4 large free-range eggs

125 g caster sugar, plus extra for dusting

1 teaspoon finely grated orange zest

125 g self-raising flour

icing sugar, for dusting

STRAWBERRY FILLING

250 g strawberries,
hulled and quartered

3 tablespoons caster sugar

150 ml double cream

2½ tablespoons crème fraîche or
mascarpone

3 tablespoons strawberry jam

2 tablespoons toasted flaked almonds

You can swap the strawberries for other soft fruit, such as raspberries or blackberries – just make the most of whatever is at its seasonal best. I love the flavour of jam in the centre, but it's not essential. Leave it out if you prefer, or replace it with something like lemon curd. Most swiss rolls will have a few cracks or splits, so don't worry about them – a sprinkling of flaked almonds and a dusting of icing sugar should cover up any problem areas.

1 Preheat the oven to 190°C (Gas Mark 5). Grease and line a swiss roll tin, leaving the edges of the baking paper sticking up around the sides.

2 Place the eggs, sugar and orange zest in a large bowl and whisk for 6–8 minutes or until the mixture is pale, creamy and tripled in volume. Sift the flour over the top in batches, carefully folding it in with a large metal spoon after each addition. Pour the mixture into the tin, spread it evenly into the corners and smooth the surface. Bake for 10–12 minutes or until the cake is golden and feels slightly springy when pressed.

3 Cut a piece of baking paper slightly larger than the size of the tin and lay it flat on the work surface. Dust with caster sugar. Remove the tin from the oven and gently pull the paper to loosen the sponge from the sides. Invert the sponge onto the sugared paper and peel away the lining.

4 Roll up the cake and the paper from the narrow end to form a neat log, then leave the sponge to cool, rolled inside the paper.

5 While the cake is cooling, make the filling. Place two-thirds of the strawberries in a bowl, sprinkle with the sugar, then squash a few of the strawberries with a fork. Leave for 5 minutes. Whip the cream until it forms soft peaks, then fold into the crème fraîche or mascarpone and add the strawberries.

6 Carefully unroll the sponge and spread with the strawberry jam, followed by the cream mixture, leaving a 2 cm border all the way around the edges. Sprinkle the flaked almonds on top, then reroll the cake to form a neat log. Place seam-side down on a plate and chill for about 30 minutes. Dust with a little icing sugar and serve with the remaining strawberries on the side. The cake will keep in the fridge for up to 3 days.

ALL-IN-ONE BANANA CAKE

PREPARATION TIME: 20 MINUTES

COOKING TIME: 1 HOUR

SERVES 8

200 g unsalted butter, diced and softened at room temperature

250 g soft brown sugar

finely grated zest of 1 lemon

pinch of salt

3 large free-range eggs, lightly beaten

3 very ripe bananas, mashed with a fork

250 ml buttermilk (or regular milk soured with a squeeze of lemon juice)

250 g self-raising flour, sifted

1 teaspoon bicarbonate of soda

½ teaspoon ground cinnamon

icing sugar, for dusting

The best bananas for this cake are over-ripe, slightly darkened and full of natural sugar – they mash easily and have much better flavour. This moist cake is perfect served with a dusting of icing sugar, or alternatively make a simple lemon cream-cheese icing (see page 313).

1 Preheat the oven to 180°C (Gas Mark 4). Grease a 22 cm round cake tin and line the base with baking paper.

2 Place the butter, sugar, lemon zest, salt, egg, banana, buttermilk, flour, bicarbonate of soda and cinnamon in an electric mixer and mix on medium speed for 2-3 minutes or until combined.

3 Spoon the batter into the tin and smooth the surface. Bake for 50-60 minutes or until golden and firm to the touch. A skewer inserted in the centre should come out clean. Cool in the tin for 10 minutes, then turn out onto a wire rack to cool completely. Dust with icing sugar and serve. The cake will keep in an airtight container for up to 5 days.

FAVOURITE CARROT CAKE

PREPARATION TIME: 25 MINUTES

COOKING TIME: 40 MINUTES

SERVES 12

250 ml vegetable oil
(sunflower oil is also good)

250 g caster sugar

finely grated zest of ½ orange

pinch of salt

3 large free-range eggs

250 g self-raising flour, sifted

250 g grated carrot (made from
about 3 large carrots)

CREAM-CHEESE ICING

400 g cream cheese
(reduced fat is also fine)

20 g softened unsalted butter

75 g icing sugar, sifted

finely grated zest of ½ orange

1 tablespoon orange juice

I have tested many carrot cakes in my time and this light, soft-textured cake is my favourite. It is based on a simple pound cake recipe, but I have replaced the butter with vegetable oil and added a luscious cream-cheese and orange icing. I like to make this in a shallow rectangular brownie tin and serve it cut into squares.

1 Preheat the oven to 180°C (Gas Mark 4). Grease a shallow 30 cm × 20 cm cake tin and line the base and sides with baking paper, extending the paper 5 cm above the tin.

2 Place the oil, sugar, orange zest and salt in an electric mixer and mix on medium speed until well combined. Transfer the beaten egg to a jug. Reduce the speed of the mixer and, with the motor running, add the egg to the mixture, followed by an occasional spoonful of the flour. Sift over the remaining flour and gently fold in with a large metal spoon until smooth. Fold in the grated carrot until just combined.

3 Spoon the batter into the tin and smooth the surface. Bake for 35–40 minutes or until golden and firm to the touch. A skewer inserted in the centre should come out clean. Cool in the tin for 10 minutes then, with the help of the overhanging baking paper, turn out onto a wire rack to cool completely.

4 To make the icing, beat all the ingredients together with hand-held electric beaters until smooth and light. Spread over the top of the cake. Cut into 12 squares and serve. The cake will keep in an airtight container for up to 5 days.

BANANA, PECAN AND COCONUT LAYER CAKE

PREPARATION TIME: 25 MINUTES

COOKING TIME: 40 MINUTES

SERVES 8

150 g unsalted butter, diced and softened at room temperature

300 g caster sugar

finely grated zest of 1 small lemon

pinch of salt

2 free-range eggs, lightly beaten

250 g plain flour, sifted

3 ripe bananas, mashed with a fork

1 teaspoon bicarbonate of soda

4 tablespoons buttermilk (or regular milk soured with a squeeze of lemon juice)

100 g ground pecans

75 g desiccated coconut

COCONUT ICING

125 g unsalted butter, softened at room temperature

500 g icing sugar

½ teaspoon vanilla extract

50 g desiccated coconut

juice of ½ lemon

2-3 tablespoons boiling water, if needed

50 g pecans, coarsely chopped

I must confess this cake was invented through necessity - friends coming for tea with very little warning and me finding only a meagre assortment of ingredients in the cupboard. I made it in two tins to reduce the baking time. I'm happy to say that as odd as the combination may seem, it has become a firm favourite.

1 Preheat the oven to 180°C (Gas Mark 4). Grease two 21 cm round cake tins and line the bases with baking paper.

2 Place the butter, sugar, lemon zest and salt in an electric mixer and mix on medium speed for 3-4 minutes or until pale and fluffy. Transfer the beaten egg to a jug. Reduce the speed of the mixer and, with the motor running, add the egg to the mixture, followed by an occasional spoonful of flour. Add the mashed banana and beat until smooth. Sift over the bicarbonate of soda and remaining flour and gently fold in with a large metal spoon until smooth. Gently mix in the buttermilk, pecans and coconut until just combined.

3 Spoon the batter evenly into the tins and smooth the surface. Bake for 35-40 minutes or until golden and firm to the touch. A skewer inserted in the centre should come out clean. Cool in the tins for 10 minutes, then turn out onto a wire rack to cool completely.

4 To make the icing, beat the butter, icing sugar and vanilla with hand-held electric beaters until pale and fluffy. Mix through the coconut and enough lemon juice to give a spreadable consistency, adding the boiling water if needed to soften the icing. Sandwich the cakes together with half the icing and spread the rest over the top. Sprinkle the chopped pecans over the cake and serve. The cake will keep in an airtight container for up to 3 days.

ANNA DEL CONTE'S ITALIAN APPLE AND RAISIN CAKE

PREPARATION TIME: 25 MINUTES, PLUS SOAKING TIME

COOKING TIME: 1 HOUR

SERVES 8

100 g seedless raisins (preferably golden raisins)

160 ml olive oil

250 g caster sugar

3 free-range eggs

320 g plain flour, sifted

1½ teaspoons bicarbonate of soda

½ teaspoon cream of tartar

1 teaspoon ground cinnamon

½ teaspoon salt

350 g apples, peeled and diced

finely grated zest of 1 lemon

Of all the apple cakes, this is my favourite - moist and full of flavour, and particularly good with a dollop of cream at the end of a meal. It is also one of the few cakes made with oil instead of butter. Use a mild extra virgin olive oil if you can, otherwise an ordinary olive oil will be fine. I owe much to food writer Anna del Conte - she is my mentor for all things Italian.

1 Preheat the oven to 180°C (Gas Mark 4). Butter and flour a 20 cm round springform tin.

2 Soak the raisins in warm water for 20 minutes.

3 Meanwhile, pour the olive oil into a bowl, add the sugar and beat with hand-held electric beaters until combined and creamy. Add the eggs one at a time and beat until the mixture has increased in volume and has the consistency of thin mayonnaise.

4 Sift the flour, bicarbonate of soda, cream of tartar, cinnamon and salt into a bowl. Gradually add the dry ingredients to the oil and sugar mixture, folding them in with a large metal spoon. Mix thoroughly and then add the apple and lemon zest.

5 Drain the raisins and pat dry. Add to the batter and mix very thoroughly - the mixture will be very stiff at this stage.

6 Spoon the batter into the tin and bake for 55-65 minutes or until a skewer inserted in the centre comes out clean. Cool in the tin for about 10 minutes, then turn out onto a wire rack to cool completely. You could also serve it just warm. The cake will keep in an airtight container for up to 3 days.

COCONUT CAKE

PREPARATION TIME: 25 MINUTES

COOKING TIME: 50 MINUTES

SERVES 8

150 g unsalted butter, diced and
softened at room temperature

250 g caster sugar

1 teaspoon vanilla extract

finely grated zest of 1 lime

pinch of salt

2 large free-range eggs

300 g self-raising flour, sifted

185 ml sour cream

3 tablespoons coconut cream

60 g shredded coconut, plus extra
for sprinkling

COCONUT AND PASSIONFRUIT ICING

100 g unsalted butter, softened
at room temperature

125 g cream cheese

120 g icing sugar, sifted

pulp of 6 passionfruit, strained

This recipe comes from my friend Diana Wilson, who insisted that I couldn't write a baking book without including her coconut cake. Who am I to argue? The addition of passionfruit to the icing is my embellishment.

1 Preheat the oven to 170°C (Gas Mark 3). Grease a 22 cm round springform tin and line the base with baking paper.

2 Place the butter, sugar, vanilla, lime zest and salt in an electric mixer and mix on medium speed for 5 minutes or until pale and fluffy. Transfer the beaten egg to a jug. Reduce the speed of the mixer and, with the motor running, add the egg to the mixture, followed by an occasional spoonful of the flour. Using a large metal spoon, fold in the sour cream, coconut cream, shredded coconut and remaining flour until just combined.

3 Spoon the batter into the tin and smooth the surface. Bake for about 50 minutes or until golden and firm to the touch. A skewer inserted in the centre should come out clean. Cool in the tin for 10 minutes, then turn out onto a wire rack to cool completely.

4 To make the icing, beat the butter and cream cheese with hand-held electric beaters until light and fluffy. Add the icing sugar and enough strained passionfruit pulp to make a spreadable icing. Spread the icing over the cake and sprinkle with extra shredded coconut. The cake will keep in the fridge for up to 3 days.

PISTACHIO CAKE WITH LIME SYRUP

PREPARATION TIME: 25 MINUTES

COOKING TIME: 45 MINUTES

SERVES 8-10

200 g whole shelled unsalted pistachios

200 g caster sugar

5 large free-range eggs, separated

50 g coarsely chopped unsalted pistachios, plus extra to garnish

whipped cream, to serve (optional)

LIME SYRUP

150 g granulated sugar

100 ml water

2 tablespoons lime juice

Ground pistachios add a wonderful colour and flavour to this moist syrup cake. If you like the flavour of rosewater, replace the fresh lime juice in the syrup with a little rosewater. This is perfect served with coffee, or as a dessert with a little whipped cream.

1 Preheat the oven to 180°C (Gas Mark 4). Grease a 23 cm springform tin and line the base with baking paper.

2 Pulse the whole pistachios and 1 tablespoon caster sugar in a food processor until finely ground. Place the egg yolks and remaining sugar in a bowl and beat with hand-held electric beaters for 5 minutes or until thick and pale. Using a large metal spoon, gently fold in the ground pistachios until combined.

3 Place the egg whites in a clean bowl and beat with clean beaters until stiff peaks form (they should still look shiny and hold their shape when the beaters are lifted from the bowl). Using a large metal spoon, gently fold the egg whites into the pistachio mixture.

4 Pour the batter into the tin and sprinkle with the chopped pistachios. Bake for 45 minutes or until firm to the touch. Cover with foil if the cake is darkening too much.

5 Meanwhile, to make the syrup, combine the sugar and water in a small saucepan and bring to the boil, stirring to dissolve the sugar. When the mixture comes to the boil, remove the pan from the heat and stir in the lime juice. Keep warm.

6 Remove the cake from the oven and pierce the top about 12 times with a skewer or toothpick. While the cake is still in the tin, gradually spoon over as much of the hot syrup as it will absorb. Remove the outside of the tin and leave the cake to cool. Scatter with extra pistachios, then serve at room temperature with whipped cream, if desired. The cake will keep in an airtight container for up to 5 days.

HONEY CAKE

PREPARATION TIME: 20 MINUTES

COOKING TIME: 1 HOUR

SERVES 10-12

220 g unsalted butter, diced

175 g runny honey

100 g soft brown sugar

300 g self-raising flour

½ teaspoon ground cardamom

pinch of salt

3 large free-range eggs, lightly beaten

icing sugar, for dusting (optional)

TOPPING

3 tablespoons runny honey

50 g flaked almonds

This dark and moist honey cake is flavoured with cardamom and finished with a sticky almond topping. The flavour is intensified if you use dark brown or muscovado sugar in place of soft brown sugar. Roughly chopped pecans or pistachios make nice variations for the topping, or leave out the topping altogether, if you like. The cake is delicious enough to stand on its own.

1 Preheat the oven to 160°C (Gas Mark 2-3). Thoroughly grease a 20 cm springform tin and line the base with baking paper.

2 Place the butter, honey and sugar in a small saucepan over low heat until melted and combined, stirring occasionally. Remove from the heat and allow to cool.

3 Sift the flour, cardamom and salt into a large bowl. Add the butter mixture and egg and beat with hand-held electric beaters until smooth.

4 Pour the batter into the tin and bake for 50-60 minutes or until risen and firm to the touch. A skewer inserted in the centre should come out clean.

5 Just before the cake is ready, make the topping. Heat the honey and almonds in a small saucepan over low heat until warm.

6 Take the cake out of the oven, remove the outside of the tin and place the cake on a wire rack. Spread the warm topping over the warm cake and leave to cool. Dust with icing sugar when cool, if liked. Store the cake in an airtight container for up to 5 days.

BLACKBERRY JAM AND POLENTA CAKE

PREPARATION TIME: 20 MINUTES

COOKING TIME: 45 MINUTES

SERVES 8

100 g plain flour

2 teaspons baking powder

pinch of salt

50 g polenta (fine cornmeal)

150 g caster sugar

finely grated zest of 1 orange

finely grated zest and juice of 1 lemon

3 free-range eggs, lightly beaten

150 g blackberry jam

juice of ½ orange

100 g unsalted butter,
melted and cooled

125 ml light olive oil

icing sugar, for dusting

Every now and then when I'm writing cake recipes, I just want to break all the rules of baking and simply combine some ingredients and see what happens. The results are usually less than successful and can only be viewed as a learning experience, but I'm happy to say that this one worked a treat. The polenta may seem like an unusual addition, but it gives the cake a lovely grainy texture.

1 Preheat the oven to 160°C (Gas Mark 2–3). Grease a 20 cm round cake tin and line the base with baking paper.

2 Sift the flour, baking powder and salt into a large bowl. Stir in the polenta, sugar and orange and lemon zest. Add the beaten egg, jam, orange juice, lemon juice, butter and olive oil and mix until combined.

3 Spoon the batter into the tin and bake for 40–45 minutes or until firm to the touch. A skewer inserted in the centre should come out clean. Remove from the oven and cool completely in the tin. Serve dusted with icing sugar. The cake will keep in an airtight container for up to 5 days.

STICKY GINGER SYRUP CAKE

PREPARATION TIME: 25 MINUTES

COOKING TIME: 1 HOUR

SERVES 8

60 g unsalted butter, diced

125 ml golden syrup

150 g self-raising flour, sifted

1 heaped teaspoon ground ginger

½ teaspoon mixed spice

110 g caster sugar

pinch of salt

125 ml milk

1 free-range egg, lightly beaten

icing sugar, for dusting (optional)

GINGER SYRUP

125 g granulated sugar

100 ml water

1 tablespoon grated ginger

If I had to choose my favourite cake, it would probably be this sticky ginger cake. I love the sweet, spicy warmth that ginger brings to baking, and I've been making this one for over twenty years. It's also good without the syrup.

1 Preheat the oven to 170ºC (Gas Mark 3). Thoroughly grease and line the base of a 20 cm × 8.5 cm loaf tin with baking paper (leave a little overhanging the two long sides). It is important to do this as this cake has a tendency to stick.

2 Place the butter and golden syrup in a small saucepan and melt over low heat, stirring occasionally. Remove from the heat.

3 Sift the flours, ginger, mixed spice, sugar and salt into a large bowl. Add the milk and egg and mix until smooth. Gradually add the melted butter mixture, stirring until well incorporated.

4 Pour the batter into the tin and bake for 50–55 minutes or until risen and firm to the touch. A skewer inserted in the centre should come out clean.

5 Just before the cake is ready, make the syrup. Combine all the ingredients in a small saucepan and bring to the boil, stirring to dissolve the sugar, then reduce the heat and simmer for 5 minutes.

6 When the cake is ready, remove and pierce all over with a skewer or toothpick. Spoon over enough of the hot syrup and ginger for it to absorb and become sticky. Dust with icing sugar when cool, if liked. The cake will keep in an airtight container for up to 5 days.

STICKY TOFFEE LOAF

PREPARATION TIME: 25 MINUTES

COOKING TIME: 45 MINUTES

SERVES 8-10

175 g pitted dates, chopped

1 teaspoon bicarbonate of soda

300 ml boiling water

75 g unsalted butter, diced and softened at room temperature

185 g caster sugar

2 free-range eggs, lightly beaten

210 g self-raising flour

pinch of salt

1 teaspoon vanilla extract

TOFFEE ICING

100 ml double cream

100 g light brown sugar

40 g unsalted butter

1 heaped tablespoon icing sugar, sifted

This cake is based on my version of a sticky toffee pudding. The main difference is that this is served at room temperature and has a toffee icing, rather than a hot toffee sauce.

1 Preheat the oven to 180°C (Gas Mark 4). Grease and line the base and sides of a 24 cm × 10 cm loaf tin.

2 Place the dates in a bowl, add the bicarbonate of soda and pour over the boiling water. Set aside.

3 Place the butter and sugar in an electric mixer and mix on medium speed for 7-8 minutes or until pale and fluffy. Add the beaten egg, a bit at a time, beating well between additions. Sift in the flour and salt. Add the dates and their soaking liquid, then the vanilla and mix well. This will be a wet mixture.

4 Spoon the batter into the tin and bake for about 45 minutes or until risen and firm to the touch. A skewer inserted in the centre should come out clean. Cool in the tin for 10 minutes, then turn out onto a wire rack to cool completely.

5 Meanwhile, to make the icing, combine the cream, sugar and butter in a small saucepan over medium heat. Bring to the boil, stirring to dissolve the sugar, then reduce the heat and simmer, without stirring, for 4-5 minutes or until nice and golden. Set aside to cool.

6 When the icing is cold, beat in the icing sugar until smooth. Spread over the cake and leave to set. The cake will keep in an airtight container for up to 3 days.

GLUTEN-FREE BLUEBERRY CAKE

PREPARATION TIME: 25 MINUTES

COOKING TIME: 1 HOUR 10 MINUTES

SERVES 10-12

250 g unsalted butter, diced and softened at room temperature

250 g caster sugar

finely grated zest of 1 large lemon

pinch of salt

3 large free-range eggs, lightly beaten

250 g ground almonds

125 g polenta (fine cornmeal)

1 teaspoon baking powder

juice of ½ large lemon

150 g blueberries, fresh or frozen

cream, mascarpone or plain yoghurt, to serve

LEMON SYRUP

finely grated zest of 1 lemon

juice of 3 lemons

100 g caster sugar

The combination of ground almonds and polenta gives this gluten-free cake an interesting texture: the almonds add softness and the polenta gives a slight crunch. This is also good served warm or at room temperature as a dessert.

1 Preheat the oven to 170°C (Gas Mark 3). Grease a 23 cm round cake tin and line the base with baking paper.

2 Place the butter, sugar, lemon zest and salt in an electric mixer and mix on medium speed for 7-8 minutes or until pale and fluffy. Transfer the beaten egg to a jug. Reduce the speed of the mixer and, with the motor running, add the egg to the mixture until combined. Sprinkle over the almonds, polenta and baking powder and carefully fold in with a large metal spoon. Add the lemon juice and mix gently to combine.

3 Spoon the batter into the tin, then sprinkle over the blueberries and press down lightly. Bake for 60-70 minutes or until a skewer inserted in the centre comes out almost clean, with a few crumbs sticking to it.

4 Just before the cake is ready, make the syrup. Combine all the ingredients in a small saucepan and bring to the boil, stirring to dissolve the sugar. Reduce the heat and simmer without stirring for about 4 minutes.

5 Remove the cake from the oven and drizzle about two-thirds of the hot syrup over the warm cake (save the rest for serving). Let the cake cool in the tin. Delicious served with cream, mascarpone or plain yoghurt, drizzled with the remaining syrup. The cake will keep in an airtight container for up to 5 days.

GLAZED CITRUS AND POPPY-SEED YOGHURT CAKE

PREPARATION TIME: 30 MINUTES

COOKING TIME: 1 HOUR

SERVES 8

200 g unsalted butter, diced and softened at room temperature

250 g caster sugar

finely grated zest of 1 lime

finely grated zest of 1 lemon

3 large free-range eggs, lightly beaten

300 g plain flour, sifted

185 ml sour cream

2 teaspoons baking powder

pinch of salt

50 g poppy seeds

juice of 1 large lemon

CITRUS GLAZE

100 ml water

zest of 1 lemon, finely sliced

125 g icing sugar

My friend Frances Foster is rightly famous for her lemon and poppy-seed cake. She's quite secretive about her recipes, but after years of asking sneaky questions I've come up with this similar cake. Frances makes hers in a bundt tin, but I've discovered it also works well in a 20 cm round tin. The syrup is more like a thin glaze and should be poured over the cake while it is still hot.

1 Preheat the oven to 180°C (Gas Mark 4). Grease and line a 24 cm bundt tin.

2 Place the butter, sugar and lemon and lime zest in an electric mixer and mix on medium speed for 5 minutes or until soft and well mixed. Transfer the beaten egg to a jug. Reduce the speed of the mixer and, with the motor running, add the egg to the mixture, followed by an occasional spoonful of flour. Reduce the speed and add the sour cream. With the motor running, gradually mix in the baking powder, salt, poppy seeds and remaining flour until combined. Stir through the lemon juice.

3 Spoon the batter into the tin and bake for 50-60 minutes or until firm to the touch. A skewer inserted in the centre should come out clean. Cool in the tin for about 10 minutes, then turn out onto a wire rack.

4 To make the glaze, combine the water, lemon zest and sugar in a small saucepan and bring to the boil over high heat, stirring to dissolve the sugar. Reduce the heat to low and simmer for 5 minutes or until the zest has softened. Allow to cool for about 5 minutes before slowly pouring over the warm cake - keep going until the cake won't absorb any more. The cake will keep in an airtight container for up to 5 days.

RICOTTA CAKE

**PREPARATION TIME: 20 MINUTES,
PLUS SOAKING TIME**

COOKING TIME: 35 MINUTES

SERVES 8-10

150 g sultanas

3 tablespoons sherry or Marsala

200 g unsalted butter, diced and
softened at room temperature

200 g caster sugar

finely grated zest of 2 lemons

3 large free-range eggs, separated

125 g self-raising flour, sifted

350 g ricotta

juice of 1 lemon

1 teaspoon baking powder

pinch of salt

icing sugar, for dusting

**This southern Italian-style cake is halfway between
a cake and a cheesecake. It is best made the day before
you want to eat it, and I usually dust it with icing sugar
just before serving. The ricotta sold in tubs at the
supermarket is fine for this, but if you find fresh
ricotta at your local deli, all the better.**

1 Place the sultanas and sherry or Marsala in a bowl
and soak for about 1 hour.

2 Preheat the oven to 170ºC (Gas Mark 3). Grease
a 23 cm springform tin and line the base and sides with
baking paper, extending the paper 3 cm above the tin.

3 Place the butter, sugar and lemon zest in an electric
mixer and mix on medium speed for 4-5 minutes until
pale and well mixed. Add the egg yolks, one at a time,
with an occasional spoonful of the flour, mixing well
between additions. Mix through the ricotta and lemon juice.

4 Whisk the egg whites in a clean, dry bowl with hand-held
electric beaters until they form firm peaks, then fold into
the batter with a large metal spoon. Fold in the baking
powder, salt, remaining flour and sultanas and soaking
liquid until smooth.

5 Spoon the batter into the tin and smooth the surface.
Bake for 30-35 minutes or until golden and firm to the
touch. A skewer inserted in the centre should come out
clean. Cool completely in the tin, then dust with icing sugar
before serving. The cake will keep in the fridge for up to
3 days.

ORANGE, SEMOLINA AND YOGHURT CAKE

PREPARATION TIME: 20 MINUTES

COOKING TIME: 1 HOUR

SERVES 8-10

250 g unsalted butter, diced and softened at room temperature

200 g caster sugar

finely grated zest of 1 orange

4 free-range eggs, lightly beaten

50 g plain flour, sifted

2 teaspoons baking powder

pinch of salt

200 g ground almonds

250 g semolina

120 g plain yoghurt

juice of 1 orange

ORANGE SYRUP

grated zest and juice of 1 large orange

150 g caster sugar

250 ml water

This is one of those lovely soft, syrupy cakes often found in the Mediterranean and northern Europe. The semolina and almonds give the cake a soft texture and the syrup adds a wonderful stickiness. Serve with tea or coffee, or as a dessert with a dollop of crème fraîche.

1 Preheat the oven to 160°C (Gas Mark 2-3). Grease a 20 cm springform tin and line the base with baking paper.

2 Place the butter, sugar and orange zest in an electric mixer and mix on medium speed for 7-8 minutes or until pale and fluffy. Transfer the beaten egg to a jug. Reduce the speed of the mixer and, with the motor running, add the egg to the mixture, followed by an occasional spoonful of flour. Reduce the speed and gradually mix in the baking powder, salt, ground almonds, semolina and remaining flour. Gently fold in the yoghurt and orange juice until combined.

3 Spoon the batter into the tin and bake for about 1 hour or until firm to the touch. A skewer inserted in the centre should come out clean.

4 Just before the cake is ready, make the syrup. Combine the orange zest and juice, sugar and water in a small saucepan and bring to the boil over low heat, stirring to dissolve the sugar. Reduce the heat and simmer gently (without stirring) for about 4 minutes.

5 Remove the cake from the oven and pierce all over with a skewer. Pour the hot syrup over the cake, then leave to cool in the tin. The cake will keep in an airtight container for up to 3 days.

PEACH YOGHURT CAKE

PREPARATION TIME: 25 MINUTES

COOKING TIME: 1 HOUR

SERVES 8

6 ripe peaches, peeled, stones removed, cut into small pieces

1 heaped tablespoon raw or demerara sugar

175 g unsalted butter, diced and softened at room temperature

175 g caster sugar

finely grated zest of 2 lemons

pinch of salt

2 large free-range eggs

175 g plain flour

175 g thick plain yoghurt

75 g semolina

2 teaspoons baking powder

This simple recipe transforms ripe peaches, nectarines, apricots or plums into a delicious and unusual cake. Enjoy it as is or serve it for dessert with cream or ice-cream.

1 Preheat the oven to 180°C (Gas Mark 4). Grease a 20 cm round cake tin and line the base with baking paper.

2 Scatter half the fruit over the base of the tin and sprinkle with the raw sugar.

3 Place the butter, sugar, lemon zest and salt in an electric mixer and mix on medium speed for 7–8 minutes or until pale and fluffy. Transfer the beaten egg to a jug. Reduce the speed of the mixer and, with the motor running, add the egg to the mixture, followed by an occasional spoonful of flour. Reduce the speed and add the yoghurt. Sprinkle over the semolina and sift in the baking powder and remaining flour. Carefully fold the ingredients together with a metal spoon, then add the remaining fruit and mix until combined.

4 Spoon the batter into the tin and bake for 50–60 minutes or until a skewer inserted in the centre comes out almost clean. Cool in the tin for about 10 minutes, then invert the cake onto a wire rack to cool completely Remove the baking paper from the (now) top of the cake and serve. The cake will keep in an airtight container for up to 3 days.

NICOLA HUMBLE'S HAZELNUT AND RASPBERRY CAKE

PREPARATION TIME: 25 MINUTES

COOKING TIME: 50 MINUTES

SERVES 8-10

220 g hazelnuts

6 large free-range eggs, separated

180 g caster sugar

250 ml double cream, whipped

150-200 g raspberries, fresh or frozen

icing sugar, for dusting

This delicious gluten-free recipe is the creation of British food writer and historian Nicola Humble. The cake is so easy to make, but be gentle when folding in the beaten egg white so you don't knock out all the air. If preferred, the batter can be baked in two shallower cake tins, then sandwiched together with the cream and raspberries. If you're doing this, reduce the baking time to 25-30 minutes.

1 Preheat the oven to 170°C (Gas Mark 3). Grease and flour a 24 cm springform tin and line the base with baking paper.

2 Place the hazelnuts in a dry frying pan and toast carefully over low heat, shaking the pan to rotate them. This can also be done in a moderate (180°C/Gas Mark 4) oven, but the nuts must be checked frequently as they burn very easily. When they are golden in patches, remove from the heat and allow to cool.

3 Grind the cooled nuts in a food processor. The aim is to reduce most of the nuts to a coarse flour, but to retain some larger chunks for texture. Be careful not to process too far or they will release their oils and turn into nut-butter.

4 Using hand-held electric beaters, whisk the egg yolks and sugar until pale, creamy and very thick. Stir in the nuts. Place the whites in a clean bowl and whisk with clean beaters until firm peaks form, then gently fold them into the yolk mixture with a large metal spoon.

5 Spoon the batter into the tin and bake for 45 minutes or until the cake begins to shrink away from the sides of the tin. Leave to cool in the tin for 10 minutes, then remove the outside of the tin and cool the cake completely on a wire rack.

6 Carefully cut the cooled cake in half horizontally, then sandwich with whipped cream and raspberries. Dust with icing sugar before serving. The cake will keep in the fridge for up to 2 days.

CLAUDIA RODEN'S FLOURLESS ORANGE AND ALMOND CAKE

PREPARATION TIME: 15 MINUTES, PLUS COOLING TIME

COOKING TIME: 2½ HOURS

SERVES 8–10

3 medium oranges, washed

5 eggs, separated

200 g caster sugar

200 g ground almonds

1 teaspoon baking powder

icing sugar, for dusting

The recipe is based on the Sephardic orange-and-almond cake in Claudia Roden's incomparable cookbook, *A New Book of Middle Eastern Food*. It was this moist, intensely flavoured cake that first ignited my lifelong passion for baking. My slight change is to separate the eggs, which makes the cake lighter and less dense than the original, but just as rich, moist and fragrant.

1 Place the clean, whole and unpeeled oranges in a saucepan of water and bring to the boil. Reduce the heat and simmer for 1½ hours or until the oranges are soft, adding more water when necessary. Drain. Cut the oranges into quarters, remove any pips and pulse the rest (including the peel) in a food processor. Allow to cool.

2 Preheat the oven to 180°C (Gas Mark 4). Grease a 23 cm springform tin and line the base with baking paper.

3 Place the egg yolks and sugar in a large bowl and beat with hand-held electric beaters for 4–5 minutes or until pale and thick. Beat in the orange mixture, almonds and baking powder.

4 Place the egg whites in a separate bowl and beat with clean, dry beaters until soft peaks form. Carefully fold into the cake mixture with a large metal spoon.

5 Pour the batter into the cake tin and bake for about 1 hour or until firm to the touch (cover with a loose sheet of foil if it starts overbrowning). Cool in the tin and dust with icing sugar to serve. The cake will keep in an airtight container for up to 5 days.

CAKES
WITH
BAKED-ON
TOPPINGS

TIPS

1 When making upside-down cakes, I often use fruits that are slightly tart as they contrast well with the sugar or caramel in the topping. The fruit slices may be arranged in a neat pinwheel or just put them in the tin randomly - this is entirely up to you and the cake will taste great either way.

2 I prefer to use a wide tin (or frying pan) a bit larger than the standard size to bake an upside-down cake as this gives a nice shallow cake with plenty of fruit topping.

3 Upside-down cakes are generally moister than regular cakes as the fruit creates lots of juice as it cooks; this makes them perfect for dessert.

4 When making a crumble-topped or streusel cake, press the topping lightly into the batter to help it stick to the cake.

5 Turning out upside-down cakes is easier than you might think. Using a sharp knife, cut and lift around the edge of the cake to loosen it from the side of the tin. Choose a serving plate that's slightly larger than the tin. Place the plate over the top of the tin, then with both hands, hold the pan and plate together firmly and invert them. The cake will gently drop onto the plate. Leave to rest for about 5 minutes, then carefully lift the tin. If anything remains stuck to the bottom of the tin, remove it and place it on top of the cake.

6 Most crumble cakes only need a dusting of icing sugar to serve.

RHUBARB CRUMBLE CAKE

PREPARATION TIME: 30 MINUTES

COOKING TIME: 1¼ HOURS

SERVES 10

185 g self-raising flour

½ teaspoon baking powder

pinch of salt

185 g unsalted butter, diced and softened at room temperature

185 g caster sugar

finely grated zest of 1 orange

3 free-range eggs, lightly beaten

juice of ½ lemon

2-3 stalks rhubarb, cut into 2 cm pieces

1 tablespoon raw sugar

icing sugar, for dusting

CRUMBLE TOPPING

50 g unsalted butter, chilled and diced

4 tablespoons plain flour

2 tablespoons demerara or raw sugar

4 tablespoons flaked almonds

Since planting rhubarb in my garden I have been experimenting with different ways to use it. In this concoction, the tartness of the rhubarb mixes well with the sweet crumble topping, giving a moist, flavoursome cake with an interesting texture. As rhubarb gives out quite a bit of liquid while it cooks, there is no need to cover the top of the cake completely. Arrange the pieces of fruit evenly over the top, spacing them out by at least 1.5 cm, then gently push them into the batter. This will enable the crumble topping to stick to the batter.

1 Preheat the oven to 180°C (Gas Mark 4). Grease a 22 cm springform tin and line the base with baking paper.

2 Sift the flour, baking powder and salt into an electric mixer. Add the butter, sugar, orange zest, egg and lemon juice. Beat on medium speed until the mixture is just combined.

3 Spoon the batter into the tin. Mix the rhubarb pieces with the raw sugar and arrange on top, gently pressing them into the batter.

4 To make the topping, rub the butter into the flour and sugar until crumbly, then mix in the almonds. Sprinkle the crumble mixture over the rhubarb and press down lightly.

5 Bake for 1-1¼ hours or until golden, risen and firm to the touch. A skewer inserted in the centre should come out clean. Cool in the tin for 10 minutes, then carefully transfer to a wire rack to cool. Dust with icing sugar and serve warm or at room temperature. Store in an airtight container for up to 3 days.

APPLE AND BLUEBERRY CAKE

PREPARATION TIME: 30 MINUTES

COOKING TIME: 1 HOUR

SERVES 8

185 g unsalted butter, diced and softened at room temperature

185 g caster sugar

1 teaspoon vanilla extract

2 free-range eggs, lightly beaten

150 g plain flour, sifted

pinch of salt

2½ tablespoons milk

100 g ground almonds

1 apple, peeled, cored and thinly sliced

100 g blueberries, fresh or frozen

1 teaspoon ground cinnamon

2 tablespoons demerara or raw sugar

This buttery cake is topped with apple and blueberries. I usually place the apple slices fairly randomly over the cake as I prefer this haphazard style, but by all means arrange them neatly if you prefer. The right apple to use is the apple you like best. Certainly, there are some differences in how various apples perform in cooking, but the final choice should be based on flavour.

1 Preheat the oven to 180°C (Gas Mark 4). Grease a 20 cm springform tin and line the base with baking paper.

2 Place the butter, sugar and vanilla in an electric mixer and mix on medium speed for 7–8 minutes or until pale and fluffy. Transfer the beaten egg to a jug. Reduce the speed of the mixer and, with the motor running, add the egg to the mixture, followed by an occasional spoonful of flour if the mixture looks as if it might separate. Using a large metal spoon, lightly fold in the remaining flour, salt, milk and ground almonds until combined.

3 Spoon the batter into the tin and top with the apple and blueberries. Combine the cinnamon and demerara or raw sugar and sprinkle over the top.

4 Bake for about 1 hour or until firm to the touch. Allow to cool completely in the tin before removing the side and base. Store in an airtight container for up to 3 days.

BLACKBERRY AND ALMOND CRUMBLE CAKE

PREPARATION TIME: 25 MINUTES

COOKING TIME: 1¼ HOURS

SERVES 10

220 g self-raising flour

½ teaspoon baking powder

pinch of salt

200 g unsalted butter, diced and softened at room temperature

250 g caster sugar

finely grated zest of 1 orange

2 tablespoons ground almonds

4 free-range eggs, lightly beaten

2½ tablespoons buttermilk (or regular milk soured with a squeeze of lemon juice)

150 g blackberries, fresh or frozen

icing sugar, for dusting

CRUMBLE TOPPING

50 g unsalted butter, chilled and diced

4 tablespoons plain flour

2 tablespoons demerara sugar

4 tablespoons flaked almonds

Juicy blackberries and crunchy almond crumble sprinkled over a classic pound cake transform something quite simple into a really memorable cake. The blackberries can be replaced with other berries, such as raspberries, if preferred. Or try other types of fruit: ripe slices of peach, pear or apple also work well.

1 Preheat the oven to 180°C (Gas Mark 4). Grease a 22 cm springform tin and line the base with baking paper.

2 Sift the flour, baking powder and salt into the bowl of an electric mixer. Add the butter, sugar, orange zest, ground almonds, egg and buttermilk. Beat on medium speed until the mixture is just combined.

3 Spoon the batter into the tin. Arrange the blackberries on top, gently pressing into the batter.

4 To make the topping, rub the butter into the flour and sugar until crumbly, then mix in the almonds. Sprinkle the crumble mixture over the blackberries and press down lightly.

5 Bake for 1-1¼ hours or until golden, risen and firm to the touch. A skewer inserted in the centre should come out clean. Cool in the tin for 10 minutes, then remove the outside of the tin and leave to cool on a wire rack. Dust with icing sugar and serve warm or at room temperature. Store in an airtight container for up to 3 days.

COFFEE STREUSEL CAKE

185 g unsalted butter, diced and softened at room temperature

185 g caster sugar

2 large free-range eggs, lightly beaten

185 g self-raising flour

1 teaspoon baking powder

pinch of salt

1 teaspoon ground cinnamon

1 tablespoon instant coffee powder

2 tablespoons boiling water

100 g sour cream

STREUSEL MIXTURE

100 g pecans, roughly chopped

120 g demerara or raw sugar

1 teaspoon instant coffee powder

This spiced coffee cake is both layered and sprinkled with a nutty streusel mixture, making it the perfect choice for a morning coffee ritual or an impressive afternoon tea.

1 Preheat the oven to 180°C (Gas Mark 4). Grease a 23 cm × 7 cm × 7cm loaf tin and line the base with baking paper.

2 Place the butter and sugar in an electric mixer and mix on medium speed for 7-8 minutes or until pale and fluffy. Transfer the beaten egg to a jug. Reduce the speed of the mixer and, with the motor running, add the egg to the mixture, beating well between additions. Sift the flour, baking powder, salt and cinnamon over the top and gently fold in with a large metal spoon. Dissolve the coffee in the boiling water, then mix into the batter with the sour cream until just combined.

3 To make the streusel mixture, combine all the ingredients in a small bowl.

4 Spoon half of the cake batter into the tin and sprinkle with half the streusel mixture. Add the rest of the batter and sprinkle over the remaining streusel.

5 Bake for 45-50 minutes or until risen and firm to the touch. Cool in the tin for 15 minutes, then turn out onto a wire rack to cool. Serve warm or cold. Store in an airtight container for up to 5 days.

PECAN AND YOGHURT CAKE

PREPARATION TIME: 25 MINUTES

COOKING TIME: 1 HOUR

SERVES 8

250 g plain flour

2 teaspoons baking powder

1 teaspoon bicarbonate of soda

1 teaspoon mixed spice

pinch of ground ginger

pinch of salt

finely grated zest of 1 orange

3 large free-range eggs, lightly beaten

250 g light brown sugar

150 g unsalted butter, melted

250 g plain yoghurt

PECAN TOPPING

3 tablespoons pouring cream

70 g unsalted butter, melted

100 g raw sugar

50 g desiccated coconut

100 g pecans, roughly chopped

This is one of those easy cakes made like a muffin, where the dry and wet ingredients are simply mixed together but still lumpy. Don't feel you have to beat the batter until smooth – if you overmix it, the cake may be heavy.

1 Preheat the oven to 160°C (Gas Mark 2–3). Grease a 23 cm springform tin and line the base with baking paper.

2 Sift the flour, baking powder, bicarbonate of soda, mixed spice, ginger and salt into a large mixing bowl. Stir in the zest and make a well in the centre. Combine the egg, sugar, melted butter and yoghurt and stir into the dry ingredients. Mix until just combined. Don't overmix – it doesn't matter if there are a few lumps.

3 Spoon the batter into the tin and bake for 50–60 minutes or until firm to the touch. A skewer inserted in the centre should come out clean. Leave to cool in the tin for about 15 minutes.

4 Meanwhile, to make the topping, combine all the ingredients in a bowl. Spread over the top of the cake and place under a preheated grill for a few minutes until golden. Remove the outside of the tin and leave to cool on a wire rack. Store in an airtight container for up to 5 days.

PLUM CAKE

PREPARATION TIME: 25 MINUTES

COOKING TIME: 1 HOUR

SERVES 8

150 g self-raising flour

pinch of salt

125 g caster sugar

1 teaspoon vanilla extract

125 g unsalted butter, diced and softened at room temperature

2 free-range eggs, lightly beaten

about 500 g ripe plums, halved and stones removed

1 tablespoon demerara or raw sugar

Depending on what I have in my fruit bowl, I often replace the plums with other stone fruit, such as ripe apricots or nectarines. If you are lucky enough to find greengages, these are also a delicious variation. Demerara or raw sugar gives the top of the cake a nice crunch, but you can also use regular granulated sugar, if preferred.

1 Preheat the oven to 180°C (Gas Mark 4). Grease a 20 cm springform tin and line the base with baking paper.

2 Sift the flour and salt into a bowl, then add the sugar, vanilla, butter and egg. Beat with hand-held electric beaters or a wooden spoon for 1-2 minutes or until the ingredients all come together. It's important not to beat the batter too much – just long enough to make it smooth.

3 Spoon the batter into the tin and level the surface. Place the plums, skin-side down, on the surface and press lightly into the batter. Sprinkle with demerara or raw sugar.

4 Bake for 50-60 minutes or until a skewer inserted in the centre comes out clean. Cool in the tin for 5 minutes, then remove the outside of the tin and leave to cool on a wire rack. Serve warm or at room temperature. Store in an airtight container for up to 3 days.

RASPBERRY AND COCONUT MACAROON CAKE

PREPARATION TIME: 35 MINUTES

COOKING TIME: 1 HOUR

SERVES 10

200 g unsalted butter, diced and softened at room temperature

175 g caster sugar

3 free-range eggs, beaten

1 teaspoon vanilla extract

250 g self-raising flour, sifted

1 teaspoon baking powder

pinch of salt

2 tablespoons ground almonds

4 tablespoons milk

100 g raspberries, fresh or frozen

MACAROON TOPPING

3 free-range egg whites

100 g caster sugar

90 g desiccated coconut

2 tablespoons ground almonds

This buttery cake is topped with raspberries and a layer of coconut macaroon. Take care not to overbeat the macaroon mixture or it will become dry, which will spoil the texture.

1 Preheat the oven to 170°C (Gas Mark 3). Grease a 22 cm springform tin and line the base with baking paper.

2 Place the butter and sugar in an electric mixer and mix on medium speed for 7-8 minutes or until pale and fluffy. Transfer the beaten egg to a jug. Reduce the speed of the mixer and, with the motor running, gradually add the egg to the mixture, beating well between additions. Using a large metal spoon, fold in the vanilla, then fold in the flour, baking powder, salt and ground almonds alternately with the milk. Spoon the batter into the tin.

3 To make the topping, whisk the egg whites with an electric mixer until they form firm peaks, then reduce the speed a little and slowly add the sugar, beating until all the sugar has been added. The meringue should be firm and shiny. Fold in the coconut and ground almonds.

4 Top the batter with the raspberries, pressing them down lightly. Carefully spread the meringue topping over the raspberries.

5 Bake for 50-60 minutes or until a skewer inserted in the centre comes out clean. Cover the cake with foil about three-quarters of the way through cooking if the top is browning too much. Cool the cake in the tin for 10 minutes, then remove the outside of the tin and leave to cool on a wire rack. Store in an airtight container for up to 3 days.

APPLE, ORANGE AND CARDAMOM CAKE

PREPARATION TIME: 35 MINUTES

COOKING TIME: 1¼ HOURS

SERVES 8

125 g unsalted butter, diced and softened at room temperature

175 g light brown sugar

juice and finely grated zest of 1 orange

2 free-range eggs, lightly beaten

125 g plain flour, sifted

125 g wholemeal flour, sifted

2 teaspoons baking powder

pinch of salt

1 teaspoon ground cardamom

2 apples, peeled, cored and grated

about 2 tablespoons milk

APPLE TOPPING

4 apples, peeled, cored, halved and thinly sliced

juice of ½ orange

1 tablespoon granulated sugar

3 tablespoons apricot jam, warmed

I often group together the flavours of apple, orange and cardamom – for instance, I love the way this combination transforms a simple apple cake into something quite exotic. Using half white and half wholemeal flour gives the cake an interesting flavour, colour and texture. As with most apple cakes, I tend to use apples that I enjoy eating. If you are able to get cooking apples (like bramleys), these will cook to a much softer texture than eating apples like golden delicious. I have successfully made this cake with both granny smiths and golden delicious.

1 Preheat the oven to 180°C (Gas Mark 4). Grease a 23 cm springform tin and line the base with baking paper.

2 Place the butter, sugar and orange zest in an electric mixer and mix on medium speed for 7–8 minutes or until pale and fluffy. Transfer the beaten egg to a jug. Reduce the speed of the mixer and, with the motor running, add the egg to the mixture, followed by an occasional spoonful of flour.

3 Sift the remaining flours, baking powder, salt and cardamom into a bowl. Place the apples in a separate bowl and toss with about 2 tablespoons of the flour mixture.

4 Add the dry ingredients to the butter mixture in three batches, alternating with the apples and milk, and gently fold in with a large metal spoon until just combined. Spoon the mixture into the tin and smooth the surface.

5 To make the topping, toss the sliced apples in the orange juice. Arrange them decoratively on the top of the batter, overlapping slightly, then press down gently. Sprinkle with the granulated sugar.

6 Bake for 1–1¼ hours or until golden and firm to the touch. Cover with a sheet of foil about three-quarters of the way through cooking if the topping starts browning too much.

7 Remove from the oven and brush the top of the cake with a little warmed apricot jam. Cool in the tin for 10 minutes, then remove the outside of the tin and leave to cool on a wire rack. Store in an airtight container for up to 3 days.

PINEAPPLE UPSIDE-DOWN CAKE

PREPARATION TIME: 25 MINUTES

COOKING TIME: 45 MINUTES

SERVES 8-10

4 tablespoons golden syrup,
plus extra for brushing (optional)

8 rings pineapple, fresh or tinned
(and drained)

300 g unsalted butter, diced and
softened at room temperature

300 g caster sugar

finely grated zest of ½ lemon

5 free-range eggs, lightly beaten

300 g self-raising flour, sifted

pinch of salt

As much as I love baking, if I can avoid icing a cake I will (anything more than a sprinkle of icing sugar and I start making excuses). So the idea of a cake with a baked-on topping is perfect for me, especially an old-fashioned favourite like this one. Sitting the tin of golden syrup in a pan of hot water will make it nice and runny, and much easier to measure and pour.

1 Preheat the oven to 180°C (Gas Mark 4). Grease a 20 cm × 30 cm slice or brownie tin and line the base with baking paper (leaving some overhanging the two long sides).

2 Warm 3-4 tablespoons of golden syrup until runny. Pour into the base of the tin and spread evenly with the back of a spoon. Arrange the pineapple rings on the top of the syrup in two rows of four.

3 Place the butter, sugar and lemon zest in an electric mixer and mix on medium speed for 7-8 minutes or until pale and fluffy. Transfer the beaten egg to a jug. Reduce the speed of the mixer and, with the motor running, add the egg to the mixture, followed by an occasional spoonful of flour. Reduce the speed and gradually mix in the salt and remaining flour.

4 Carefully spoon the batter into the tin and bake for about 45 minutes or until firm to the touch. Cool in the tin for about 10 minutes, then ease the cake out of the tin using the overhanging paper and invert onto a large platter or board. Brush the pineapple top with a little extra warmed golden syrup, if desired. Serve warm or at room temperature. Store in an airtight container for up to 3 days.

PEACH UPSIDE-DOWN CAKE

PREPARATION TIME: 30 MINUTES

COOKING TIME: 40 MINUTES

SERVES 6-8

240 g unsalted butter, diced and softened at room temperature

85 g granulated sugar

6 ripe peaches or apricots, halved, stones removed and cut into wedges

175 g golden caster sugar

2 free-range eggs

140 g plain flour, sifted

140 g self-raising flour, sifted

pinch of salt

2 tablespoons ground almonds

75 ml milk

For ease of preparation, I make this moist and sticky cake in a deep frying pan - the same pan that I make the caramel in. You end up with a cross between a torte and an upside-down cake. Serve it warm as a dessert with a little cream, ice-cream or crème fraîche, or enjoy it at room temperature at tea time.

1 Preheat the oven to 180°C (Gas Mark 4).

2 Melt 40 g butter in a heavy-based 21 cm frying pan with an ovenproof handle (cast iron works well). Add the granulated sugar and cook over low heat, stirring, until the sugar has melted and started to bubble gently. Keep an eye on the pan as the sugar can burn quite quickly; remove it as soon as it looks golden and set aside to cool slightly. Arrange the peaches or apricots in the caramelised sugar. Set aside.

3 To make the cake batter, cream the golden caster sugar and remaining butter with hand-held electric beaters. Beat in the eggs one at a time. Fold in the flours, salt and ground almonds and then the milk, using a large metal spoon.

4 Spoon dollops of the batter over the peaches or apricots and smooth the surface with the back of a spoon. Bake for 40 minutes or until puffed up and golden. Remove from the oven and leave to sit for 10 minutes. Invert the cake onto a plate and leave to cool. Cut into wedges to serve. Store in an airtight container for up to 3 days.

UPSIDE-DOWN BANANA CAKE

PREPARATION TIME: 30 MINUTES

COOKING TIME: 50 MINUTES

SERVES 8

125 g unsalted butter, diced and softened at room temperature

200 g soft brown sugar

1 teaspoon vanilla extract

2 free-range eggs, lightly beaten

185 g self-raising flour

1 teaspoon baking powder

pinch of salt

2 large ripe bananas, mashed

BANANA TOPPING

50 g unsalted butter

125 g soft brown sugar

5 ripe bananas, halved lengthways

The aroma of this cake wafting from the oven as it bakes is almost as good as the taste. The brown sugar and butter caramelise to give it a sweet, moist banana topping. If you like a bit of spice, replace the vanilla with a teaspoon of ground cinnamon or mixed spice. Serve warm with thick cream for dessert, or at room temperature for an afternoon treat.

1 Preheat the oven to 180°C (Gas Mark 4). Grease a 20 cm round cake tin and line the base with baking paper.

2 To make the topping, melt the butter in a saucepan, add the brown sugar and cook, stirring, over low heat until the sugar has melted and started to bubble gently. Pour evenly over the base of the tin. Arrange the bananas, cut-side down, in a single layer over the caramel (so they look like the spokes of a wheel), covering most of the base.

3 Place the butter, sugar and vanilla in an electric mixer and mix on medium speed for 7–8 minutes or until pale and fluffy. Transfer the beaten egg to a jug. Reduce the speed of the mixer and, with the motor running, add the egg to the mixture, followed by an occasional spoonful of flour. Sift the baking powder, salt and remaining flour into the bowl and fold in using a large metal spoon. Fold in the mashed banana.

4 Spoon the batter over the top of the bananas and bake for 45–50 minutes or until firm to the touch. Cool in the tin for 10 minutes, then remove the outside of the tin and leave to cool on a wire rack. Serve warm or at room temperature. Store in an airtight container for up to 3 days.

'WHATEVER IS IN SEASON' UPSIDE-DOWN CAKE

PREPARATION TIME: 30 MINUTES

COOKING TIME: 50 MINUTES

SERVES 6-8

175 g unsalted butter, diced and softened at room temperature

175 g soft brown sugar

your choice of sliced fruit (see recipe introduction)

150 g caster sugar

1 teaspoon vanilla extract

2 large free-range eggs, lightly beaten

220 g plain flour

1½ teaspoons baking powder

pinch of salt

125 ml buttermilk (or regular milk soured with a squeeze of lemon juice)

I have successfully made this cake with most seasonal fruit: plums, apricots, pears, peaches, nectarines, pitted cherries and even orange segments. If using plums or apricots you will need about eight, cut into quarters, or three to four sliced pears, large peaches or nectarines. The most important thing is to make sure there is enough fruit to cover the base of the pan – I sometimes tuck raspberries or blackberries into any gaps between the fruit slices. If you want to make this in advance but still serve it warm, just leave it in the pan and rewarm it in a low oven before serving.

1 Preheat the oven to 180°C (Gas Mark 4).

2 Melt 50 g butter in a heavy-based 25 cm frying pan with an ovenproof handle (cast iron works well). Add the brown sugar and cook, stirring, over low heat until the sugar has melted and started to bubble gently. Set aside to cool slightly. Arrange the fruit over the caramelised sugar.

3 Place the sugar, vanilla and remaining butter in an electric mixer and mix on medium speed for 7-8 minutes or until pale and fluffy. Transfer the beaten egg to a jug. Reduce the speed of the mixer and, with the motor running, add the egg to the mixture, followed by an occasional spoonful of flour. Sift the baking powder, salt and half the remaining flour into the bowl and fold in using a large metal spoon. Fold in half the buttermilk. Repeat with the remaining flour and buttermilk, being careful not to overmix; fold just until the flour is incorporated into the batter.

4 Spoon dollops of the batter over the fruit and smooth the surface with the back of a spoon. Bake for 40-45 minutes or until firm to the touch. Remove from the oven and leave to sit for 20 minutes. Invert the cake onto a plate, being careful of any escaping hot syrup, and leave to cool slightly. Cut into wedges and serve warm. Store in an airtight container for up to 3 days.

FRUIT CAKES

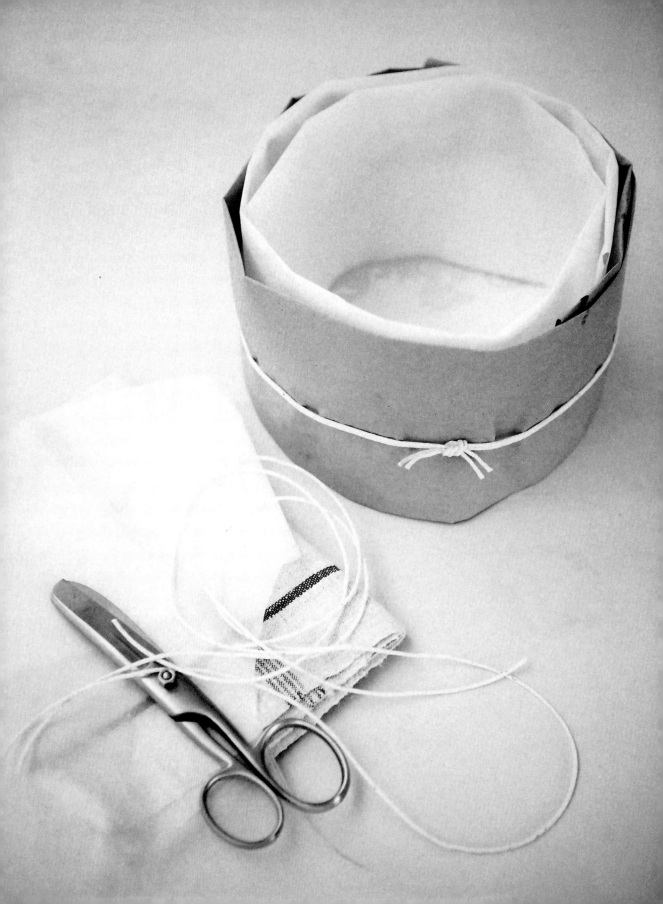

TIPS

1 As with most other cakes, it isn't easy to make a good fruit cake without scales - weighing the ingredients is more accurate than using cup measurements. Unless stated otherwise, spoon measures are based on level spoonfuls.

2 For best results, make sure the cake tin is the size specified in the recipe and check the oven temperature with a thermometer prior to baking.

3 The varieties of fruit can easily be adapted to suit individual tastes - if you prefer raisins to currants, or dried cherries to dates, then go ahead and use them. The important thing is that the total weight of fruit and nuts should be approximately the same as the weight given in the recipe. Always soak the fruit in alcohol overnight as this will plump it up, adding to the moisture of the cake.

4 Before baking, push any exposed fruit below the surface of the batter, otherwise it will burn.

5 Generally speaking, fruit cakes cook for a longer time than most butter cakes so it is important to line the tins correctly. In addition, I often wrap the outside of the tin with a couple of layers of baking or brown paper to prevent the cake from burning.

6 The cooking times given in the recipes are only a guide as every oven is different. Your first clue that a fruit cake is ready is that it smells fantastic. It will be lightly coloured and firm to the touch - a wooden skewer inserted in the centre should come out clean. If you find the cake is browning too fast, place a sheet of foil loosely on top for the remainder of the baking time.

7 Once the cake is baked, leave it to cool overnight and then wrap it in baking paper and foil. Store it in a cool, dry place until you are ready to decorate the cake.

8 The best fruit cakes are matured for at least a month and 'fed' from time to time with alcohol. To do this, every week or so insert a skewer in the base of the cake about 10 times and then feed a tablespoon or two of brandy, rum or sherry into each small hole. Wrap well after feeding.

BOILED FRUIT CAKE

PREPARATION TIME: 35 MINUTES,
PLUS COOLING TIME

COOKING TIME: 2¾ HOURS

SERVES 20

250 g unsalted butter, diced

200 g soft brown sugar

125 ml brandy

125 ml water

1 kg mixed dried fruit

100 g mixed peel

100 g red or green glacé cherries,
halved

5 free-range eggs, lightly beaten

2 tablespoons treacle

2 teaspoons finely grated lemon zest

2 tablespoons finely grated orange zest

250 g plain flour

70 g self-raising flour

1 teaspoon bicarbonate of soda

pinch of salt

1½ teaspoons mixed spice

150 g blanched almonds

This recipe first appeared in *The Perfect Cookbook* and I give it again as it is such a versatile and much-loved recipe. It's the cake I make as a gift or for a festive occasion, especially when I want something that is very moist and will keep well. I usually make the cake in two stages: boiling the fruit on the first day and then mixing the ingredients and baking the cake on the second day. Vary the selection of dried fruit to suit your tastes: a good basic combination is 375 g chopped raisins, 250 g sultanas, 250 g currants and 125 g chopped mixed dates, figs and prunes. But keep a look out for other types of dried fruit, such as dried cherries, blackberries or cranberries, to add a little variety to the mixture.

1 Place the butter, brown sugar, brandy, water, dried fruit, mixed peel and glacé cherries in a large saucepan. Cook, stirring frequently, over medium heat until the mixture comes to the boil. Reduce the heat to low and simmer, stirring, for 10 minutes. Set aside to cool completely.

2 Preheat the oven to 150°C (Gas Mark 2). Grease a 23 cm round cake tin. Line the base and sides with a double layer of baking paper, extending the paper 5 cm above the tin.

3 Transfer the cooled fruit mixture to a large mixing bowl. Add the egg, treacle and lemon and orange zest and mix well with a wooden spoon. Sift the flours, bicarbonate of soda, salt and mixed spice into the bowl and mix until well combined. Roughly chop half the almonds and stir these into the mixture.

4 Spoon the batter into the tin. Decorate the top with the remaining whole almonds. Wrap the outside of the cake tin in a double or triple layer of brown paper, extending the paper 5 cm above the cake tin to match the baking paper. Tie the paper securely with string.

5 Bake for 1 hour. Cover the top of the cake with baking paper and cook for a further 1–1½ hours or until the cake is firm to the touch and a skewer inserted in the centre comes out clean. Allow to cool in the tin. Remove from the tin, then wrap in foil and store for up to 3 months in an airtight container in a cool, dark place.

GLACÉ FRUIT CAKE

PREPARATION TIME: 25 MINUTES

COOKING TIME: 1¾ HOURS

SERVES 12

100 g seedless golden raisins

100 g dried tropical fruit

175 g glacé pineapple

175 g glacé red cherries

150 g glacé green cherries

100 g brazil nuts

50 g blanched almonds

50 g macadamias

2 teaspoons finely grated lemon zest

50 g caster sugar

3 tablespoons plain flour

1 tablespoon self-raising flour

2 free-range eggs, lightly beaten

40 g unsalted butter, melted

This cake is also known as 'stained-glass-window cake' as it is full of large pieces red, green and yellow fruit - colours often seen in a stained-glass window. There is just enough cake batter to hold the fruit in place as it cooks, giving a lovely translucent effect when the cake is cut into slices and served.

1 Preheat the oven to 150ºC (Gas Mark 2). Grease a 21 cm × 5 cm × 7 cm loaf tin and line the base with baking paper.

2 Place all the fruit and nuts in a large bowl, add the lemon zest and mix together well. Combine the sugar and flours and sift into the bowl. Mix well, then add the egg and butter, stirring to combine.

3 Spoon the batter into the tin and smooth the top. It helps if you add the batter bit by bit, pressing down as you go - this is to avoid any air pockets (which will spoil the stained-glass effect of the sliced cake).

4 Bake for 1½-1¾ hours or until a skewer inserted in the centre of the cake comes out clean. (You may need to insert the skewer several times to make sure as fruit can stick to it and be mistaken for uncooked cake batter.) Allow to cool in the tin. Remove from the tin, then wrap in foil and baking paper and store for up to 2 weeks in an airtight container in a cool, dark place.

MINCEMEAT CAKE

PREPARATION TIME: 15 MINUTES

COOKING TIME: 55 MINUTES

SERVES 10-12

175 g self-raising flour, sifted

pinch of salt

150 g soft brown sugar

100 g unsalted butter, diced and softened at room temperature

100 ml milk

200 g mincemeat

2 free-range eggs, lightly beaten

finely grated zest of 1 orange

icing sugar, for dusting (optional)

CRUMBLE TOPPING

200 g mincemeat

50 g demerara or raw sugar

3 tablespoons pine nuts

2 tablespoons plain flour

This dark and fruity cake with a crumble topping is so simple to make – it falls into that stress-free 'all in one bowl' category of baking. Rather than weighing out various types of dried fruit, one jar of good-quality mincemeat is all that is needed. In fact, this is a perfect way to use any leftover mincemeat you may have lurking in your pantry at Christmas time. It is important to be gentle with the cake when removing it from the oven and adding the topping, so I usually place the cake tin on a baking sheet before putting it in the oven – it makes transporting the cake to and from the oven much easier.

1 Preheat the oven to 170°C (Gas Mark 3). Grease a 21 cm round cake tin and line the base with baking paper.

2 Place all the cake ingredients in a large bowl and mix with a wooden spoon until combined. Spoon into the tin and bake for 30 minutes.

3 Meanwhile, to make the topping, combine all the ingredients in a bowl.

4 Carefully remove the cake from the oven and gently spoon over the topping (don't go all the way to the edges) – take care with this as you don't want the topping to sink into the cake. Return to the oven and bake for a further 20-25 minutes or until a skewer inserted in the centre comes out clean. Cover the cake loosely with foil or baking paper for the last 10 minutes of cooking to prevent it from colouring too much.

5 Cool the cake in the tin for about 15 minutes, then turn out onto a wire rack to cool completely. Dust with icing sugar, if liked. The cake will keep in the fridge for up to 4 days.

CHOCOLATE FRUIT CAKE

PREPARATION TIME: 35 MINUTES,
PLUS COOLING TIME

COOKING TIME: 2 HOURS 40 MINUTES

SERVES 20

350 g sultanas

100 g dried cherries, roughly chopped

100 g dried blueberries

175 g glacé cherries, halved

175 g dark chocolate chips

200 g unsalted butter, diced

125 g soft brown sugar

150 ml sweet sherry

4 large free-range eggs, lightly beaten

finely grated zest of 1 orange

175 g dark chocolate chips, extra

200 g plain flour

2 tablespoons self-raising flour

½ teaspoon bicarbonate of soda

pinch of salt

This cake is based on one that was served when a friend of mine married into a large Italian family. The wedding was great fun, but the memory I took with me was of this delicious fruit cake full of chocolate chips. The Italian cook wouldn't part with her secret recipe, but after much trial and error I've come up with my own version, which comes pretty close. It may be iced with white icing like a classic wedding cake, if desired (see page 314). You can make the cake in two stages: boiling the fruit, sugar, sherry, chocolate and butter on the first day, and then mixing the ingredients and baking the cake on the second day.

1 Place all the dried fruit in a large saucepan. Add the chocolate, butter, brown sugar and sherry and heat over low heat, stirring occasionally, until the chocolate and butter have melted. Increase the heat and bring to a boil, then reduce the heat and simmer gently for 5 minutes. Set aside to cool completely.

2 Preheat the oven to 150°C (Gas Mark 2). Grease a 20 cm square cake tin. Line the base and sides with a double layer of baking paper, extending the paper 5 cm above the tin.

3 Transfer the cooled fruit mixture to a large mixing bowl. Add the egg, orange zest and extra chocolate chips and mix well with a wooden spoon. Sift the flours, bicarbonate of soda and salt into the bowl and mix until well combined.

4 Spoon the batter into the tin. Wrap the outside of the tin in a double or triple layer of brown paper, extending the paper 5 cm above the tin to match the baking paper. Tie the paper securely with string.

5 Bake for 1 hour. Cover the top of cake with baking paper and cook for a further 1–1½ hours or until the cake is firm to the touch and a skewer inserted in the centre comes out clean. Allow to cool in the tin. Remove from the tin, then wrap in foil and store for up to 3 months in an airtight container in a cool, dark place.

CLASSIC RICH FRUIT CAKE

PREPARATION TIME: 35 MINUTES,
PLUS SOAKING TIME

COOKING TIME: 2½ HOURS

SERVES 20

750 g dried mixed fruit

100 g mixed peel

100 g glacé cherries, halved

3 tablespoons brandy

250 g unsalted butter, diced and
softened at room temperature

250 g dark brown sugar

finely grated zest of 1 orange

finely grated zest of 1 lemon

4 free-range eggs, lightly beaten

250 g plain flour, sifted

½ teaspoon mixed spice

½ teaspoon ground nutmeg

½ teaspoon ground ginger

pinch of salt

50 g toasted flaked almonds

This heavily fruited cake is the perfect choice for Christmas or for a classic wedding cake. It can be made well before the event and decorated just before you are ready to serve. For the traditional marzipan and white icing treatment, see page 314. I usually use a mixture of 250 g sultanas, 250 g currants and 250 g other mixed dried fruit such as chopped dates, figs or prunes. Use walnuts instead of the almonds, if desired.

1 Place the dried fruit, mixed peel and glacé cherries in a bowl and pour over the brandy. Leave to soak for 6 hours or overnight.

2 Preheat the oven to 150ºC (Gas Mark 2). Grease a 20 cm round cake tin (or an 18 cm square cake tin). Line the base and sides with a double layer of baking paper, extending the paper 5 cm above the tin.

3 Place the butter, sugar and orange and lemon zest in an electric mixer and mix on medium speed for 7–8 minutes or until pale and fluffy. Transfer the beaten egg to a jug. Reduce the speed of the mixer and, with the motor running, add the egg to the mixture, followed by an occasional spoonful of flour. Using a large metal spoon, fold in the mixed spice, nutmeg, ginger, salt and remaining flour alternately with the soaked fruit and brandy and flaked almonds.

4 Spoon the batter into the cake tin. Wrap the outside of the tin in a double or triple layer of brown paper, extending the paper 5 cm above the cake tin to match the baking paper. Tie the paper securely with string.

5 Bake for 1 hour. Cover the top of cake with baking paper and cook for a further 1–1½ hours or until the cake is firm to the touch and a skewer inserted in the centre comes out clean. Allow to cool in the tin. Remove from the tin, then wrap in foil and store for up to 3 months in an airtight container in a cool, dark place.

FRUITY CHOCOLATE TEA BREAD

PREPARATION TIME: 30 MINUTES

COOKING TIME: 1 HOUR

SERVES 8

50 g dark chocolate, broken into pieces

250 g self-raising flour

pinch of salt

125 g unsalted butter, chilled and diced

125 g caster sugar

50 g seedless raisins

50 g currants

50 g chopped mixed peel

2 free-range eggs, lightly beaten

3-4 tablespoons milk

I love the simplicity of tea bread - a no-nonsense loaf that keeps well and is delicious served simply with butter and freshly brewed tea. This one contains the classic combination of raisins, currants and peel, but I have also added melted chocolate to give an interesting depth of flavour.

1 Preheat the oven to 180°C (Gas Mark 4). Grease a 20 cm × 8.5 cm loaf tin and line the base with baking paper.

2 Melt the chocolate in a bowl set over a saucepan of barely simmering water, stirring occasionally (make sure the bowl doesn't touch the water). Remove from the heat and leave to cool for about 10 minutes.

3 Sift the flour and salt into a large bowl. With your fingertips, rub the butter into the flour until the mixture resembles breadcrumbs. Stir in the sugar, raisins, currants and mixed peel. Add the egg and melted chocolate and mix well, adding enough milk to give the batter a dropping consistency.

4 Spoon the batter into the tin and bake for about 1 hour or until golden. A skewer inserted in the centre should come out clean. Cool in the tin for 5 minutes, then turn out onto a wire rack to cool completely. Store in an airtight container for up to 7 days.

CHERRY, GINGER AND PISTACHIO CAKE

PREPARATION TIME: 25 MINUTES,
PLUS SOAKING TIME

COOKING TIME: 1 HOUR

SERVES 10

100 g dried cherries, coarsely chopped

100 g glacé cherries, halved

4 tablespoons Grand Marnier or brandy

150 g unsalted butter, diced and
softened at room temperature

150 g dark brown sugar

finely grated zest of 1 orange

2 large free-range eggs, lightly beaten

125 g plain flour, sifted

100 g self-raising flour, sifted

1 teaspoon bicarbonate of soda

pinch of salt

4 tablespoons golden syrup

5 pieces stem ginger (preserved
in syrup), chopped

50 g unsalted pistachio kernels

100 ml milk

Since dried cherries appeared on the market a few years ago I've been including them in various fruit cakes as they add an interesting flavour and texture. In this recipe I have left out traditional mixed dried fruit altogether and replaced it with dried and glacé cherries and preserved ginger. I've made it in a loaf tin here, but you could also use a ring tin (a tin with a hollow centre), which allows the cake to cook a little more quickly and also gives a nice shape for icing and decorating. Serve it as a tea cake or dress it up as a nice alternative to Christmas cake.

1 Place the dried and glacé cherries in a bowl and pour over the Grand Marnier or brandy. Leave to soak for 6 hours or overnight.

2 Preheat the oven to 160°C (Gas Mark 2-3). Grease a 23 cm × 7 cm × 7 cm loaf tin and dust the inside with flour. Tap the tin to coat with the flour, then discard any excess.

3 Place the butter, sugar and orange zest in an electric mixer and mix on medium speed for 7-8 minutes or until pale and fluffy. Transfer the beaten egg to a jug. Reduce the speed of the mixer and, with the motor running, add the egg to the mixture, followed by an occasional spoonful of flour. Using a large metal spoon, fold in the bicarbonate of soda, salt and remaining flours alternately with the soaked fruit and soaking liquid, golden syrup, ginger, pistachios and milk.

4 Spoon the batter into the tin and bake for 50-60 minutes or until it springs back when lightly touched. Cool in the tin for about 10 minutes, then turn out onto a wire cake rack to cool completely. The cake will keep in the fridge for up to 7 days.

SOUTHERN HEMISPHERE FRUIT CAKE

PREPARATION TIME: 25 MINUTES

COOKING TIME: 1 HOUR 20 MINUTES

SERVES 12

250 g unsalted butter, diced and softened at room temperature

250 g soft brown sugar

finely grated zest of 1 orange

finely grated zest of 1 lemon

2 free-range eggs, lightly beaten

200 g self-raising flour, sifted

2 tablespoons lemon juice

2 tablespoons orange juice

50 g ground almonds

pinch of salt

175 g dried tropical fruit, chopped

With an abundance of all sorts of beautiful dried tropical fruit available in most supermarkets, I thought it was time to create a fruit cake featuring these great flavours. Choose from dried mango, pineapple, papaya, dragonfruit or guava, or use a combination.

1 Preheat the oven to 170°C (Gas Mark 3). Grease a 20 cm springform tin and line the base with baking paper.

2 Place the butter, sugar and orange and lemon zest in an electric mixer and mix on medium speed for 7–8 minutes or until pale and fluffy. Transfer the beaten egg to a jug. Reduce the speed of the mixer and, with the motor running, add the egg to the mixture, followed by an occasional spoonful of flour. Gently fold in the lemon and orange juice, ground almonds, salt and remaining flour with a large metal spoon, then fold in the fruit.

3 Spoon the batter into the tin and bake for about 1 hour 20 minutes or until golden and firm to the touch. Cool in the tin for about 10 minutes, then turn out onto a wire cake rack to cool completely. The cake will keep in the fridge for up to 10 days.

FRUIT AND NUT LOAF

PREPARATION TIME: 30 MINUTES

COOKING TIME: 1 HOUR

SERVES 10-12

175 g unsalted butter, diced and softened at room temperature

250 g caster sugar (or brown sugar if you prefer a darker cake)

juice and finely grated zest of 1 small orange

4 free-range eggs, lightly beaten

250 g plain flour

½ teaspoon baking powder

pinch of salt

100 g dried apricots, chopped

75 g dried figs, chopped

75 g fresh or dried dates, pitted and chopped

50 g toasted hazelnuts, roughly chopped

50 g toasted pecans, roughly chopped

1 teaspoon vanilla extract

Roughly chopped nuts add a wonderful flavour and texture to this cake. Mixing the fruit and nuts with the flour helps to stop them sinking to the bottom of the cake during cooking. If you want to decorate the cake, arrange some whole pecans or almonds on top of the batter before baking, then brush with warmed apricot jam or marmalade after removing the cake from the oven.

1 Preheat the oven to 170°C (Gas Mark 3). Grease a 23 cm × 12 cm loaf tin and line the base with baking paper.

2 Place the butter, sugar and orange zest in an electric mixer and mix on medium speed for 7-8 minutes or until pale and fluffy. Transfer the beaten egg to a jug. Reduce the speed of the mixer and, with the motor running, add the egg to the mixture, followed by an occasional spoonful of flour.

3 Sift the baking powder, salt and remaining flour into a bowl and stir in the fruit and nuts until coated in the flour. Gently fold the fruit and flour mixture, orange juice and vanilla into the butter mixture with a large metal spoon.

4 Spoon the batter into the tin and bake for about 1 hour or until golden and firm to the touch. Cool in the tin for 10 minutes, then turn out onto a wire cake rack to cool completely. The cake will keep in an airtight container for up to 7 days.

EARL GREY FRUIT LOAF

PREPARATION TIME: 20 MINUTES,
PLUS SOAKING TIME

COOKING TIME: 1½ HOURS

SERVES 10–12

250 g currants

250 g sultanas

1 earl grey tea bag

375 ml boiling water

500 g self-raising flour

1 teaspoon baking powder

1 teaspoon mixed spice

finely grated zest of 1 lemon

250 g soft brown sugar

1 large free-range egg, lightly beaten

This is one of those uncomplicated, old-fashioned loaf cakes that was once found in many cafes, but is rarely seen these days. Using earl grey tea to soak the fruit infuses the cake with an interesting flavour – the longer the fruit soaks the better, so start this the night before you want to bake the cake. It is also low in fat as there is no oil or butter in the recipe. Good served warm or cold with butter and a cup of tea or coffee.

1 Place the fruit in a large heatproof bowl. Make a pot of earl grey tea using the tea bag and boiling water. Let it steep for about 2 minutes, then remove the tea bag and pour the hot tea over the fruit. Leave to soak for 8 hours or overnight.

2 Preheat the oven to 170°C (Gas Mark 3). Grease a 23 cm × 12 cm loaf tin and line the base with baking paper.

3 Sift the flour, baking powder and mixed spice into a large bowl and stir in the lemon zest and brown sugar. Add the beaten egg and cold tea and fruit and mix until well combined.

4 Spoon the batter into the tin and bake for 1½ hours or until golden. Cover the cake loosely with foil or baking paper for the last 15 minutes to prevent it colouring too much. Cool in the tin for about 10 minutes, then turn out onto a wire cake rack to cool completely. Because there is so little fat in this cake, it needs to be wrapped well in plastic film and foil if you are going to store it. It will keep for about 4 days.

CHOCOLATE CAKES AND BROWNIES

TIPS

1 When buying chocolate for use in cooking, read the list of ingredients and check the percentage of cocoa solids, which is basically all the bits that are from the cocoa pod rather than the additives such as sugar, milk, lecithin, vanilla and so on. Look for a minimum of 35% cocoa solids.

....

2 Be guided by what you're making and the amount of chocolate specified in the recipe. For simple chocolate cakes I use a dark chocolate with about 35% cocoa solids. For rich brownies, where you want a more intense chocolate flavour, I use a chocolate with 50-70% cocoa solids. The higher the percentage of cocoa solids, the less sweet the chocolate.

....

3 Avoid storing chocolate in the fridge; a cool, dark cupboard is a better option. Sometimes after being stored for a length of time or being kept in the fridge, chocolate may develop a white surface which simply means the cocoa butter has separated. This is nothing to worry about and the chocolate is still good for cooking.

....

4 When you are melting chocolate, use gentle heat and don't let any water or steam come into contact with it. Chocolate doesn't like to be overheated so it should never be melted over direct heat, except when it is combined with other ingredients. The best method is to break the chocolate into small pieces or chop it using a large clean sharp knife. Place the chopped chocolate in a clean heatproof bowl and set it over a saucepan of very hot water (it should not be boiling - just barely simmering). The base of the bowl shouldn't touch the water. Stir the chocolate as it starts to melt. When melted and completely smooth, remove the bowl from the heat and set aside to cool slightly before using.

....

5 You can also melt chocolate in a microwave. Keep it on a low setting and just do a minute at a time so you can closely monitor its progress. Place equal-sized pieces of chocolate in a glass bowl, so you can keep an eye on it. For 50-125 grams of chocolate try 3-4 minutes; for anything over 125 grams try 5 minutes. The thing to watch out for is that the pieces will often keep their form and not look melted, even when they are. Check regularly by stirring, which is a good thing to do anyway.

....

6 Brownies freeze well, either cut into squares or as the whole piece - just make sure they have cooled completely before wrapping and freezing. For best results, take them out of the freezer several hours before you're planning to serve them and let them thaw out at room temperature.

....

CHOCOLATE FUDGE CAKE

PREPARATION TIME: 25 MINUTES

COOKING TIME: 1 HOUR

SERVES 10

100 g unsalted butter, diced and softened at room temperature

2 large free-range eggs, lightly beaten

250 g caster sugar

100 g dark chocolate, melted (see page 91)

280 g self-raising flour

1 teaspoon bicarbonate of soda

pinch of salt

2 tablespoons cocoa

250 ml milk

1 tablespoon lemon juice

CHOCOLATE GANACHE

100 g unsalted butter

250 g dark chocolate, chopped

Fudge cakes are often quite heavy in texture, but thanks to the self-raising flour and bicarbonate of soda, this cake does not fall into that category. It is delicious simply dusted with icing sugar, but when I'm in need of a big chocolate fix, I also love to cover it with chocolate ganache icing.

1 Preheat the oven to 180°C (Gas Mark 4). Grease a 20 cm springform tin and line the base with baking paper.

2 Combine the butter, egg, sugar and melted chocolate in a large bowl. Sift in the flour, bicarbonate of soda, salt and cocoa. Combine the milk and lemon juice in a jug (it should curdle slightly) and pour into the bowl. Beat with a wooden spoon or hand-held electric beaters for 1-2 minutes or until smooth.

3 Spoon the batter into the tin. Bake for 50-60 minutes or until firm in the centre. Cool in the tin for about 10 minutes, then turn out onto a wire rack to cool completely.

4 Once the cake is cool, make the ganache. Melt the butter and chocolate in a heatproof bowl set over a saucepan of barely simmering water, stirring occasionally (make sure the bowl doesn't touch the water). Cool for about 20 minutes or until the icing has thickened slightly. Spread the icing over the top and side of the cake. Store the cake in an airtight container for up to 5 days.

CHOCOLATE CHERRY CAKE

PREPARATION TIME: 45 MINUTES

COOKING TIME: 40 MINUTES

SERVES 10

675 g caster sugar

250 g unsalted butter, diced

40 g cocoa

1 teaspoon bicarbonate of soda

pinch of salt

500 ml boiling water

450 g self-raising flour, sifted

4 free-range eggs, lightly beaten

500 ml double cream, lightly whipped

500 g jar preserved pitted cherries, drained

10 chocolate truffles (optional)

CHOCOLATE ICING

400 g dark chocolate, chopped

350 g unsalted butter, diced and softened at room temperature

This tall layered cake is an updated version of a black forest cake. It takes a little assembling, but is great as a celebration cake or to serve as a special dessert. You can make the cake the day before if you like, and put it all together a couple of hours before serving. When assembling the cake, press down on the layers to help keep the cake steady. Use a warm knife (dip it in hot water and wipe dry) to cut the cake.

1 Preheat the oven to 180°C (Gas Mark 4). Grease three 18 cm sandwich tins and line the bases with baking paper.

2 Place the sugar, butter, cocoa, bicarbonate of soda, salt and boiling water in a large saucepan. Place over low heat and bring to the boil, stirring to dissolve the sugar. Set aside to cool for 20 minutes.

3 Transfer the chocolate mixture to a large bowl and add the flour and egg, beating until smooth. Spoon the batter into the tins and bake for 30-40 minutes or until firm to the touch. Cool in the tins for 10 minutes, then turn out onto a wire rack to cool completely.

4 To make the chocolate icing, place the chocolate in a heatproof bowl set over a saucepan of barely simmering water (make sure the bowl doesn't touch the water), stirring until melted. Using hand-held electric beaters, beat the butter in a separate bowl until pale and creamy, then beat in the warm melted chocolate until glossy and smooth. Set aside.

5 To assemble the cake, place one cake on a serving plate and top with half the whipped cream and half the cherries. Repeat with another cake and the remaining cream and cherries. Place the final cake on top. Using a flat-bladed knife, spread the chocolate icing over the side and top of the cake. Decorate with chocolate truffles, if liked. The cake will keep in the fridge for 3 days.

SIMPLE CHOCOLATE LAYER CAKE

PREPARATION TIME: 25 MINUTES

COOKING TIME: 25 MINUTES

SERVES 8

250 g unsalted butter, diced and softened at room temperature

250 g caster sugar

4 free-range eggs, lightly beaten

250 g plain flour

3 tablespoons cocoa

pinch of salt

CHOCOLATE FILLING

250 g icing sugar

3 tablespoons cocoa

120 g unsalted butter, diced and softened at room temperature

1 teaspoon hot water, if needed

This delicious cake is made like a pound cake and has a nice crumb similar to a classic butter cake. It is made with cocoa, rather than melted chocolate, which gives the cake a good rich flavour – perfect for birthday parties and other celebrations.

1 Preheat the oven to 170°C (Gas Mark 3). Grease two 20 cm sandwich tins and line the bases with baking paper.

2 Place the butter and sugar in an electric mixer and mix on medium speed for 7–8 minutes or until pale and fluffy. Transfer the beaten egg to a jug. Reduce the speed of the mixer and, with the motor running, add the egg to the mixture, followed by an occasional spoonful of flour. Sift the remaining flour, cocoa and salt onto the mixture and fold in gently with a large metal spoon.

3 Spoon the batter into the tins and level the surface. Bake for about 25 minutes or until firm to the touch. A skewer inserted in the centre should come out clean. Cool in the tins for 5 minutes, then turn out onto a wire rack to cool completely.

4 To make the filling, sift the icing sugar and cocoa into a bowl. Add the butter and beat until smooth with a wooden spoon. Add the hot water if needed – the mixture should be thick but easily spreadable. Use about two-thirds of the filling to sandwich the cakes together and spread the rest over the top. Store the cake in an airtight container for up to 5 days.

CHOCOLATE PEANUT BUTTER CAKE

PREPARATION TIME: 25 MINUTES

COOKING TIME: 1¼ HOURS

SERVES 12-14

125 g dark chocolate (at least 70% cocoa solids), broken into pieces

225 g jar crunchy peanut butter

250 g unsalted butter, diced and softened at room temperature

500 g soft brown sugar

250 g plain flour

2 teaspoons baking powder

pinch of salt

5 large free-range eggs

125 ml milk

PEANUT BUTTER ICING

25 g unsalted butter

2 tablespoons smooth peanut butter

3 tablespoons pure maple syrup

175 g dark chocolate (at least 70% cocoa solids), broken into pieces

2 tablespoons hot water

The combination of peanut butter and chocolate is too good to resist. Be warned: this cake is quite rich and not one for the calorie counters - but as with all good things, a little bit won't hurt too much. This recipe is a simplified version of a cake in *The Ultimate Encyclopedia of Chocolate* by Christine McFadden. I have used crunchy peanut butter as I like the nutty texture it brings, but you can use smooth if you prefer. Leave out the icing if you like and just serve the cake with a dusting of icing sugar.

1 Preheat the oven to 170°C (Gas Mark 3). Grease a large ring tin or better still, a kugelhopf or savarin tin, with a capacity of at least 2.6 litres.

2 Place the chocolate in a heatproof bowl set over a saucepan of barely simmering water (make sure the bowl doesn't touch the water) until melted.

3 Meanwhile, place the peanut butter, butter and sugar in an electric mixer and mix on medium speed for 7-8 minutes or until pale and fluffy. Sift in the flour, baking powder and salt and continue to beat slowly while adding the combined eggs and milk. When well mixed, add the melted chocolate and beat until smooth.

4 Spoon the batter into the tin and bake for 60-70 minutes or until firm and springs back when touched. Cover the cake with a piece of foil after about 45 minutes to stop it browning too much. Cool in the tin for 15 minutes, then turn out onto a wire rack to cool completely.

5 To make the icing, combine all the ingredients in a small saucepan over low heat and whisk until melted and smooth. Cool until it is barely liquid, then pour over the cake. Store the cake in an airtight container for up to 5 days.

CHOCOLATE BEETROOT CAKE

PREPARATION TIME: 40 MINUTES

COOKING TIME: 1 HOUR 10 MINUTES

SERVES 8

2 large beetroots, trimmed

50 g cocoa

200 g plain flour

1½ teaspoons baking powder

pinch of salt

300 g caster sugar

250 ml corn or vegetable oil

1 teaspoon vanilla extract

3 free-range eggs, lightly beaten

2 tablespoons finely chopped walnuts

icing sugar, for dusting

This unusual cake became a firm favourite from the very first time I made it. The idea of adding beetroot to a chocolate cake came from a newspaper article by Jill Dupleix that I cut out a few years ago. It gives the cake plenty of moisture and an interesting texture.

1 Cook the whole unpeeled beetroots in a large saucepan of boiling salted water for about 20 minutes or until tender. Drain and, when cool enough to handle, slip off their skins. Chop into smaller pieces and either mash well or purée in a food processor - you should have about 250 ml of purée.

2 Preheat the oven to 190°C (Gas Mark 5). Grease and flour an 18 cm *deep* round cake tin.

3 Sift the cocoa, flour, baking powder and salt into a large bowl, then mix in the sugar.

4 Add the oil, vanilla, egg, walnuts and beetroot puree and stir well - the mixture will become a glorious purple colour.

5 Pour the batter into the tin and bake for 50 minutes or until a skewer inserted in the centre comes out clean. Cool in the tin for 15 minutes, then turn out onto a wire rack to cool completely. Dust with icing sugar to serve. Store the cake in an airtight container for up to 5 days.

NB. don't use a loose bottomed cake tin – it'll seep out & make a mess of the oven!

CHOCOLATE AND ALMOND TORTE

PREPARATION TIME: 20 MINUTES

COOKING TIME: 45 MINUTES

SERVES 10-12

400 g dark chocolate, broken into pieces

250 g unsalted butter, diced

6 free-range eggs

400 g caster sugar

pinch of salt

100 g ground almonds

cocoa, for dusting (optional)

cream or ice-cream, to serve (optional)

This gluten-free cake is so rich and dense it is more of a dessert than a cake. All it needs is a dusting of cocoa or icing sugar before serving with cream or ice-cream.

1 Preheat the oven to 180°C (Gas Mark 4). Grease a 23 cm springform tin and line the base with baking paper.

2 Place the chocolate and butter in a heatproof bowl set over a saucepan of barely simmering water (make sure the bowl doesn't touch the water) until melted. Remove from the heat and leave to cool for about 10 minutes.

3 Place the eggs, sugar and salt in an electric mixer and mix on medium speed for 7-8 minutes or until thick and pale. Add the melted chocolate and then the ground almonds and fold in with a large metal spoon.

4 Spoon the batter into the tin and bake for 45 minutes - the middle of the cake will still be a little soft, but that's fine. Leave to cool in the tin (it will sink while cooling). Dust with cocoa (if using) and serve slightly chilled with cream or ice-cream, if liked. Wrap the cake well in plastic film and store in the fridge for up to 3 days.

ALAPHIA'S CHOCOLATE CAKE

PREPARATION TIME: 20 MINUTES

COOKING TIME: 50 MINUTES

SERVES 10

300 g dark chocolate, broken into pieces

250 g unsalted butter, diced

5 free-range eggs, separated

120 g caster sugar

50 g plain flour, sifted

pinch of salt

1 teaspoon baking powder

icing sugar, for dusting

During a working holiday to London in 1989, I helped out in the kitchen at 'Books for Cooks', a wonderful specialist cookbook shop and cafe in Notting Hill. Often wafting through the shelves was the smell of freshly baked cakes and biscuits. The kitchen was run by the very talented Alaphia Bidwell, and this simple, almost flourless, chocolate cake was one of her most popular creations.

1 Preheat the oven to 170°C (Gas Mark 3). Grease a 21 cm springform tin and line the base with baking paper.

2 Place the chocolate and butter in a heatproof bowl set over a saucepan of barely simmering water (make sure the bowl doesn't touch the water) until melted. Remove from the heat and leave to cool for about 10 minutes, then transfer to a large bowl.

3 Using hand-held electric beaters, beat the egg yolks into the chocolate mixture, followed by the caster sugar, flour, salt and baking powder.

4 In a clean bowl, using clean, dry beaters, whisk the egg whites until they form firm peaks. Carefully fold the egg whites into the chocolate mixture with a large metal spoon.

5 Pour the mixture into the tin and bake for 45-50 minutes or until firm to the touch. Cool completely in the tin, then dust with icing sugar before serving. Store the cake in an airtight container for up to 3 days.

RED VELVET CHOCOLATE CAKE

PREPARATION TIME: 40 MINUTES

COOKING TIME: 25 MINUTES

SERVES 10

150 g unsalted butter, diced and softened at room temperature

300 g caster sugar

1 teaspoon vanilla extract

2 large free-range eggs, lightly beaten

270 g plain flour

30 g cocoa

pinch of salt

200 ml buttermilk (or regular milk soured with a squeeze of lemon juice)

½ teaspoon red food colour paste

1 tablespoon white wine vinegar

1 teaspoon bicarbonate of soda

WHITE CHOCOLATE ICING

350 g white chocolate, broken into pieces

250 g cream cheese

1 teaspoon vanilla extract

250 g unsalted butter, diced and softened at room temperature

Red velvet cake was a signature dessert at the Waldorf-Astoria Hotel in New York during the 1920s. According to an urban legend of the 1960s, a woman once asked for the recipe, and was billed a large amount for the privilege. Her indignant response was to spread the recipe in a chain letter! I use red food colour paste, rather than food colouring in bottles, as the paste is more concentrated and gives a better colour.

1 Preheat the oven to 180°C (Gas Mark 4). Grease three 20 cm sandwich tins and line the bases with baking paper.

2 Place the butter, sugar and vanilla in an electric mixer and mix on medium speed for 7–8 minutes or until pale and fluffy. Transfer the beaten egg to a jug. Reduce the speed of the mixer and, with the motor running, add the egg to the mixture, followed by an occasional spoonful of flour.

3 Sift the remaining flour, cocoa and salt into the mixture and fold in gently with a large metal spoon, alternating with the buttermilk until incorporated. Stir in the food colouring. Combine the vinegar and bicarbonate of soda until it fizzes, then stir into the batter.

4 Spoon the batter evenly into the three tins and level the surface. Bake for about 25 minutes or until firm to the touch. (I usually arrange two shelves in the oven, one just above and one below the centre, and place two cake tins on the top and one underneath. The cake on the bottom shelf may need an extra few minutes cooking.) A skewer inserted in the centre should come out clean. Cool in the tins for 10 minutes, then turn out onto a wire rack to cool completely.

5 To make the icing, place the chocolate in a heatproof bowl set over a saucepan of barely simmering water (make sure the bowl doesn't touch the water) until melted. Allow to cool until lukewarm. In a large bowl, beat the cream cheese and vanilla with hand-held electric beaters until pale and fluffy. Gradually beat in the melted chocolate and butter until the mixture is the consistency of whipped cream.

6 Once the cakes are completely cold, sandwich them together with half the icing. Spread the remaining icing over the top of the cake and around the side. The cake will keep in the fridge for 3 days.

FLUFFY AND MOIST CHOCOLATE CAKE

PREPARATION TIME: 20 MINUTES

COOKING TIME: 1 HOUR

SERVES 6–8

175 g plain flour

275 g caster sugar

75 g cocoa

1½ teaspoons baking powder

½ teaspoon bicarbonate of soda

pinch of salt

50 g tapioca flour

375 ml milk

100 g dark chocolate, broken into pieces

1 large free-range egg, plus 1 large yolk

75 ml sunflower oil

25 g treacle

squeeze of lemon juice

2 teaspoons vanilla extract

If you love the fluffy softness and long-lasting moist texture of a chocolate packet cake (but have now advanced to making your own from scratch), this is the recipe for you. It's all down to the tapioca flour, which swells with moisture when baked, leaving you with a delicate, moist crumb that stays soft for days. I read this recently on a torn-out piece of newspaper and was excited to try it for myself. This is my adapted version of that (sadly) unaccredited recipe. Tapioca flour is usually available from Asian food shops. If you can't find it, you can grind pearl tapioca or sago to a powder in an electric blender (100 grams at a time) and then sieve it. This cake is lovely finished with a simple chocolate icing

1 Preheat the oven to 180ºC (Gas Mark 4). Grease a 20 cm round cake tin and line the base with baking paper.

2 Sift the flour, sugar, cocoa, baking powder, bicarbonate of soda, salt and tapioca flour into a large mixing bowl.

3 Bring the milk to the boil in a small saucepan, then remove from the heat and add the chocolate, stirring until melted and smooth. Leave to cool. When cool, beat the egg and yolk, oil, treacle, lemon juice and vanilla into the chocolate and milk mixture.

4 Whisk the wet ingredients into the dry ingredients until well combined and smooth.

5 Pour the batter into the tin and bake for about 1 hour or until a skewer inserted in the centre comes out clean. Cool in the tin for 15 minutes, then turn out onto a wire rack to cool completely. Store the cake in an airtight container for up to 5 days.

CHOCOLATE MARBLE CAKE

PREPARATION TIME: 25 MINUTES

COOKING TIME: 50 MINUTES

SERVES 6-8

75 g dark chocolate, broken into pieces

200 g unsalted butter, softened
at room temperature

200 g caster sugar

½ teaspoon vanilla extract

3 large free-range eggs

220 g self-raising flour, sifted

pinch of salt

Marble cakes are always fun to make and eat due to their random pattern and flavour. After placing alternate spoonfuls of each coloured batter into the tin, run a flat knife in a figure of eight through the batter for a more interesting marbled effect.

1 Preheat the oven to 180°C (Gas Mark 4). Grease an 18 cm round cake tin and line the base with baking paper.

2 Place the chocolate in a heatproof bowl set over a saucepan of barely simmering water (make sure the bowl doesn't touch the water) until melted. Set aside to cool slightly while you make the batter.

3 Put the remaining ingredients in a large bowl and beat with a wooden spoon or hand-held electric beaters for 1 minute or until just combined. It's important not to beat the batter too much – just long enough to make it smooth. Transfer half the mixture to a separate bowl and beat in the melted chocolate.

4 Spoon alternate spoonfuls of the plain and chocolate batter into the tin, smooth the top and bake for about 45-50 minutes or until risen and golden. A skewer inserted in the centre should come out clean. Cool in the tin for 5 minutes, then turn out onto a wire rack to cool completely. Store the cake in an airtight container for up to 5 days.

CHOCOLATE CHIP ORANGE CAKE

PREPARATION TIME: 30 MINUTES

COOKING TIME: 1¼ HOURS

SERVES 8

175 g unsalted butter, diced and softened at room temperature

250 g caster sugar

finely grated zest of 1 orange

4 free-range eggs, lightly beaten

300 g plain flour

1 teaspoon baking powder

pinch of salt

100 g dark chocolate chips

DARK CHOCOLATE ICING

150 g dark chocolate, broken into pieces

3 tablespoons water

1 teaspoon canola or sunflower oil

2 tablespoons caster sugar

Chocolate and orange is a classic flavour combination and works well in this chocolate chip butter cake. The icing is simply poured over the top, giving the cake a delicious soft glaze. Don't use a dark chocolate with a high cocoa butter content for the icing as it may make it too bitter.

1 Preheat the oven to 180°C (Gas Mark 4). Grease an 18 cm round cake tin and line the base with baking paper.

2 Place the butter, sugar and orange zest in an electric mixer and mix on medium speed for 7-8 minutes or until pale and fluffy. Transfer the beaten egg to a jug. Reduce the speed of the mixer and, with the motor running, add the egg to the mixture, followed by an occasional spoonful of flour.

3 Sift the baking powder, salt and remaining flour into the mixture and fold in gently with a large metal spoon. Stir in the chocolate chips.

4 Spoon the batter into the tin and level the surface. Bake for 60-70 minutes or until firm to the touch. A skewer inserted in the centre should come out clean. Cool in the tin for 5 minutes, then turn out onto a wire rack to cool completely.

5 To make the icing, place all the ingredients in a small saucepan and heat very gently over low heat, stirring until smooth. Cool for 5 minutes, then carefully pour over the cake. Store the cake in an airtight container for up to 5 days.

CHOCOLATE PECAN SPONGE

PREPARATION TIME: 1 HOUR

COOKING TIME: 30 MINUTES

SERVES 8-10

200 g dark chocolate,
broken into pieces

200 g unsalted butter, diced

4 free-range eggs

150 g caster sugar

pinch of salt

125 g plain flour

1 heaped teaspoon baking powder

PECAN GANACHE

250 g dark chocolate,
broken into pieces

250 ml double cream

30 g unsalted butter, diced

100 g pecans, crushed

CHOCOLATE ICING

200 g dark chocolate, broken into pieces

125 g unsalted butter, diced

This is one of those great American-style chocolate layer cakes, so naturally it is completely 'over the top', with both a pecan ganache filling and a rich chocolate icing. It's the perfect party cake.

1 Preheat the oven to 180°C (Gas Mark 4). Grease a deep 20 cm round cake tin and line the base with baking paper.

2 Place the chocolate and butter in a heatproof bowl set over a saucepan of barely simmering water (make sure the bowl doesn't touch the water) until melted. Remove from the heat and leave to cool for about 10 minutes.

3 Using hand-held electric beaters, beat the eggs, sugar and salt for about 7 minutes or until thick and pale. Sift in the flour and baking powder and fold in gently with a large metal spoon. Add the melted chocolate and carefully fold through.

4 Pour the batter into the tin and bake for 25-30 minutes or until firm to the touch. A skewer inserted in the centre should come out clean. Cool in the tin for 10 minutes, then turn out onto a wire rack to cool completely. When cold, cut the cake horizontally into three layers.

5 To make the pecan ganache, place the chocolate, cream and butter in a small saucepan and heat over low heat. Mix well to melt and combine, then set aside to cool. Add the pecans and beat the mixture with a wooden spoon to lighten it. Sandwich the cake layers together with the pecan ganache.

6 To make the icing, place the chocolate and butter in a heatproof bowl set over a saucepan of barely simmering water (make sure the bowl doesn't touch the water) until melted. Whisk together until fluffy and smooth, then leave to cool and thicken slightly. Spread the icing over the top and side of the cake. The cake will keep in the fridge for 3 days.

CHOCOLATE MERINGUE MOUSSE CAKE

PREPARATION TIME: 50 MINUTES,
PLUS COOLING TIME

COOKING TIME: 50 MINUTES

SERVES 8-10

5 free-range eggs, separated

250 g caster sugar,
plus 3 tablespoons extra

3 tablespoons cocoa

200 g dark chocolate, roughly chopped

2 teaspoons instant coffee powder

1 tablespoon boiling water

600 ml double cream, lightly whipped

icing sugar or cocoa, for dusting

In this cake, thin layers of meringue are sandwiched together with a lovely mocha-flavoured mousse. The meringues can be made a day or two ahead, then wrapped in plastic film and stored until needed.

1 Preheat the oven to 150°C (Gas Mark 2). Line three baking sheets with baking paper, then mark a 22 cm circle on each bit of paper.

2 Using an electric mixer, whisk the egg whites until they form stiff peaks. Add the sugar, a tablespoon at a time, beating constantly after each addition, then keep whisking for a further 5-10 minutes or until the mixture is thick and glossy. Sift in the cocoa and gently fold in with a large metal spoon.

3 Divide the mixture into three even portions and thinly spread over the circles on the trays (they should have a thickness of about 1 cm).

4 Bake for 50 minutes or until pale and crisp (you may need to do this in two batches if your oven isn't big enough to fit all the trays at once). Turn off the oven, open the door and leave the meringues inside to cool completely.

5 To make the mousse, place the chocolate in a heatproof bowl set over a saucepan of barely simmering water (make sure the bowl doesn't touch the water) until melted. Allow to cool slightly, then gradually whisk in the egg yolks and extra caster sugar. Dissolve the coffee powder in the boiling water, add to the bowl and beat until smooth. Fold in the whipped cream with a large metal spoon until combined. Chill until you're ready to assemble the cake.

6 To assemble, place one round of meringue on a cake stand and spread with half the chilled mousse. Repeat with another meringue round and the remaining mousse. Place the final piece of meringue on top. Dust with a little icing sugar or cocoa before serving. The cake will keep in the fridge for up to 2 days.

SIMPLE STICKY CHOCOLATE LOAF CAKE

PREPARATION TIME: 20 MINUTES

COOKING TIME: 1 HOUR

SERVES 8

125 g unsalted butter

250 ml golden syrup

125 g plain flour

125 g self-raising flour

20 g cocoa

125 g caster sugar

pinch of salt

150 ml milk

1 large free-range egg

icing sugar, for dusting

The method for this cake is based on my ginger syrup cake recipe (see page 37), where the ingredients are simply combined - no beating necessary. The result is a lovely moist cake that will keep well for a few days - in fact, I think it is better the day after it is baked. It is important to grease and line the base of the tin as this cake batter is quite runny and has a tendency to stick.

1 Preheat the oven to 170°C (Gas Mark 3). Thoroughly grease a 21 cm × 11 cm loaf tin and line the base with baking paper.

2 Place the butter and golden syrup in a small saucepan over low heat and stir occasionally until melted and combined. Remove from the heat.

3 Sift the flour, cocoa, sugar and salt into a large bowl. Add the milk and egg and mix until smooth. Gradually add the melted butter mixture, stirring until well incorporated.

4 Pour the batter into the tin and bake for 45–55 minutes, or until risen and firm to the touch. A skewer inserted in the centre should come out clean. Cool in the tin for 5 minutes, then turn out onto a wire rack to cool completely. Dust with icing sugar and serve. Store the cake in an airtight container for up to 5 days.

CLASSIC FUDGE BROWNIES

PREPARATION TIME: 20 MINUTES

COOKING TIME: 40 MINUTES

MAKES 15-18

300 g dark chocolate, roughly chopped

300 g unsalted butter, diced

5 free-range eggs

400 g caster sugar

1 teaspoon vanilla extract

150 g plain flour

50 g cocoa

½ teaspoon baking powder

pinch of salt

100 g dark chocolate chips (_milk_)

icing sugar or cocoa, for dusting (optional)

Cherries 180g

Do you like your brownies fudgy and soft in the centre, or cake-like and full of nuts? There are probably more variations on the basic brownie than any other chocolate treat, but just so you know, these are definitely the gooey, fudgy version. Brownies need no decorating – I love them as they are or with a dusting of cocoa or icing sugar.

1 Preheat the oven to 180°C (Gas Mark 4). Grease a shallow 30 cm × 20 cm baking tin and line with baking paper (leave a little overhanging the two long sides to help remove the brownies from the tin).

2 Melt the chocolate and butter in a bowl set over a saucepan of barely simmering water, stirring occasionally until smooth (make sure the bowl doesn't touch the water). Allow to cool.

3 Place the eggs, sugar and vanilla in an electric mixer and beat for 3-4 minutes or until pale and fluffy. Beat in the cooled chocolate mixture. Sift in the flour, cocoa, baking powder and salt and fold in with a large metal spoon until smooth. Gently fold in the chocolate chips.

4 Spoon the mixture into the tin and smooth the surface. Bake for 35-40 minutes or until the top is dark brown and has formed a crust. It should be firm to the touch but still a bit fudgy. Allow to cool in the tin. Dust with icing sugar or cocoa (if using), then remove and cut into squares. Store in an airtight container for up to 2 days.

160° for 35 mins check after 30 mins

CHOCOLATE AND ORANGE BROWNIES WITH WHITE CHOCOLATE CHIPS

PREPARATION TIME: 20 MINUTES

COOKING TIME: 30 MINUTES

MAKES 15-18

250 g dark chocolate, roughly chopped

250 g unsalted butter, diced

4 large free-range eggs

300 g caster sugar

1 teaspoon vanilla extract

finely grated zest of 1 orange

2 tablespoons orange juice

150 g plain flour

1 teaspoon baking powder

pinch of salt

100 g white chocolate chips

This is a soft and chewy fudge-style brownie, flavoured with orange and chunks of white chocolate. Make sure you don't overcook them, or you will lose the wonderful gooey centre. When cooked, the brownies will have developed a delectable crust on the top.

1 Preheat the oven to 180°C (Gas Mark 4). Grease a shallow 30 cm × 20 cm baking tin and line with baking paper (leave a little overhanging the two long sides to help remove the brownies from the tin).

2 Melt the chocolate and butter in a bowl set over a saucepan of barely simmering water, stirring occasionally until smooth (make sure the bowl doesn't touch the water). Allow to cool.

3 Place the eggs, sugar, vanilla, orange zest and orange juice in an electric mixer and beat for 3-4 minutes or until pale and fluffy. Beat in the cooled chocolate mixture. Sift in the flour, baking powder and salt and mix until smooth. Gently fold in the white chocolate chips.

4 Spoon the mixture into the tin and smooth the surface. Bake for 25-30 minutes or until the top is dark brown and has formed a crust. It should be firm to the touch but still a bit fudgy (check by inserting a skewer in the middle - some of the chocolate centre should stick to it). Allow to cool in the tin, then remove and cut into squares. Store in an airtight container for up to 2 days.

ONE-BOWL NUTTY BROWNIES

PREPARATION TIME: 15 MINUTES

COOKING TIME: 30 MINUTES

MAKES 15-18

120 g self-raising flour

60 g cocoa

pinch of salt

250 g caster sugar

250 g unsalted butter, melted

4 free-range eggs, lightly beaten

1 teaspoon vanilla extract

250 g dark chocolate chips

125 g pecans or walnuts,
roughly chopped

icing sugar, for dusting

This one-bowl recipe is easy to make and results in a moist, cake-like brownie. The cocoa adds a deep chocolate flavour, which is enhanced by a generous serve of dark chocolate chips. Both pecans or walnuts work here, so use whichever you prefer. Keep the nuts coarsely chopped to add texture. If you have time, toast the whole nuts first to enhance their flavour – either in an 180°C (Gas Mark 4) oven for 5 minutes or in a frying pan over low heat, stirring until golden.

1 Preheat the oven to 180°C (Gas Mark 4). Grease a shallow 30 cm × 20 cm baking tin and line with baking paper (leave a little overhanging the two long sides to help remove the brownies from the tin).

2 Sift the flour, cocoa and salt into a large bowl and stir through the sugar. Add the butter, egg and vanilla and beat with a wooden spoon until smooth and combined. Stir in the chocolate chips and nuts.

3 Spoon the mixture into the tin and smooth the surface. Bake on the middle shelf of the oven for 25-30 minutes or until a skewer inserted in the centre comes out clean. Cool in the tin for 10 minutes, the carefully lift out onto a wire rack to cool completely. Cut into squares and dust with icing sugar before serving. Store in an airtight container for up to 3 days.

PECAN AND BANANA BROWNIES

PREPARATION TIME: 20 MINUTES

COOKING TIME: 30 MINUTES

MAKES 15-18

200 g dark chocolate, roughly chopped

200 g unsalted butter, diced

125 g self-raising flour

1 teaspoon baking powder

pinch of salt

300 g soft brown sugar

100 g pecans, toasted and
roughly chopped

2 ripe bananas, mashed with a fork

3 large free-range eggs, lightly beaten

drinking chocolate, for dusting

Bananas and brown sugar keep these nutty brownies nice and moist and add a lovely, almost caramel flavour. The riper the bananas the better. The simplest way to toast the pecans is by heating them in a dry frying pan, stirring occasionally until lightly coloured.

1 Preheat the oven to 180°C (Gas Mark 4). Grease a shallow 30 cm × 20 cm baking tin and line with baking paper (leave a little overhanging the two long sides to help remove the brownies from the tin).

2 Melt the chocolate and butter in a bowl set over a saucepan of barely simmering water, stirring occasionally until smooth (make sure the bowl doesn't touch the water). Remove from the heat.

3 Sift the flour, baking powder and salt into a bowl. Fold in the sugar, pecans, banana and egg, then pour in the warm butter and chocolate mixture. Mix until combined.

4 Spoon the mixture into the tin and smooth the surface. Bake for 25-30 minutes or until the top is dark brown and has formed a crust. It should be firm to the touch but still a bit fudgy. Allow to cool in the tin. Dust with drinking chocolate, then remove and cut into squares. Store in an airtight container for up to 3 days.

WHITE CHOCOLATE AND MACADAMIA BROWNIES

PREPARATION TIME: 20 MINUTES

COOKING TIME: 25 MINUTES

MAKES 15–18

150 g unsalted butter, diced

300 g white chocolate, roughly chopped

150 g caster sugar

3 large free-range eggs

1 teaspoon vanilla extract

80 g macadamias, roughly chopped

finely grated zest of 1 orange

1 tablespoon lemon juice

200 g self-raising flour, sifted

pinch of salt

These are often called blondies as they are made with white chocolate and have a golden colour when cooked. They have more of a cake-like texture than regular brownies.

1 Preheat the oven to 180°C (Gas Mark 4). Grease a shallow 30 cm × 20 cm baking tin and line with baking paper (leave a little overhanging the two long sides to help remove the brownies from the tin).

2 Melt the butter and 200 g of the chocolate in a large bowl set over a saucepan of barely simmering water, stirring occasionally until smooth (make sure the bowl doesn't touch the water). Remove from the heat. Stir in the sugar, then gradually beat in the eggs, one at a time, until combined. Add the remaining ingredients and mix with a wooden spoon until smooth and combined. Stir in the remaining white chocolate.

3 Spoon the mixture into the tin and smooth the surface. Bake on the middle shelf of the oven for 20–25 minutes or until slightly risen and the top is a pale golden colour. It should be firm to the touch but still a bit fudgy. Allow to cool in the tin, then remove and cut into squares. Store in an airtight container for up to 3 days.

TRIPLE CHOCOLATE BROWNIES

PREPARATION TIME: 20 MINUTES

COOKING TIME: 35 MINUTES

MAKES 15-18

250 g dark chocolate, roughly chopped

250 g unsalted butter, diced

4 free-range eggs

250 g caster sugar

1 teaspoon vanilla extract

150 g plain flour

1 tablespoon cocoa

½ teaspoon baking powder

pinch of salt

100 g milk chocolate chips

100 g white chocolate chips

These over-the-top fudgy brownies are made with melted dark chocolate and contain both milk and white chocolate chips – a chocolate lover's dream.

1 Preheat the oven to 180°C (Gas Mark 4). Grease a shallow 20 cm × 30 cm baking tin and line with baking paper (leave a little overhanging the two long sides to help remove the brownies from the tin).

2 Melt the chocolate and butter in a bowl set over a saucepan of barely simmering water, stirring occasionally until smooth (make sure the bowl doesn't touch the water). Allow to cool.

3 Place the eggs, sugar and vanilla in an electric mixer and beat for 3-4 minutes or until pale and fluffy. Beat in the cooled chocolate mixture. Sift in the flour, cocoa and salt and fold in with a large metal spoon until smooth. Gently fold in the chocolate chips.

4 Spoon the mixture into the tin and smooth the surface. Bake for 25-30 minutes or until the top is dark brown and has formed a crust. It should be firm to the touch but still a bit fudgy. Allow to cool in the tin, then remove and cut into squares. Store in an airtight container for up to 3 days.

SMALL CAKES

TIPS

1 Cupcakes, fairy cakes and friands are some of the easiest and cutest treats you can bake. For me, the appeal is that you can have an indulgent cake in miniature – all to yourself. The finishing touches can also be fun; they can be baked in colourful paper cases and then simply dusted with icing sugar, or finished with all sorts of rich icings and decorations.

2 Paper liners look pretty, and they are also inexpensive, easy to use and make for less washing up. If you are not using liners, you will need to butter and flour the individual holes of your tin.

3 Don't overmix the batter – too much beating will overwork the gluten in the mixture, resulting in a less tender cake.

4 Fill each little cake tin to two-thirds full; any more and it may rise too high or spill when baking.

5 Set a timer so you don't forget about your cakes. Bake for the minimum time suggested, then test them to see if they're done. They are ready when a fine skewer or toothpick inserted in the middle comes out clean and dry.

6 Let the cupcakes cool completely before you decorate them.

7 Fairy cakes and cupcakes are best eaten on the day they are made. Undecorated cakes can be frozen up to 3 months. Thaw at room temperature before icing or eating.

BASIC CUPCAKES

PREPARATION TIME: 15 MINUTES

COOKING TIME: 20 MINUTES

MAKES 12

200 g self-raising flour

pinch of salt

125 g unsalted butter, diced and softened at room temperature

185 g caster sugar

1 teaspoon vanilla extract

2 free-range eggs, lightly beaten

100 ml milk

This is my basic cupcake recipe. It couldn't be easier – you simply place all in the ingredients in a bowl and beat with a wooden spoon until combined.

1 Preheat the oven to 180°C (Gas Mark 4). Line a 12-hole cupcake tin with paper patty cases.

2 Sift the flour and salt into a large bowl. Add the remaining ingredients and beat with a wooden spoon or hand-held electric beaters on low speed for 2 minutes or until combined.

3 Spoon the batter evenly into the patty cases and bake for 15–20 minutes or until golden and firm to the touch. A skewer inserted in the centre should come out clean. Cool completely on a wire rack, then ice and decorate as desired. Store in an airtight container for up to 5 days.

TOPPING IDEAS
Lemon icing
Combine 150 g sifted icing sugar, 20 g softened unsalted butter and 1-2 tablespoons lemon juice. Beat until smooth and spread over the cooled cupcakes.

Strawberry icing
Mash 3-4 large ripe strawberries with a fork. Combine with 150 g sifted icing sugar and 1-2 drops pink food colouring (optional) and mix well (leaving the strawberries lumpy). Spread over the cupcakes.

PISTACHIO CUPCAKES

PREPARATION TIME: 20 MINUTES

COOKING TIME: 20 MINUTES

MAKES 12

50 g unsalted pistachio kernels

125 g unsalted butter, diced and softened at room temperature

125 g caster sugar

1 teaspoon vanilla extract

2 free-range eggs

125 g self-raising flour, sifted

pinch of salt

2 tablespoons milk

Ground pistachios give these cupcakes a lovely pale-green crumb and a sweet, nutty flavour. They are delicious simply dusted with icing sugar, but they also work well with a simple royal icing (see page 314). You'll only need half the quantity to ice these. Leave the icing as white or colour as desired (in this case, using a small amount of green food colouring to make a pale green colour) and top each with a pistachio nut.

1 Preheat the oven to 180°C (Gas Mark 4). Line a 12-hole cupcake tin with paper patty cases.

2 Place the pistachios in a food processor and pulse until ground.

3 Place the butter, sugar and vanilla in an electric mixer and beat on medium speed for 4-5 minutes or until light and well mixed. Add the eggs one at a time, beating well between additions. Add the flour, salt and ground nuts and gently fold through with a large metal spoon. Stir in the milk.

4 Spoon the batter evenly into the patty cases and bake for 15-20 minutes or until golden and firm to the touch. A skewer inserted in the centre should come out clean. Cool completely on a wire rack, then ice and decorate as desired. Store in an airtight container for up to 5 days.

PASSIONFRUIT FAIRY CAKES

PREPARATION TIME: 30 MINUTES,
PLUS REFRIGERATING TIME

COOKING TIME: 20 MINUTES

MAKES 12

3 small passionfruit

250 g self-raising flour

pinch of salt

125 g unsalted butter, diced and
softened at room temperature

200 g caster sugar

1 teaspoon vanilla extract

2 free-range eggs, lightly beaten

1 tablespoon milk

icing sugar, for dusting

PASSIONFRUIT ICING

1 passionfruit

250 g mascarpone

125 g icing sugar, sifted

Fairy cakes were probably the first thing I baked as a child, tempted by the way the little wings transform them into something magical. In this slightly more grown-up version, I've replaced the traditional whipped-cream filling with a combination of passionfruit and mascarpone.

1 Preheat the oven to 180°C (Gas Mark 4). Line a 12-hole cupcake tin with paper patty cases.

2 Scoop the flesh of the passionfruit into a sieve set over a bowl. Press on the seeds with the back of a spoon to extract as much juice as possible. Discard the seeds.

3 Sift the flour and salt into a large bowl. Add the remaining ingredients and beat with a wooden spoon or hand-held electric beaters on low speed for 2 minutes or until combined. Stir in the passionfruit juice.

4 Spoon the batter evenly into the patty cases and bake for 15–20 minutes or until golden and firm to the touch. A skewer inserted in the centre should come out clean. Cool completely on a wire rack.

5 Meanwhile, to make the icing, scoop the flesh of the passionfruit into a sieve set over a bowl. Press on the seeds with the back of a spoon to extract as much juice as possible. Add the mascarpone, icing sugar and a few passionfruit seeds, if desired, and mix with a wooden spoon until combined. Cover and refrigerate for about 45 minutes.

6 Slice off the top of each cupcake, then cut these pieces in half (to make the wings). Spoon a tablespoon of icing onto the top of each cake and press in the 'wings'. Dust with extra icing sugar before serving. Store in an airtight container for up to 3 days.

LITTLE MOCHA SYRUP CAKES

PREPARATION TIME: 25 MINUTES

COOKING TIME: 20 MINUTES

MAKES 12

185 g self-raising flour

pinch of salt

185 g caster sugar

185 g unsalted butter, diced and
softened at room temperature

3 large free-range eggs, lightly beaten

3 tablespoons espresso-strength
coffee, cooled

75 g pecans, roughly chopped

COFFEE SYRUP

50 g soft brown sugar

2–3 tablespoons hot espresso-
strength coffee

CHOCOLATE TOPPING

50 g milk chocolate, chopped

100 g mascarpone,
at room temperature

We all know that coffee and chocolate make a good marriage. Here, little coffee cupcakes are drizzled with a coffee syrup and then topped with mascarpone flavoured with milk chocolate.

1 Preheat the oven to 180°C (Gas Mark 4). Line a 12-hole cupcake tin with paper patty cases.

2 Sift the flour, salt and caster sugar into a large bowl. Add the butter, egg, coffee and pecans and beat with a wooden spoon or hand-held electric beaters on low speed for 2 minutes or until combined.

3 Spoon the batter evenly into the patty cases and bake for 15–20 minutes or until golden and firm to the touch. A skewer inserted in the centre should come out clean.

4 Meanwhile, make the syrup by stirring the brown sugar and hot coffee together until the sugar has dissolved. As soon as the cakes come out of the oven, pierce them in several places with a skewer and drizzle over the syrup. Leave to cool on a wire rack.

5 To make the topping, place the chocolate in a heatproof bowl set over a saucepan of barely simmering water (make sure the bowl doesn't touch the water) until melted, stirring occasionally until smooth. Set aside to cool to room temperature. Using a whisk, beat the mascarpone and cooled chocolate together until smooth. Spread over the cakes. Store in the fridge for up to 3 days.

DOUBLE CHOCOLATE AND HAZELNUT CUPCAKES

PREPARATION TIME: 30 MINUTES

COOKING TIME: 20 MINUTES

MAKES 12

75 g dark chocolate,
broken into pieces

100 g self-raising flour

pinch of salt

100 g unsalted butter, softened
at room temperature

100 g caster sugar

2 free-range eggs, lightly beaten

3 tablespoons ground hazelnuts

100 g chocolate and hazelnut spread

CHOC HAZELNUT ICING

100 g dark chocolate,
broken into pieces

2 tablespoons chocolate
and hazelnut spread

100 ml double cream

Chocolate and hazelnut spread is one of my addictions (like peanut butter) so there is always a jar in the fridge. Spooning a little into the centre of these cakes gives them a wonderfully gooey texture.

1 Preheat the oven to 180°C (Gas Mark 4). Line a 12-hole cupcake tin with paper patty cases.

2 Place the chocolate in a heatproof bowl set over a saucepan of barely simmering water (make sure the bowl doesn't touch the water) until melted.

3 Sift the flour and salt into a large bowl. Add the butter, sugar, egg, ground hazelnuts and melted chocolate. Beat with a wooden spoon or hand-held electric beaters on low speed for 2 minutes or until combined.

4 Spoon a heaped tablespoon of the batter into each patty case, followed by a teaspoon of chocolate spread. Top each with the remaining batter and bake for 15-20 minutes or until firm to the touch. Cool completely on a wire rack.

5 Meanwhile, to make the icing, place the chocolate and chocolate spread in a heatproof bowl. Bring the cream to the boil in a small saucepan, then pour over the chocolate mixture, stirring until melted and smooth. Cool until thickened, then spread over the cakes. Store in an airtight container for up to 3 days.

STICKY COCONUT AND LIME CAKES

PREPARATION TIME: 25 MINUTES

COOKING TIME: 20 MINUTES

MAKES 12

185 g unsalted butter, diced and softened at room temperature

finely grated zest of 1 lime

185 g caster sugar

3 free-range eggs

2 tablespoons desiccated coconut

155 g self-raising flour, sifted

pinch of salt

2 tablespoons lime juice

shredded lime zest or coconut, to garnish (optional)

LIME SYRUP

100 ml water

100 g caster sugar

juice of 1 lime

LIME ICING

150 g icing sugar, sifted

1 tablespoon lime juice

A little coconut, lime and syrup cake is my idea of heaven. These moist cakes can also be made without the icing - simply dust them with icing sugar, if desired.

1 Preheat the oven to 180°C (Gas Mark 4). Line a 12-hole cupcake tin with paper patty cases.

2 Place the butter, lime zest and sugar in an electric mixer and beat for 4-5 minutes or until light and well mixed. Add the eggs one at a time, beating well between additions. Using a large metal spoon, gently fold in the desiccated coconut, flour and salt until smooth, then stir in the lime juice.

3 Spoon the batter evenly into the patty cases and bake for 15-20 minutes or until firm to the touch. A skewer inserted in the centre should come out clean. Cool completely on a wire rack.

4 Meanwhile, to make the syrup, place all the ingredients in a small saucepan and stir over medium heat until the sugar has dissolved. Simmer for 3 minutes. As soon as the cakes come out of the oven, pierce them in several places with a skewer and spoon over the hot syrup. Leave to cool.

5 To make the lime icing, sift the icing sugar into a small bowl and then beat in enough lime juice to make a thin, pourable icing. Spread the icing over the cakes. Sprinkle with shredded lime zest or coconut, if desired. Store in an airtight container for up to 5 days.

LITTLE BLUEBERRY, ORANGE AND POLENTA CAKES

PREPARATION TIME: 20 MINUTES

COOKING TIME: 20 MINUTES

MAKES 12

250 g unsalted butter, diced and softened at room temperature

250 g caster sugar

4 free-range eggs, lightly beaten

grated zest and juice of 1 large orange

150 g polenta (or fine cornmeal)

150 g plain flour, sifted

pinch of salt

2 teaspoons baking powder

150 g blueberries, fresh or frozen

icing sugar, for dusting

Polenta gives these little cakes a nice texture with a coarse crumb. They can also be made with semolina instead of polenta, if desired, and the regular flour may be replaced with gluten-free flour.

1 Preheat the oven to 180°C (Gas Mark 4). Line a 12-hole cupcake tin with paper patty cases.

2 Place the butter, sugar, egg, orange zest and juice and polenta in a large bowl. Sift in the flour, salt and baking powder. Beat with a wooden spoon or hand-held electric beaters for 2 minutes or until just combined. It's important not to beat the batter too much – just long enough to make it smooth.

3 Spoon the batter evenly into the patty cases. Poke three or four blueberries into the top of each cupcake, pressing them gently into the batter. Bake for 15–20 minutes or until risen and golden. Transfer to a wire rack to cool completely. Dust with icing sugar to serve. Store in an airtight container for up to 5 days.

BANANA AND WHITE CHOCOLATE CUPCAKES

PREPARATION TIME: 15 MINUTES

COOKING TIME: 20 MINUTES

MAKES 12

250 g plain flour

1 teaspoon bicarbonate of soda

½ teaspoon mixed spice

pinch of salt

200 g unsalted butter, diced and softened at room temperature

250 g caster sugar

3 free-range eggs, lightly beaten

3 ripe bananas, mashed

3 tablespoons hot milk

150 g white chocolate chips

To give these cakes maximum banana flavour, it is important to use really ripe bananas. This is the perfect way to use up any lurking in the fruit bowl that have been left to go dark. A fine dusting of icing sugar is all that is needed, but a white chocolate ganache (see page 316) is also good.

1 Preheat the oven to 180°C (Gas Mark 4). Line a 12-hole cupcake tin with paper patty cases.

2 Sift the flour, bicarbonate of soda, mixed spice and salt into a large bowl. Add the butter, sugar, egg, mashed banana and milk. Beat with a wooden spoon or hand-held electric beaters on low speed for 2 minutes or until combined. Fold in the white chocolate chips with a large metal spoon.

3 Spoon the batter evenly into the patty cases and bake for 15-20 minutes or until golden and firm to the touch. A skewer inserted in the centre should come out clean. Cool completely on a wire rack, then ice and decorate as desired. Store in an airtight container for up to 5 days.

PEACH CUPCAKES

PREPARATION TIME: 15 MINUTES

COOKING TIME: 20 MINUTES

MAKES 12

125 g self-raising flour

1 teaspoon baking powder

pinch of salt

125 g unsalted butter, diced and softened at room temperature

125 g caster sugar

2 free-range eggs, lightly beaten

1 tablespoon lemon juice

3 tablespoons sour cream

2 tablespoons peach jam

2 ripe peaches, halved and stones removed

icing sugar, for dusting

If you are lucky enough to have some sweet, ripe summer peaches, they make a great baked-on topping for cupcakes, and the peach jam and sour cream in the batter give a delicious 'peaches and cream' flavour. These are perfect dusted with icing sugar, or brush them with some warmed peach jam to glaze.

1 Preheat the oven to 180°C (Gas Mark 4). Line a 12-hole cupcake tin with paper patty cases.

2 Sift the flour, baking powder and salt into a large bowl. Add the butter, sugar and egg. Beat with a wooden spoon or hand-held electric beaters on low speed for 2 minutes or until combined. Fold in the lemon juice, sour cream and jam.

3 Spoon the batter evenly into the patty cases. Cut each peach half into six thin wedges, then place two wedges on top of each cupcake. Bake for about 20 minutes or until golden and firm to the touch. A skewer inserted in the centre should come out clean. Cool completely on a wire rack, then dust with icing sugar and serve. Store in an airtight container for up to 3 days.

MINI CHOCOLATE DEVIL'S FOOD CAKES

PREPARATION TIME: 15 MINUTES

COOKING TIME: 20 MINUTES

MAKES 6

125 g plain flour

2 tablespoons cocoa

1 teaspoon baking powder

pinch of salt

150 g soft brown sugar

100 g unsalted butter, diced and softened at room temperature

1 large free-range egg

125 ml milk

½ teaspoon vanilla extract

This recipe comes from Michael Fox, an American friend who makes one of the best (and easiest) devil's food cakes I have ever tasted. With Michael's blessing, I have adjusted the recipe to make mini cupcake versions. The mixture is a little like muffin batter so don't overbeat it or the cakes will be heavy. Enjoy them as they are, or finish them off with a chocolate ganache icing (see page 316).

1 Preheat the oven to 180°C (Gas Mark 4). Line a 6-hole cupcake tin with paper patty cases.

2 Sift the flour, cocoa, baking powder and salt into an electric mixer. Add the sugar and butter and beat for about 2 minutes or until combined.

3 Whisk together the egg, milk and vanilla and gradually add to the cake batter. Don't overmix though – just beat until combined.

4 Spoon the batter evenly into the patty cases and bake for 18-20 minutes or until firm to the touch. A skewer inserted in the centre should come out clean. Cool completely on a wire rack, then ice and decorate as desired. Store in an airtight container for up to 5 days.

APPLE AND HAZELNUT MINI LOAF CAKES

PREPARATION TIME: 20 MINUTES

COOKING TIME: 20 MINUTES

MAKES 6

125 g unsalted butter, diced and softened at room temperature

60 g caster sugar

60 g dark muscovado or brown sugar

2 free-range eggs

125 g self-raising flour

1 teaspoon baking powder

pinch of salt

1 apple, peeled, cored and grated

60 g skinned hazelnuts, toasted and chopped

4 tablespoons pure maple syrup

icing sugar, for dusting (optional)

I make these apple cakes in baby loaf tins, but you could also use a regular muffin tin (this recipe will make about nine) or little fluted baby brioche moulds (makes 12). These tins are available in specialist baking shops.

1 Preheat the oven to 180°C (Gas Mark 4). Grease and line the base of six mini loaf tins (about 10 cm × 5 cm × 5 cm).

2 Place the butter, caster sugar and muscovado or brown sugar in an electric mixer and beat for 4–5 minutes or until light and well mixed. Add the eggs one at a time, beating well between additions. Sift in the flour, baking powder and salt and gently fold in with a large metal spoon. Stir in the grated apple, hazelnuts and half the maple syrup.

3 Spoon the batter evenly into the tins and bake for about 15–20 minutes or until firm to the touch. A skewer inserted in the centre should come out clean.

4 Warm the remaining maple syrup with 1 tablespoon water in a small saucepan over low heat and drizzle over the warm cakes. Cool completely on a wire rack. Dust with icing sugar before serving, if desired. Store in an airtight container for up to 5 days.

FIG AND APRICOT CAKES

PREPARATION TIME: 25 MINUTES

COOKING TIME: 25 MINUTES

MAKES 12

100 g dried figs, chopped

100 g dried apricots, chopped

1 teaspoon bicarbonate of soda

300 ml boiling water

60 g unsalted butter, diced and softened at room temperature

2 tablespoons golden syrup

125 g soft brown sugar

2 free-range eggs, lightly beaten

210 g self-raising flour

pinch of salt

1 teaspoon vanilla extract

These little cakes are an adaptation of the classic sticky date pudding. They are delicious served warm for dessert with a toffee sauce and ice-cream, or dust the cooled cakes with icing sugar and enjoy them with an afternoon cup of tea or coffee. If you want to serve them warm, make them ahead of time and remove them from the tin, then reheat in a moderate (180°C/Gas Mark 4) oven just before serving. Serve the warmed sauce on the side.

1 Preheat the oven to 180°C (Gas Mark 4). Grease and line the bases of a 12-hole regular muffin tin.

2 Place the dried fruit in a bowl, add the bicarbonate of soda and pour over the boiling water. Set aside.

3 Place the butter, golden syrup and brown sugar in an electric mixer and mix on medium speed for 7–8 minutes or until pale and fluffy. Transfer the beaten egg to a jug. Reduce the speed of the mixer and, with the motor running, gradually add the egg to the mixture, beating well after each addition. Sift in the flour and salt and fold in gently with a large metal spoon. Add the dried fruit and juices and then the vanilla. Mix well. This will be a wet batter.

4 Spoon the batter evenly into the muffin holes and bake for about 25 minutes or until risen and firm to the touch. A skewer inserted in the centre should come out clean. These are better if you let them cool in the tin. To remove them, run a small butter knife around the edge of each little cake and then carefully lift them out with the edge of the knife. Store in an airtight container for up to 5 days.

TOFFEE SAUCE
Make a toffee sauce by combining 100 g unsalted butter, 200 g soft brown sugar and 125 ml pouring cream in a small saucepan. Bring to the boil and simmer for 5 minutes. Pour over the warm cakes and serve.

BASIC FRIANDS

PREPARATION TIME: 20 MINUTES

COOKING TIME: 25 MINUTES

MAKES 8

180 g unsalted butter

4 tablespoons plain flour

pinch of salt

180 g icing sugar, plus extra for dusting

100 g ground almonds

2 teaspoons finely grated lemon zest

5 free-range egg whites

These delicious, moist almond cakes are easy to make at home, and are so adaptable that you can use a variety of baking tins. I often use fluted baby brioche tins, but you can use the classic oval friand tins or even muffin tins, if desired. To make berry friands, follow the recipe, then top each friand with a few fresh or frozen raspberries, blackberries or blueberries before baking.

1 Preheat the oven to 200°C (Gas Mark 6). Lightly grease eight friand tins.

2 Melt the butter in a small saucepan over low heat, then cook for a further minute, until golden. Be careful not to let it burn.

3 Sift the flour, salt and icing sugar into a bowl. Stir in the ground almonds and lemon zest.

4 Lightly beat the egg whites with a fork, then pour over the dry ingredients. Add the warm butter and mix with a wooden spoon until smooth.

5 Spoon the batter evenly into the tins, to about three-quarters full. Bake for 5 minutes, then reduce the heat to 180°C (Gas Mark 4) and cook for a further 10-15 minutes or until golden and risen. Cool in the tins for 5 minutes, then turn out onto a wire rack to cool completely. Dust with extra icing sugar and serve. Store in an airtight container for up to 5 days.

VANILLA, BLUEBERRY AND ORANGE FRIANDS

PREPARATION TIME: 20 MINUTES

COOKING TIME: 25 MINUTES

MAKES 8

180 g unsalted butter

4 tablespoons plain flour

pinch of salt

180 g icing sugar, plus extra for dusting

100 g ground almonds

2 teaspoons finely grated orange zest

5 free-range egg whites

1 teaspoon vanilla extract

16 blueberries, fresh or frozen

Blueberries, orange and almonds are another one of those happy combinations in the baking world. However, you could replace the blueberries with fresh or frozen raspberries or blackberries.

1 Preheat the oven to 200°C (Gas Mark 6). Lightly grease eight friand tins.

2 Melt the butter in a small saucepan over low heat, then cook for a further minute or until golden. Be careful not to let it burn.

3 Sift the flour, salt and icing sugar into a bowl. Stir in the ground almonds and orange zest.

4 Lightly beat the egg whites with a fork, then pour over the dry ingredients. Add the vanilla and warm butter and mix with a wooden spoon until smooth.

5 Spoon the batter evenly into the tins, to about three-quarters full. Place two blueberries on top of each friand, pressing down gently into the batter. Bake for 5 minutes, then reduce the heat to 180°C (Gas Mark 4) and cook for a further 10-15 minutes or until golden and risen. Cool in the tins for 5 minutes, then turn out onto a wire rack to cool completely. Dust with extra icing sugar and serve. Store in an airtight container for up to 5 days.

RASPBERRY AND WHITE CHOCOLATE FRIANDS

PREPARATION TIME: 20 MINUTES

COOKING TIME: 30 MINUTES

MAKES 8

100 g unsalted butter

100 g white chocolate chips

4 tablespoons plain flour

pinch of salt

125 g icing sugar, plus extra for dusting

100 g ground almonds

2 teaspoons finely grated lemon zest

5 free-range egg whites

125 g raspberries, fresh or frozen

In my early days of making friends, I preferred the simplicity of the plain almond version, but I was inspired to make these after trying something similar in my local cafe. I have replaced some of the butter with white chocolate, which makes the friands quite sweet, but the sweetness is balanced nicely by the freshness of the raspberries and lemon zest.

1 Preheat the oven to 180°C (Gas Mark 4). Lightly grease eight friand tins.

2 Melt the butter and white chocolate chips in a small saucepan over low heat, stirring occasionally until smooth.

3 Sift the flour, salt and icing sugar into a bowl. Stir in the ground almonds and lemon zest.

4 Lightly beat the egg whites with a fork, then pour over the dry ingredients. Crush half the raspberries with a fork and add to the bowl with the melted butter mixture and mix with a wooden spoon until smooth.

5 Spoon the batter evenly into the tins, to about three-quarters full. Gently press the remaining raspberries into the batter. Bake for 20-25 minutes or until golden and risen. Cool in the tins for 5 minutes, then turn out onto a wire rack to cool completely. Dust with extra icing sugar and serve. Store in an airtight container for up to 5 days.

TRIPLE CHOCOLATE FRIANDS

PREPARATION TIME: 25 MINUTES, PLUS COOLING TIME

COOKING TIME: 25 MINUTES

MAKES 12

175 g unsalted butter

100 g dark chocolate, broken into pieces

6 free-range egg whites

125 g ground almonds

250 g icing sugar, plus extra for dusting

30 g cocoa

80 g plain flour

pinch of salt

100 g dark chocolate chips

I invented these friands as part of a challenge after a friend suggested that friands should be plain or fruity and wouldn't work at all with dark chocolate. The proof is in the pudding, I think.

1 Preheat the oven to 190°C (Gas Mark 5). Lightly grease 12 friand tins.

2 Place the butter and chocolate in a heatproof bowl set over a saucepan of barely simmering water (make sure the bowl doesn't touch the water) until melted. Remove from the heat and leave to cool for about 10 minutes.

Lightly beat the egg whites with a fork, then gently stir in the melted butter and chocolate. Add the ground almonds, then sift in the icing sugar, cocoa, flour and salt. Add the chocolate chips and mix until well combined.

3 Spoon the batter evenly into the tins, to about three-quarters full. Bake for 25 minutes or until golden and risen. Cool in the tins for 5 minutes, then turn out onto a wire rack to cool completely. Dust with extra icing sugar and serve. Store in an airtight container for up to 5 days.

LAMINGTONS

PREPARATION TIME: 35 MINUTES

COOKING TIME: 50 MINUTES

MAKES 18

275 g self-raising flour

pinch of salt

175 g caster sugar

150 g unsalted butter, diced and softened at room temperature

3 free-range eggs, lightly beaten

1 teaspoon vanilla extract

125 ml milk

about 300 g desiccated coconut

CHOCOLATE COATING

375 g icing sugar

40 g cocoa

30 g unsalted butter, melted

185 ml milk

This recipe first appeared in my *Perfect Cookbook* and I still use it. I have included it again here as you can't have a baking book without this Australian national treasure. The cake is easier to cut if you make it a day ahead, although if you're pushed for time, you can make the lamingtons with bought sponge cake.

1 Preheat the oven to 180°C (Gas Mark 4). Grease and line the base of a 30 cm × 20 cm shallow cake tin.

2 Sift the flour, salt and sugar into a large bowl. Add the butter, egg, vanilla and milk and beat with hand-held electric beaters for 2–3 minutes or until the mixture is smooth and drops easily off a spoon.

3 Spoon the mixture into the tin and smooth the surface. Bake for 45–50 minutes or until golden and firm to the touch. A skewer inserted in the centre should come out clean. Cool in the tin for 5 minutes, then turn out onto a wire rack to cool completely.

4 To make the chocolate coating, sift the icing sugar and cocoa into a heatproof bowl, then stir in the melted butter and milk. Set the bowl over a saucepan of barely simmering water and stir until smooth, shiny and runny. Remove from the heat.

5 Pour the desiccated coconut into a shallow bowl.

6 Trim away the edges of the cooled cake and cut it into 18 squares. Using two forks, dip a piece of cake into the chocolate coating, then roll in the coconut. Transfer to a wire rack to dry. Repeat with the remaining pieces of cake, thinning the icing if necessary with a little extra milk and adding more coconut if needed. Store in an airtight container for up to 3 days.

MADELEINES

PREPARATION TIME: 20 MINUTES

COOKING TIME: 10 MINUTES

MAKES 12-18

2 free-range eggs

60 g caster sugar, plus extra
for sprinkling

grated zest of ½ orange

4 tablespoons plain flour

pinch of salt

50 g unsalted butter, melted

These little cakes can be baked in a flash, so this is the recipe I turn to when I'm pushed for time and visitors are due. The traditional shell-shaped madeleine tins are definitely worth the investment.

1 Preheat the oven to 180°C (Gas Mark 4). Lightly grease a 12-hole madeleine tin or shallow patty tin and dust lightly with flour.

2 Place the eggs, sugar and orange zest in a bowl and beat with hand-held electric beaters for 3-4 minutes or until the sugar has dissolved and the mixture has increased in volume and is thick and pale. (You could also do this in an electric mixer.) Sift the flour and salt on top and gently fold in with a large metal spoon. Fold in the melted butter until just combined.

3 Spoon the mixture evenly into the madeleine holes to about three-quarters full. Bake for 8-10 minutes or until risen and firm to the touch. Cool in the tin for 2 minutes, then transfer to a wire rack. Sprinkle lightly with sugar while still warm. Repeat with any remaining batter and serve within a couple of hours of baking. They don't really keep for more than a day.

CHOCOLATE MADELEINES

PREPARATION TIME: 20 MINUTES

COOKING TIME: 10 MINUTES

MAKES ABOUT 15

2 large free-range eggs

175 g caster sugar

140 g plain flour

3 tablespoons cocoa

pinch of salt

175 g unsalted butter, melted

1 teaspoon vanilla extract

icing sugar, for dusting

These little chocolate sponge cakes can be made in the classic shell-shaped madeleine tins or in shallow patty tins. They are best eaten on the day they are made.

1 Preheat the oven to 180°C (Gas Mark 4). Lightly grease a 12-hole madeleine tin or shallow patty tin and dust with flour.

2 Place the eggs and sugar in a bowl and whisk with hand-held electric beaters for 3-4 minutes or until the sugar has dissolved and the mixture has increased in volume and is thick and pale. (You could also do this in an electric mixer.) Sift the flour, cocoa and salt on top and gently fold in with a large metal spoon. Fold in the melted butter and vanilla until just combined.

3 Spoon the mixture evenly into the madeleine holes to about three-quarters full. Bake for 8-10 minutes or until risen and firm to the touch. Cool in the tin for 2 minutes, then transfer to a wire rack. Sprinkle lightly with icing sugar while still warm. Repeat with any remaining batter and serve within a couple of hours of baking. They don't really keep for more than a day.

WHOOPIE PIES

PREPARATION TIME: 30 MINUTES

COOKING TIME: 15 MINUTES

MAKES 8

120 g unsalted butter, diced and
softened at room temperature

120 g caster sugar

2 large free-range eggs, lightly beaten

4 tablespoons cocoa

225 g self-raising flour, sifted

½ teaspoon salt

1 teaspoon vanilla extract

120 ml milk

icing sugar, for dusting

MARSHMALLOW FILLING

100 g white marshmallows

2 tablespoons milk

125 g unsalted butter, diced and
softened at room temperature

After reading that whoopie pies were hailed by the US food press as 'the new cupcake', I had to investigate. Basically, they are pairs of flattish cakes that are filled with a marshmallow or buttercream filling. The batter can be either piped or dropped and spread with the back of a spoon to achieve a nice round shape. Traditionally, the cakes are flavoured with cocoa.

1 Preheat the oven to 180°C (Gas Mark 4). Grease and line two baking trays with baking paper.

2 Place the butter, sugar, egg, cocoa, flour, salt, vanilla and milk in a large bowl and beat with a wooden spoon or hand-held electric beaters until just combined. It's important not to beat the batter too much - just long enough to make it smooth.

3 Drop 2 heaped tablespoons of cake batter onto the baking trays and spread out with the back of a spoon to a 7 cm round. You should get eight per tray.

4 Bake for 10-15 minutes or until firm to the touch and a skewer inserted in the centre comes out clean. Cool on the trays for 2 minutes, then transfer to a wire rack to cool completely.

5 To make the filling, place the marshmallows and milk in a saucepan over low heat and stir until melted and smooth. Set aside to cool. In a separate bowl, beat the butter with hand-held electric beaters until creamy and soft, then gradually beat in the cooled marshmallow mixture until smooth.

6 Sandwich the cakes together with the marshmallow filling. There should be enough filling to form a deep layer which is clearly visible between the two layers. Dust with icing sugar before serving. Store in an airtight container for up to 3 days.

KATIE STEWART'S ROCK CAKES

PREPARATION TIME: 20 MINUTES

COOKING TIME: 15 MINUTES

MAKES 12

225 g self-raising flour

pinch of salt

pinch of mixed spice

75 g unsalted butter, chilled and diced

75 g caster sugar

75 g sultanas

1 large free-range egg

2 tablespoons milk

This recipe comes from British food writer (and one of my mentors) Katie Stewart, and I hasten to add that the 'rock' in the title should apply to the rough appearance only. The cakes should be light and crumbly. According to Katie, rock cakes are dry and boring if the recipe is too lean (that is, made with too little butter). You can use either sultanas or currants in this recipe, or try 2 tablespoons of mixed peel.

1 Preheat the oven to 200°C (Gas Mark 6). Lightly grease a large baking tray and line with baking paper.

2 Sift the flour, salt and mixed spice into a large bowl. Using your fingertips, rub the butter into the flour until the mixture resembles coarse breadcrumbs. Stir in the sugar and sultanas.

3 Whisk together the egg and milk and pour into the dry ingredients. Using a fork, mix to form a rough dough that clings together in clumps (these clumps make them rock cakes - it's a mistake to add too much liquid).

4 Pile the mixture into 12 rough heaps on the baking tray, not too close together as they will flatten out slightly on baking. Bake on the middle shelf of the oven for about 10-15 minutes or until lightly golden. Transfer to a wire rack to cool. Store in an airtight container for up to 2 days.

STRAWBERRY POWDER PUFFS

PREPARATION TIME: 30 MINUTES

COOKING TIME: 12 MINUTES

MAKES 12

3 free-range eggs, separated

185 g caster sugar

1 teaspoon finely grated orange zest

1 teaspoon vanilla extract

75 g plain flour

60 g cornflour

2 teaspoons baking powder

250 ml double cream

24 strawberries, hulled and sliced

icing sugar, for dusting

These are a lovely way to enjoy the luscious sweetness of ripe strawberries when they're in season, but you can use raspberry or strawberry jam in place of the fresh fruit, if preferred.

1 Preheat the oven to 180°C (Gas Mark 4). Line two baking sheets with baking paper.

2 Place the egg whites in an electric mixer and mix on high speed for 3-4 minutes or until stiff peaks form. With the motor running, gradually add the sugar and continue beating for another minute or until thick and glossy. Beat in the egg yolks, one at a time, until combined. Fold in the orange zest and vanilla with a large metal spoon.

3 Sift the flours and baking powder into a small bowl, then gently fold into the egg mixture until no white streaks remain. Be careful not to overmix.

4 Spoon tablespoons of the batter onto the prepared trays (you'll need 24 rounds), leaving room for spreading, and bake for 10-12 minutes or until puffed and golden. Cool on the baking sheets for a few minutes, then transfer to a wire rack to cool completely.

5 Whip the cream until soft peaks form.

6 To serve, place a dollop of whipped cream on the base of 12 rounds and top with some slices of strawberry. Sandwich with the remaining rounds and dust with icing sugar. These are best eaten within a few hours of baking.

TIPS

1 A mixing bowl, a large metal spoon and a muffin tin are all you need to make muffins. The method is simplicity itself, but it is important that you do not overmix the batter. It doesn't need to be smooth - for once, a few lumps are OK.

2 You need a little acidity in the mixture for the raising agents to work. This is achieved in most of the recipes by using buttermilk, yoghurt or milk soured with a squeeze of lemon juice. If a recipe calls for buttermilk and you can't locate any, just use the soured milk instead.

3 Have all the ingredients at room temperature. Place the dry ingredients in a bowl, whisk together the wet ingredients, then use a large metal spoon to gently stir the two mixtures until everything just comes together - remember, lumps are fine.

4 Add any extras like fruit or nuts after combining the wet and dry ingredients and fold in with just a couple of turns of the spoon. The batter should be thick and lumpy.

5 You can make your own paper tin liners by cutting rounds of baking paper about 5 cm wider than the diameter of the holes in the muffin tin. Grease the tins and line each with the rounds, leaving the folded edges standing up - they look irregular and pretty!

6 The simplest way to test if muffins are cooked is to lightly touch the top of one - it should feel firm to the touch. You can also insert a skewer or toothpick into the centre of the muffin; it should come out clean.

7 You can make bite-sized muffins by using mini muffin tins and reducing the cooking time by about a third. These make great snacks, and mini savoury muffins are a great nibble to serve with drinks.

8 Muffins are delicious eaten warm and are best eaten on the day they are made, but they can be stored if necessary. Let them cool to room temperature and keep them in an airtight container for a day or two. Wrap day-old muffins in foil and warm them in a preheated 150°C (Gas Mark 2) oven for about 10 minutes. Alternatively, split them lengthways, toast them under a hot grill and serve with butter.

9 If you need to store them for longer, muffins can be frozen. Wrap them individually in plastic film or place in plastic bags and freeze for up to 2 months. To reheat from frozen, wrap each muffin loosely in foil and place in a preheated 180°C (Gas Mark 4) oven for 15-20 minutes.

BASIC MUFFINS

PREPARATION TIME: 20 MINUTES

COOKING TIME: 25 MINUTES

MAKES 12

310 g plain flour

2 teaspoons baking powder

½ teaspoon bicarbonate of soda

pinch of salt

300 ml buttermilk (or regular milk
soured with a squeeze of lemon juice)

2 free-range eggs

1 teaspoon vanilla extract

200 g caster sugar

125 g unsalted butter, melted

My basic mixture is wetter than a lot of other muffin recipes. They don't rise as high as commercial muffins so you won't get that famous muffin top, but these muffins will stay moist for longer and have a nice cake-like crumb. If you can't find buttermilk, use regular milk and add a squeeze of lemon juice to make it sour. Sprinkle the tops with raw or demerara sugar before baking for a nice crunchy topping.

1 Preheat the oven to 190°C (Gas Mark 5). Grease a 12-hole muffin tin or line with paper muffin cases.

2 Sift the flour, baking powder, bicarbonate of soda and salt into a large bowl and make a well in the centre.

3 Whisk together the buttermilk, eggs, vanilla, sugar and melted butter. Pour into the well in the flour mixture and stir until the ingredients are just combined. Do not overmix - the batter should not be smooth.

4 Spoon the batter evenly into the muffin holes and bake for 20-25 minutes or until the tops are golden. A skewer inserted in the centre should come out clean. Cool in the tin for 5 minutes, then turn out onto a wire rack. Serve warm or at room temperature. Store in an airtight container for up to 2 days.

CLASSIC BLUEBERRY MUFFINS

PREPARATION TIME: 20 MINUTES

COOKING TIME: 25 MINUTES

MAKES 12

310 g plain flour

2 teaspoons baking powder

½ teaspoon bicarbonate of soda

pinch of salt

150 g caster sugar

1 teaspoon finely grated orange zest

300 ml buttermilk (or regular milk
soured with a squeeze of lemon juice)

2 free-range eggs

100 g unsalted butter, melted

250 g blueberries, fresh or frozen

**Both fresh and frozen blueberries work beautifully
in these much-loved muffins. If you are using frozen
berries, don't thaw them first otherwise they will streak
the batter. These are best enjoyed warm or at room
temperature.**

1 Preheat the oven to 190°C (Gas Mark 5). Grease a 12-hole
muffin tin or line with paper muffin cases.

2 Sift the flour, baking powder, bicarbonate of soda, salt
and sugar into a large bowl. Add the orange zest and make
a well in the centre.

3 Whisk together the buttermilk, eggs and melted butter.
Pour into the well in the flour mixture and stir until the
ingredients are just combined. Do not overmix – the batter
should not be smooth. Quickly fold in the blueberries with
a large metal spoon.

4 Spoon the batter evenly into the muffin holes and bake
for 20-25 minutes or until the tops are golden. A skewer
inserted in the centre should come out clean. Cool in the tin
for 5 minutes, then turn out onto a wire rack. Serve warm
or at room temperature. Store in an airtight container for
up to 3 days.

RASPBERRY MUFFINS WITH STREUSEL TOPPING

PREPARATION TIME: 25 MINUTES

COOKING TIME: 25 MINUTES

MAKES 12

310 g plain flour

2 teaspoons baking powder

½ teaspoon bicarbonate of soda

pinch of salt

150 g caster sugar

1 teaspoon finely grated orange zest

300 ml buttermilk (or regular milk soured with a squeeze of lemon juice)

2 free-range eggs

100 g unsalted butter, melted

150 g raspberries, fresh or frozen

icing sugar, for dusting (optional)

STREUSEL TOPPING

40 g unsalted butter, chilled and chopped

4 tablespoons plain flour

1 teaspoon mixed spice

2 tablespoons raw or demerara sugar

2 tablespoons roughly chopped pecans

The streusel topping gives these muffins a delicious nutty flavour and crunchy texture. I have used pecans, but the recipe works just as well with walnuts or slivered almonds. Serve warm or at room temperature.

1 Preheat the oven to 190°C (Gas Mark 5). Grease a 12-hole muffin tin or line with paper muffin cases.

2 To make the topping, rub the butter into the flour and mixed spice with your fingertips until it clumps together and resembles coarse breadcrumbs. Stir in the sugar and pecans.

3 Sift the flour, baking powder, bicarbonate of soda, salt and sugar into a large bowl. Add the orange zest and make a well in the centre.

4 Whisk together the buttermilk, eggs and melted butter. Pour into the well in the flour mixture and stir until the ingredients are just combined. Do not overmix - the batter should not be smooth. Quickly fold in the raspberries with a large metal spoon.

5 Spoon the batter evenly into the muffin holes. Sprinkle over the topping and bake for 20-25 minutes or until the tops are golden. A skewer inserted in the centre should come out clean. Cool in the tin for 5 minutes, then turn out onto a wire rack. Dust with icing sugar (if using) and serve warm or at room temperature. Store in an airtight container for up to 3 days.

PEAR AND YOGHURT MUFFINS

PREPARATION TIME: 20 MINUTES

COOKING TIME: 25 MINUTES

MAKES 12

310 g plain flour

2 teaspoons baking powder

½ teaspoon bicarbonate of soda

pinch of salt

pinch of ground ginger

250 g plain yoghurt

2 free-range eggs

1 teaspoon vanilla essence

200 g caster sugar

125 g unsalted butter, melted

2 small ripe pears, peeled,
cored and diced

Most muffin recipes use buttermilk, soured milk or yoghurt as one of the ingredients because the sourness reacts with the rising agents to give nice light results. Here I have used yoghurt as it gives a good rise and a lovely flavour when combined with the pears.

1 Preheat the oven to 190°C (Gas Mark 5). Grease a 12-hole muffin tin or line with paper muffin cases.

2 Sift the flour, baking powder, bicarbonate of soda, salt and ginger into a large bowl and make a well in the centre.

3 Whisk together the yoghurt, eggs, vanilla, sugar and melted butter. Pour into the well in the flour mixture, add the diced pear and stir until the ingredients are just combined. Do not overmix - the batter should not be smooth.

4 Spoon the batter evenly into the muffin holes and bake for 20-25 minutes or until the tops are golden. A skewer inserted in the centre should come out clean. Cool in the tin for 5 minutes, then turn out onto a wire rack. Serve warm or at room temperature. Store in an airtight container for up to 3 days.

GINGER, FIG AND WALNUT MUFFINS

164

PREPARATION TIME: 20 MINUTES

COOKING TIME: 25 MINUTES

MAKES 12

310 g plain flour

2 teaspoons baking powder

½ teaspoon bicarbonate of soda

pinch of salt

175 g soft brown sugar

8 dried figs, chopped

100 g walnuts, chopped

3 tablespoons chopped stem
or glacé ginger

300 ml buttermilk (or regular milk
soured with a squeeze of lemon juice)

2 free-range eggs

1 teaspoon vanilla extract

125 g unsalted butter, melted

raw or demerara sugar, for sprinkling

I love stem ginger that comes in a jar with lots of ginger syrup – and it's perfect in this recipe. The syrup is also good drizzled over the warm muffins when they come out of the oven.

1 Preheat the oven to 190°C (Gas Mark 5). Grease a 12-hole muffin tin or line with paper muffin cases.

2 Sift the flour, baking powder, bicarbonate of soda and salt into a large bowl. Stir in the sugar, figs, walnuts and ginger and make a well in the centre.

3 Whisk together the buttermilk, eggs, vanilla and melted butter. Pour into the well in the flour mixture and stir until the ingredients are just combined. Do not overmix – the batter should not be smooth.

4 Spoon the batter evenly into the muffin holes. Sprinkle with raw or demerara sugar and bake for 20–25 minutes or until the tops are golden. A skewer inserted in the centre should come out clean. Cool in the tin for 5 minutes, then turn out onto a wire rack. Serve warm or at room temperature. Store in an airtight container for up to 2 days.

CARROT AND GINGER MUFFINS

PREPARATION TIME: 20 MINUTES

COOKING TIME: 25 MINUTES

MAKES 12

310 g plain flour

1 teaspoon ground ginger

2 teaspoons baking powder

½ teaspoon bicarbonate of soda

pinch of salt

300 ml buttermilk (or regular milk soured with a squeeze of lemon juice)

2 free-range eggs

1 teaspoon vanilla extract

200 g soft brown sugar

125 g unsalted butter, melted

120 g grated carrot (about 1 large carrot)

Carrot muffins are great with a little spice, and I've always thought ginger works particularly well. These little beauties make excellent lunchbox treats.

1 Preheat the oven to 190°C (Gas Mark 5). Grease a 12-hole muffin tin or line with paper muffin cases.

2 Sift the flour, ginger, baking powder, bicarbonate of soda and salt into a large bowl and make a well in the centre.

3 Whisk together the buttermilk, eggs, vanilla, sugar and melted butter. Pour into the well in the flour mixture and stir until the ingredients are just combined. Do not overmix – the batter should not be smooth. Quickly fold in the grated carrot with a large metal spoon.

4 Spoon the batter evenly into the muffin holes and bake for 20-25 minutes or until the tops are golden. A skewer inserted in the centre should come out clean. Cool in the tin for 5 minutes, then turn out onto a wire rack. Serve warm or at room temperature. Store in an airtight container for up to 2 days.

OATY FRUIT MUFFINS

PREPARATION TIME: 20 MINUTES

COOKING TIME: 25 MINUTES

MAKES 6

185 g self-raising flour

½ teaspoon bicarbonate of soda

pinch of salt

1 teaspoon mixed spice

50 g rolled oats (porridge oats)

150 g dried fruit (such as dried cranberries or blueberries or chopped dried apricots or dates)

150 g soft brown sugar

150 ml buttermilk (or regular milk soured with a squeeze of lemon juice)

1 large free-range egg

1 teaspoon vanilla extract

100 ml vegetable oil

These are great breakfast muffins. I usually make them with dried cranberries (craisins) or chopped dried apricots, but you can use whatever dried fruit you have to hand. This recipe makes six muffins, but you can easily double the quantities if you are feeding a crowd.

1 Preheat the oven to 190°C (Gas Mark 5). Grease a 6-hole muffin tin or line with paper muffin cases.

2 Sift the flour, bicarbonate of soda, salt and mixed spice into a large bowl. Stir in the oats, dried fruit and sugar and make a well in the centre.

3 Whisk together the buttermilk, egg, vanilla and oil. Pour into the well in the flour mixture and stir until the ingredients are just combined. Do not overmix - the batter should not be smooth.

4 Spoon the batter evenly into the muffin holes (fill them to the top - these don't rise very much) and bake for 20-25 minutes or until the tops are golden. A skewer inserted in the centre should come out clean. Cool in the tin for 5 minutes, then turn out onto a wire rack. Serve warm or at room temperature. Store in an airtight container for up to 3 days.

YOGHURT AND COFFEE MUFFINS

PREPARATION TIME: 20 MINUTES

COOKING TIME: 25 MINUTES

MAKES 12

2 teaspoons instant coffee powder

150 ml boiling water

310 g plain flour

2 teaspoons baking powder

½ teaspoon bicarbonate of soda

pinch of salt

150 ml plain yoghurt

2 free-range eggs

200 g caster sugar

125 g unsalted butter, melted

These are delicious served just as they are or dusted with a little icing sugar, but if you want to gild the lily finish them off with some coffee buttercream (see page 313).

1 Preheat the oven to 190°C (Gas Mark 5). Grease a 12-hole muffin tin or line with paper muffin cases.

2 Dissolve the coffee powder in the boiling water and set aside to cool.

3 Sift the flour, baking powder, bicarbonate of soda and salt into a large bowl and make a well in the centre.

4 Whisk together the yoghurt, eggs, sugar, melted butter and coffee. Pour into the well in the flour mixture and stir until the ingredients are just combined. Do not overmix – the batter should not be smooth.

5 Spoon the batter evenly into the muffin holes and bake for 20–25 minutes or until the tops are golden. A skewer inserted in the centre should come out clean. Cool in the tin for 5 minutes, then turn out onto a wire rack. Serve warm or at room temperature. Store in an airtight container for up to 2 days.

MRS MAIETTA'S CORN MUFFINS

PREPARATION TIME: 20 MINUTES

COOKING TIME: 25 MINUTES

MAKES 12

185 g plain flour

2 teaspoons baking powder

½ teaspoon bicarbonate of soda

pinch of salt

125 g polenta (or fine cornmeal)

300 ml buttermilk (or regular milk soured with a squeeze of lemon juice)

2 free-range eggs

75 g caster sugar

100 ml vegetable oil

The first time I came across corn muffins was when an American friend served them for breakfast, alongside fried eggs and bacon. The slight sweetness of the muffins contrasted beautifully with the salty bacon, although I soon discovered they are also delicious served warm with butter. This recipe was generously provided by my friend's mother.

1 Preheat the oven to 190°C (Gas Mark 5). Grease a 12-hole muffin tin or line with paper muffin cases.

2 Sift the flour, baking powder, bicarbonate of soda and salt into a large bowl. Stir in the polenta and make a well in the centre.

3 Whisk together the buttermilk, eggs, sugar and vegetable oil. Pour into the well in the flour mixture and stir until the ingredients are just combined. Do not overmix – the batter should not be smooth.

4 Spoon the batter evenly into the muffin holes and bake for 20-25 minutes or until the tops are golden. A skewer inserted in the centre should come out clean. Cool in the tin for 5 minutes, then turn out onto a wire rack. Serve warm or at room temperature. Store in an airtight container for up to 2 days.

ZUCCHINI AND PINE NUT MUFFINS

PREPARATION TIME: 25 MINUTES

COOKING TIME: 25 MINUTES

MAKES 12

225 g plain flour

2 teaspoons baking powder

½ teaspoon bicarbonate of soda

½ teaspoon salt

40 g rolled oats (porridge oats)

8 large basil leaves, shredded

80 g parmesan, coarsely grated

freshly ground black pepper

250 g plain yoghurt

2 free-range eggs

4 tablespoons light olive oil

2 medium zucchini (courgettes), coarsely grated

50 g pine nuts, toasted

This recipe was born out of necessity. I recently grew zucchini from seed and raised far too many plants. I am not ruthless by nature and, after giving away as many seedlings as I could, I just couldn't bear to discard the excess. Naturally, I ended up with a glut and have been trying ever since to think of inventive ways to use them all up. A little chopped fresh chilli makes a nice addition to these muffins, if you like a little heat.

1 Preheat the oven to 200°C (Gas Mark 6). Grease a 12-hole muffin tin or line with paper muffin cases.

2 Sift the flour, baking powder, bicarbonate of soda and salt into a large bowl. Stir in the oats, basil, 60 g of the parmesan and a couple of grindings of black pepper. Make a well in the centre.

3 Whisk together the yoghurt, eggs and olive oil. Pour into the well in the flour mixture and stir until the ingredients are just combined. Do not overmix - the batter should not be smooth. Fold in the zucchini and pine nuts with a large metal spoon.

4 Spoon the batter evenly into the muffin holes, sprinkle with the remaining parmesan and bake for 20-25 minutes or until the tops are golden. A skewer inserted in the centre should come out clean. Cool in the tin for 5 minutes, then turn out onto a wire rack. Serve warm or at room temperature. These muffins are best eaten on the day they are made, spread with a little butter.

THREE-CHEESE AND SEMI-DRIED TOMATO MUFFINS

PREPARATION TIME: 25 MINUTES

COOKING TIME: 30 MINUTES

MAKES 12

350 g self-raising flour

½ teaspoon bicarbonate of soda

pinch of salt

75 g semi-dried tomatoes,
roughly chopped

50 g parmesan, grated

50 g mozzarella, chopped or grated

freshly ground black pepper

75 g cheddar, grated

300 ml buttermilk (or regular milk
soured with a squeeze of lemon juice)

2 free-range eggs, lightly beaten

100 g butter, melted

These muffins are perfect served warm alongside a steaming bowl of soup, or as a savoury snack. Look for the sunblush or semi-dried tomatoes, which have a bit more give to them than the fully dried variety. A pinch of powdered English mustard is a nice addition to the mixture.

1 Preheat the oven to 190°C (Gas Mark 5). Grease a 12-hole muffin tin or line with paper muffin cases.

2 Sift the flour, bicarbonate of soda and salt into a large bowl. Stir in the semi-dried tomato, parmesan, mozzarella, a couple of grindings of black pepper and most of the cheddar (save a little bit to sprinkle over the batter). Make a well in the centre.

3 Whisk together the buttermilk, eggs and melted butter. Pour into the well in the flour mixture and stir until the ingredients are just combined. Do not overmix - the batter should not be smooth.

4 Spoon the batter evenly into the muffin holes. Sprinkle with the reserved cheddar and bake for 25-30 minutes or until the tops are golden. A skewer inserted in the centre should come out clean. Cool in the tin for 5 minutes, then turn out onto a wire rack. Serve warm or at room temperature. These muffins are best eaten on the day they are made, spread with a little butter.

SCONES AND QUICKBREADS

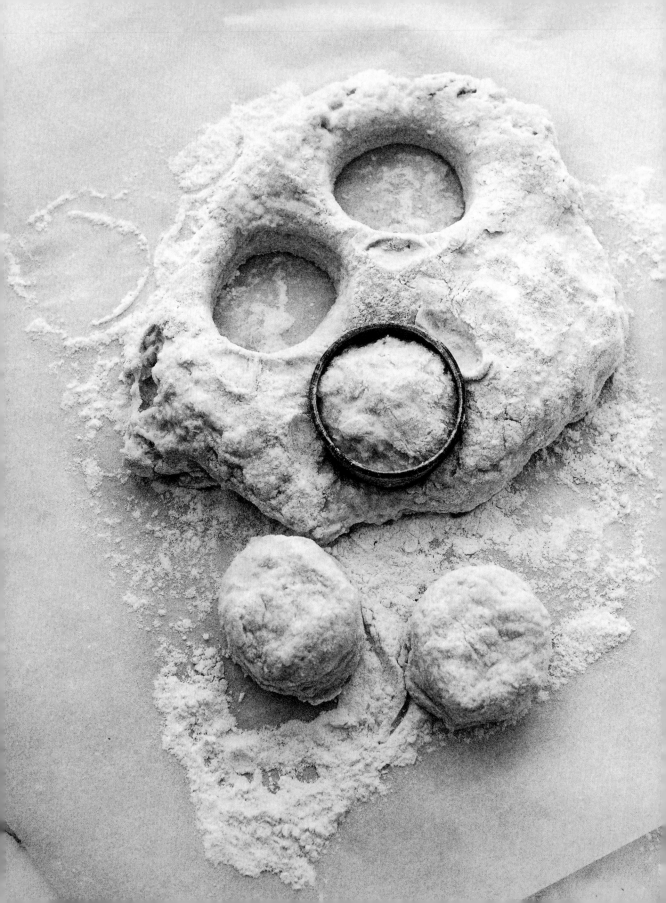

TIPS

1 Baking is generally an exact science so it is important to measure your ingredients accurately. Remember that all the spoonfuls of raising agents are level - too much baking powder or bicarbonate of soda will leave a chemical taste and make the dough rise too much.

2 For scones, the butter should be well chilled and cut into small dice before rubbing into the flour. Warm butter won't distribute properly.

3 Scones need a light touch and don't like to be overmixed or handled too much. A flat-bladed knife or a large metal spoon are best for mixing.

4 The dough should be very lightly kneaded on a floured surface, just enough to shape the scones. The lighter and quicker this is the better (some cooks just pat out the dough). Make sure the dough is not too dry - it should be stickier than a shortcrust pastry.

5 Avoid twisting the scone cutter when stamping out the shapes. This can cause them to rise lopsided.

6 Bake scones, damper and quickbreads as soon as you can after combining the dry and liquid ingredients. If you want to prepare ahead, rub the butter and other dry ingredients together, but don't add the liquids until just before shaping and baking.

7 Scones, damper and quickbreads need to be put into a nice hot oven as this initial blast of heat activates the ingredients and helps them to rise.

8 To keep scones soft, wrap them in a clean tea towel immediately after baking. For crisper scones, cool them uncovered on a wire rack.

9 Scones are best eaten on the day they are made, but they do freeze well. Thaw them at room temperature and brush with a little milk before reheating in a 180°C (Gas Mark 4) oven for 5-10 minutes.

10 If buttermilk is listed in the recipe and you don't have any, you can simply use the same quantity of soured milk (made by adding a squeeze of lemon juice to regular milk).

11 I think quickbreads often have a better flavour and texture the day after baking, but they will store for up to 5 days. Let the loaves cool, then wrap them in foil or plastic film and store them in the fridge. They can also be frozen for up to 2 months - thaw them overnight in the fridge.

12 Most of the quickbread recipes can be made in a muffin tin rather than the usual loaf tin, if desired. You will need to bake them for 20-25 minutes.

PLAIN SCONES

PREPARATION TIME: 20 MINUTES

COOKING TIME: 15 MINUTES

MAKES 12

400 g self-raising flour

½ teaspoon salt

2 tablespoons caster sugar

70 g unsalted butter,
chilled and diced

250 ml milk, plus extra for brushing

1 free-range egg, lightly beaten

butter or cream and jam, to serve

As a child, I watched both my grandmother and mother making scones. Something must have rubbed off, even at that tender age, as I still hold those memories and follow their method to this day. Handle the dough as little as possible – no rolling allowed. To make simple fruit scones, add 60 g sultanas and some finely grated orange zest to the dough when mixing.

1 Preheat the oven to 220°C (Gas Mark 7). Dust a baking tray with flour.

2 Sift the flour, salt and sugar into a large bowl. Add the butter and, using your fingertips, rub it into the flour until it resembles fine breadcrumbs.

3 Whisk together the milk and egg and pour into the flour mixture. Mix gently with a flat-bladed knife just until a dough forms – be careful not to overwork the dough. Gather into a rough ball shape, then turn out onto a lightly floured surface and knead very lightly. The dough should feel slightly wet and sticky.

4 Gently flatten out the dough to a thickness of 3 cm, then cut out 12 rounds with a floured 5 cm round cutter. Brush the tops with a little extra milk.

5 Place the rounds on the baking tray 2 cm apart and bake for 10–15 minutes or until risen and golden. Remove from the tray and wrap the scones in a clean tea towel to keep them warm and soft. Serve warm with butter or cream and jam. Scones are best eaten on the day they are made.

KATIE'S HONEY AND RAISIN SCONES

PREPARATION TIME: 20 MINUTES

COOKING TIME: 12 MINUTES

MAKES 8-10

250 g self-raising flour,
plus extra for dusting

½ teaspoon salt

30 g unsalted butter, chilled and diced

1 tablespoon caster sugar

2 tablespoons seedless raisins

1 tablespoon runny honey

1 free-range egg

about 200 ml milk, plus extra
for brushing

butter, to serve

This delightful recipe comes from a (sadly) out-of-print book called *The Pooh Cook Book* by Katie Stewart, one of my favourite English cookery writers. This lovely little book, full of tea-time treats that Winnie the Pooh himself would have appreciated, is worth looking for in second-hand bookshops.

1 Preheat the oven to 220°C (Gas Mark 7). Dust a baking tray with flour.

2 Sift the flour and salt into a large bowl. Add the butter and, using your fingertips, rub it into the flour until it resembles fine breadcrumbs. Add the sugar and raisins, mix well and then make a well in the centre.

3 Place the honey and egg in a measuring jug and add enough milk to make 150 ml of liquid. Whisk well with a fork. Pour into the well in the flour mixture and mix gently with a flat-bladed knife just until a dough forms – be careful not to overwork the dough. Gather into a rough ball shape, then turn out onto a lightly floured surface and knead very lightly to form a smooth dough.

4 Gently flatten out the dough to a thickness of about 1 cm and cut out eight to ten rounds with a floured 5 cm round cutter (don't waste the trimmings). Alternatively, cut the dough neatly into squares with a sharp knife. Brush the tops with a little extra milk.

5 Place the rounds on the baking tray 2 cm apart and lightly dust with flour. Bake for about 12 minutes or until risen and golden. Serve warm with butter. Scones are best eaten on the day they are made.

SPICED MINCEMEAT SCONES

400 g self-raising flour

2 tablespoons caster sugar

½ teaspoon salt

1 teaspoon mixed spice

70 g unsalted butter,
chilled and diced

250 ml milk, plus extra for brushing

1 small free-range egg, lightly beaten

4 heaped tablespoons mincemeat

butter or cream and jam, to serve

These scones are perfect for Boxing Day as they're a great way to use up any leftover mincemeat. They are best served warm from the oven but also freeze well.

1 Preheat the oven to 220°C (Gas Mark 7). Dust a baking tray with flour.

2 Sift the flour, sugar, salt and mixed spice into a large bowl. Add the butter and, using your fingertips, rub it into the flour until it resembles fine breadcrumbs.

3 Whisk together the milk and egg and pour into the flour mixture. Add the mincemeat and mix gently with a flat-bladed knife just until a dough forms – be careful not to overwork the dough. Gather into a rough ball shape, then turn out onto a lightly floured surface and knead very lightly. The dough should feel slightly wet and sticky.

4 Gently flatten out the dough to a thickness of 3 cm and cut out 12 rounds with a floured 5 cm round cutter. Brush the tops with a little extra milk.

5 Place the rounds on the baking tray 2 cm apart and bake for 10-15 minutes or until risen and golden. Remove from the tray and wrap the scones in a clean tea towel to keep them warm and soft. Serve warm with butter or cream and jam. Scones are best eaten on the day they are made.

APRICOT SCONES WITH GINGER CREAM

PREPARATION TIME: 20 MINUTES

COOKING TIME: 12 MINUTES

MAKES 8

250 g self-raising flour

½ teaspoon salt

50 g unsalted butter, chilled and diced

2 tablespoons caster sugar

85 g dried apricots, roughly chopped

1 tablespoon runny honey

1 free-range egg, lightly beaten

about 150 ml milk

GINGER CREAM

150 double cream

2 pieces stem ginger (in syrup), drained and finely chopped

2 tablespoons syrup from the stem ginger jar

I usually prefer to spread scones with butter rather than whipped cream, but as with every rule there's always an exception. These honey and apricot scones are perfect served with ginger-flavoured cream.

1 Preheat the oven to 220°C (Gas Mark 7). Dust a baking tray with flour.

2 Sift the flour and salt into a large bowl. Add the butter and, using your fingertips, rub it into the flour until it resembles fine breadcrumbs. Add the sugar and apricot and mix well, breaking up any pieces of chopped apricot that clump together. Make a well in the centre.

3 Place the honey and egg in a measuring jug and add enough milk to make 150 ml of liquid. Whisk well with a fork. Pour into the well in the flour mixture and mix gently with a flat-bladed knife just until a dough forms - be careful not to overwork the dough. Gather into a rough ball shape, then turn out onto a lightly floured surface and knead very lightly to form a smooth dough.

4 Gently flatten out the dough to a thickness of 2.5 cm and cut out six to eight rounds with a floured 5 cm round cutter (don't waste the trimmings). Alternatively, cut the dough neatly into squares with a sharp knife. Brush the tops with milk.

5 Place the rounds on the baking tray 2 cm apart and bake for 10-12 minutes or until risen and golden. Remove from the tray and wrap the scones in a clean tea towel to keep them warm and soft.

6 Meanwhile, to make the ginger cream, lightly whip the cream and then fold through the ginger and syrup. Serve with the warm scones. Scones are best eaten on the day they are made.

PUMPKIN SCONES

PREPARATION TIME: 25 MINUTES,
PLUS COOLING TIME

COOKING TIME: 30 MINUTES

MAKES 12

250 g peeled, seeded pumpkin,
cut into 2 cm chunks

350 g self-raising flour

1 teaspoon baking powder

pinch of mixed spice

pinch of salt

2 tablespoons soft brown sugar

30 g unsalted butter, chilled and diced

2 tablespoons milk,
plus extra if needed

1 large free-range egg, beaten

1 teaspoon lemon juice

milk, extra, for brushing

butter, to serve

The dough for these classic Australian scones can also be formed into one large scone. Shape the dough into a 3 cm thick round and then use a sharp knife to mark out wedges (without cutting all the way through the dough). Brush the top with milk and bake for 20-25 minutes or until risen and golden.

1 Preheat the oven to 200°C (Gas Mark 6). Lightly grease a baking tray.

2 Steam the pumpkin over a saucepan of boiling water for 15 minutes or until soft when pierced with a knife. Mash with a potato masher or purée with a stick blender (you'll need about 250 ml). Allow to cool.

3 Sift the flour, baking powder, mixed spice and salt into a large bowl and stir in the sugar. Add the butter and, using your fingertips, rub it into the flour until it resembles fine breadcrumbs. Stir in the mashed pumpkin.

4 Whisk together the milk, egg and lemon juice and pour into the flour mixture. Mix gently with a flat-bladed knife just until a dough forms - be careful not to overwork the dough. If the dough is too dry, gradually add another tablespoon or two of milk. The dough should feel slightly damp. Gather into a rough ball shape, then turn out onto a lightly floured surface.

5 Gently flatten out the dough to a thickness of 3 cm and cut out 12 rounds with a floured 5 cm round cutter. Brush the tops with a little extra milk.

6 Place the rounds on the baking tray 2 cm apart and bake for 12-15 minutes or until risen and golden. Remove from the tray and wrap the scones in a clean tea towel to keep them warm and soft. Serve warm with butter. Scones are best eaten on the day they are made.

SPICED DATE AND BUTTERMILK SCONES

PREPARATION TIME: 20 MINUTES

COOKING TIME: 12 MINUTES

MAKES 12

400 g self-raising flour

½ teaspoon salt

1 teaspoon mixed spice

2 tablespoons soft brown sugar

70 g unsalted butter, chilled and diced

50 g pitted dates, chopped

½ small granny smith apple,
peeled and grated

250 ml buttermilk (or regular milk
soured with a squeeze of lemon juice)

1 free-range egg, beaten

milk, for brushing

butter or cream, to serve

The buttermilk not only gives good flavour to these lightly spiced dates scones, but also helps the scones to rise; the acidity of the buttermilk works to assist the raising agent in the flour.

1 Preheat the oven to 220ºC (Gas Mark 7). Dust a baking tray with flour.

2 Sift the flour, salt and mixed spice into a large bowl and stir in the sugar. Add the butter and, using your fingertips, rub it into the flour until it resembles fine breadcrumbs. Stir in the date and apple.

3 Whisk together the buttermilk and egg and pour into the flour mixture. Mix gently with a flat-bladed knife just until a dough forms – be careful not to overwork the dough. Gather into a rough ball shape, then turn out onto a lightly floured surface and knead very lightly. The dough should feel slightly wet and sticky.

4 Gently flatten out the dough to a thickness of 3 cm and cut out 12 rounds with a floured 5 cm round cutter. Brush the tops with a little milk.

5 Place the rounds on the baking tray 2.5 cm apart and bake for 10–12 minutes or until risen and golden. Remove from the tray and wrap the scones in a clean tea towel to keep them warm and soft. Serve warm with butter or cream. Scones are best eaten on the day they are made.

CHEESE SCONES

PREPARATION TIME: 25 MINUTES

COOKING TIME: 15 MINUTES

MAKES 9

250 g self-raising flour

1 teaspoon baking powder

½ teaspoon mustard powder

pinch of salt

50 g butter, chilled and diced,
plus extra to serve

3 tablespoons grated parmesan

100 g cheddar, grated

200 ml milk, plus extra for brushing

1 teaspoon lemon juice

When friends are coming for afternoon tea I always try to offer both savoury and sweet dishes, and these are the best cheese scones I have ever tasted. Serve them warm with butter. Cheese scones also make a delicious accompaniment to tomato or vegetable soup and are sensational served with a herb and chilli butter.

1 Preheat the oven to 200°C (Gas Mark 6). Line a baking tray with baking paper.

2 Sift the flour, baking powder, mustard powder and salt into a large bowl. Add the butter and, using your fingertips, rub it into the flour until it resembles fine breadcrumbs. Mix in the parmesan and about two-thirds of the cheddar.

3 Whisk together the milk and lemon juice (it will curdle slightly) and pour into the flour mixture. Mix gently with a flat-bladed knife just until a dough forms. It will be quite a soft wet dough; this is fine, but be careful not to overwork it. Gather into a rough ball shape, then turn out onto a lightly floured surface and knead very lightly. The dough should feel slightly wet and sticky.

4 Gently flatten out the dough to a thickness of 3 cm and cut out 9 rounds with a floured 5 cm round cutter (don't waste the trimmings). Brush the tops with a little extra milk.

5 Place the rounds on the baking tray 2.5 cm apart and sprinkle with the remaining cheddar. Bake for 12–15 minutes or until risen and golden. Serve warm with butter. Scones are best eaten on the day they are made.

GEM SCONES

PREPARATION TIME: 10 MINUTES

COOKING TIME: 10 MINUTES

MAKES ABOUT 18

40 g unsalted butter, softened
at room temperature

2 tablespoons caster sugar

pinch of salt

1 free-range egg

250 g self-raising flour, plus extra
if needed

250 ml milk, plus extra if needed

butter or jam, to serve

Gem scones are a cross between an English Yorkshire pudding and an American popover, only smaller and slightly sweetened. They seem to be a particularly Australian thing. I found this recipe among my grandmother's handwritten notes and, judging by the amount of mess on the page, she made them regularly. The perfect gem scone is almost spherical in shape with a soft, light, melt-in-the-mouth texture. Eat them hot from the oven, split and buttered. Jam is also good (although my granny's recipe says to serve them with butter and golden syrup). For best results you will need to buy a gem scone pan (called an iron) – a heavy metal tray with hemispherical indents. Second-hand versions are still available: look for them at garage sales or charity shops, or try online auction sites.

1 Preheat the oven to 240°C (Gas Mark 9). Grease the irons well with butter, then place the irons on a baking tray in the oven to preheat.

2 Beat the butter, sugar and salt with a wooden spoon until light. Add the egg and beat well until combined. Sift the flour over the mixture and fold in with a metal spoon, then stir through the milk until smooth. The mixture should be like a pancake batter – add a little extra flour or milk if needed.

3 Remove the baking tray and irons from the oven and place on a chopping board. Quickly drop about 1 tablespoon of mixture into each mould and then return to the oven. Cook for 4–6 minutes or until risen and golden. Tip the scones onto a wire rack, then serve immediately with butter and jam (or golden syrup!). Gem scones are best eaten warm on the day they are made.

MARMALADE AND GINGER TEA LOAF

PREPARATION TIME: 20 MINUTES

COOKING TIME: 1¼ HOURS

SERVES 8-10

250 g self-raising flour

½ teaspoon baking powder

1 teaspoon ground cinnamon

1 teaspoon ground ginger

pinch of salt

175 g soft brown sugar

50 g pecans, roughly chopped

3 free-range eggs, lightly beaten

120 g chunky orange marmalade

175 g unsalted butter, diced and softened at room temperature

Tea loaves are delicious things and so quick to make. Keep an eye on this one as it bakes and cover loosely with foil after about 45 minutes if it starts colouring too much. Once cool, you can brush the top with a little warmed marmalade, if you like. I think tea loaves are better the day after baking; the texture improves and the flavour develops overnight.

1 Preheat the oven to 170°C (Gas Mark 3). Grease a 21 cm × 11 cm loaf tin and line the base and sides with baking paper (leave a little overhanging the sides to help remove the bread from the tin).

2 Sift the flour, baking powder, cinnamon, ginger and salt into a large bowl. Stir in the sugar and pecans, then add the egg, marmalade and butter and beat with a wooden spoon until just combined.

3 Transfer the mixture to the tin and smooth the top. Bake for 1-1¼ hours or until the top is firm and golden brown. A skewer inserted in the centre should come out clean. Cool in the tin for 10 minutes, then turn out onto a wire rack to cool completely. Store in an airtight container for up to 2 days.

WALNUT, BANANA AND HONEY LOAF

PREPARATION TIME: 20 MINUTES

COOKING TIME: 1¼ HOURS

SERVES 8-10

250 g self-raising flour

½ teaspoon ground cinnamon

pinch of salt

125 g soft brown sugar

175 g unsalted butter, diced and softened at room temperature

2 free-range eggs, lightly beaten

2 tablespoons runny honey

100 g dates, pitted and chopped

2 ripe bananas, mashed with a fork

50 g walnuts, roughly chopped

icing sugar, for dusting (optional)

This lovely old-fashioned loaf is comfort food at its best, and so easy to make. The ingredients are simply combined in a bowl and mixed with a wooden spoon until smooth. If the top starts browning too much, cover it with a sheet of foil or baking paper during the last 20 minutes of cooking time.

1 Preheat the oven to 160°C (Gas Mark 2-3). Grease a 21 cm × 11 cm loaf tin and line the base and sides with baking paper (leave a little overhanging the sides to help remove the bread from the tin).

2 Place all the ingredients (except the walnuts) in a large bowl and beat with a wooden spoon for 1-2 minutes or until combined.

3 Transfer the mixture to the tin and smooth the top. Sprinkle over the walnuts, pressing them gently into the batter, and bake for 1-1¼ hours or until the top is firm and golden brown. Cool in the tin for 10 minutes, then turn out onto a wire rack to cool completely. Dust with a little icing sugar, if desired. Store in an airtight container for up to 3 days.

WHITE DAMPER

PREPARATION TIME: 15 MINUTES

COOKING TIME: 50 MINUTES

MAKES 1 MEDIUM LOAF

500 g plain flour, plus extra
for sprinkling

1 teaspoon salt

1 teaspoon bicarbonate of soda

30 g butter, chilled and diced

400 ml buttermilk (or regular milk
soured with a squeeze of lemon juice),
plus extra if needed

**Damper (or soda bread) is one of those dishes that
I remember from my childhood. When fresh bread
wasn't available, my grandmother would quickly whip
up a damper to accompany a warming bowl of homemade
soup. Damper is best eaten on the day it is made,
preferably while still warm from the oven.**

1 Preheat the oven to 200°C (Gas Mark 6). Sprinkle
a baking tray with a little extra flour.

2 Sift the flour, salt and bicarbonate of soda into a large
bowl. Rub the butter into the flour mixture with your
fingertips until it resembles breadcrumbs, then make
a well in the centre.

3 Pour the buttermilk into the well in the flour mixture.
Using a large metal spoon (or your hand), stir in large
strokes until a soft dough forms - it should be soft, but
not too wet or sticky. If it is a bit dry, add more milk
(a tablespoon at a time) and gently mix.

4 Gather into a rough ball shape, then turn out onto a
lightly floured surface and gently shape into a round loaf
(about 4 cm deep). The dough should feel slightly damp.
If it's a bit dry, add more milk (a tablespoon at a time)
and gently mix. Place the loaf on the baking tray, sprinkle
with a little extra flour and slash a cross in the top with
a sharp knife.

5 Bake for about 40 minutes or until risen and golden and
the loaf sounds hollow when tapped on the base. If the loaf
is still a bit damp underneath, turn it upside-down on the
tray and cook for a further 5-10 minutes. Remove from the
tray and wrap in a clean tea towel. Serve warm or at room
temperature.

WHOLEMEAL SODA BREAD

PREPARATION TIME: 15 MINUTES

COOKING TIME: 55 MINUTES

MAKES 1 LARGE LOAF

300 g plain flour, plus extra
for sprinkling

200 g wholemeal flour

1 teaspoon salt

1 teaspoon bicarbonate of soda

30 g butter, chilled and diced

about 400 ml buttermilk (or regular
milk soured with a squeeze of lemon
juice), plus extra if needed

A mixture of plain and wholemeal flour makes a healthy, yet deliciously more-ish loaf. The dough should be kneaded very lightly on a floured surface, just enough to shape the loaf.

1 Preheat the oven to 200°C (Gas Mark 6). Sprinkle a baking tray with a little extra flour.

2 Sift the flours, salt and bicarbonate of soda into a large bowl (tipping any husks back into the bowl). Rub the butter into the flour mixture with your fingertips until it resembles breadcrumbs, then make a well in the centre.

3 Pour the buttermilk into the well in the flour mixture. Using a large metal spoon (or your hand), stir in large strokes until a soft dough forms - it should be soft, but not too wet or sticky. If it is a bit dry, add more milk (a tablespoon at a time) and gently mix.

4 Gather into a rough ball shape, then turn out onto a lightly floured surface and gently shape into a round loaf (about 5 cm deep). The dough should feel slightly damp. If it's a bit dry, add more milk (a tablespoon at a time) and gently mix. Place the loaf on the baking tray, sprinkle with a little extra flour and slash a cross in the top with a sharp knife.

5 Bake for about 45 minutes or until risen and golden and the loaf sounds hollow when tapped on the base. If the loaf is still a bit damp underneath, turn it upside-down on the tray and cook for a further 5-10 minutes. Remove from the oven and wrap in a clean tea towel. Serve warm or cold. The loaf is best eaten on the day it is made.

MEDITERRANEAN DAMPER

PREPARATION TIME: 20 MINUTES

COOKING TIME: 1 HOUR 20 MINUTES

MAKES 1 LARGE LOAF

1 red capsicum (pepper)

1 yellow capsicum (pepper)

olive oil, for drizzling

450 g self-raising flour, plus extra for sprinkling

2 teaspoons salt

1 teaspoon bicarbonate of soda

125 g butter, chilled and diced

50 g good-quality seeded black olives, halved

3 tablespoons grated parmesan

250 ml buttermilk or (or regular milk soured with a squeeze of lemon juice), plus extra if needed

Damper or soda bread also works well with additions. Here I've added red and yellow capsicum and olives to create a Mediterranean variation. Thinly sliced, it makes delicious sandwiches.

1 Preheat the oven to 200°C (Gas Mark 6).

2 Halve the capsicums, removing any seeds or white pith, and place in a roasting tin. Drizzle with olive oil and roast for 20-25 minutes or until soft and coloured. Allow to cool, then slip off their skins. Roughly chop the flesh.

3 Sift the flour, salt and bicarbonate of soda into a large bowl. Rub the butter into the flour mixture with your fingertips. Add the chopped capsicum, olives and parmesan, then make a well in the centre.

4 Pour the buttermilk into the well in the flour mixture. Using a large metal spoon (or your hand), stir in large strokes until a soft dough forms – it should be soft, but not too wet or sticky. If it is a bit dry, add more milk (a tablespoon at a time) and gently mix.

5 Turn out onto a lightly floured surface and gently shape into a large loaf (about 4 cm deep). The dough should feel slightly damp.

6 Sprinkle a baking tray with a little flour. Place the loaf on the tray, sprinkle with a little extra flour and slash a cross in the top with a sharp knife.

7 Bake for 45-55 minutes or until risen and golden and the loaf sounds hollow when tapped on the base. If the loaf is still a bit damp underneath, turn it upside-down on the tray and cook for a further 5-10 minutes. Remove from the tray and wrap in a clean tea towel. Serve warm or cold. The loaf is best eaten on the day it is made.

SLICES

TIPS

1 Slices are wonderful old-fashioned, all-occasion treats, loved by beginners and experienced cooks alike. Simple to make, they are equally at home in a lunchbox, alongside your morning coffee or as part of a fancy afternoon tea spread. Slices also make great gifts (especially for friends who haven't worked out how easy they are to bake). I sometimes give them in the tin they were baked in, but you could also present them in pretty biscuit tins or brightly coloured cardboard boxes, or pile them up in an oversized tea cup.

2 When preparing the tin for slices, I always grease the base and sides and then line the base with baking paper, leaving 4–5 cm overhanging the two long sides – this makes it easier to remove when cool.

3 As a general rule, if making a slice that has a separately cooked base, don't add the topping or filling until the base has cooled completely.

4 Slices may be cut into squares, rectangles or diamonds. The portion size is up to you. Most of these recipes are baked in a rectangular 30 cm × 20 cm tin and I usually cut them into 15 portions by dividing the cake into three on the short end and five on the long end. Trim the edges straight and square. If you want to make sure the pieces are a consistent size, use a tape measure or ruler and mark the cuts with a knife. Use a sharp serrated knife to cut all the way through the base of the slice.

5 Un-iced slices freeze well, either cut into squares or as the whole piece – just make sure they have cooled completely before wrapping and freezing. For best results, take them out of the freezer several hours before you're planning to serve them and let them thaw out at room temperature.

CHEWY CRANBERRY BARS

PREPARATION TIME: 15 MINUTES

COOKING TIME: 35 MINUTES

MAKES 12-20

4 tablespoons self-raising flour

pinch of salt

300 g rolled oats (porridge oats)

50 g desiccated coconut

4 tablespoons sesame seeds

100 g pumpkin seeds

125 g dried cranberries (craisins)

200 g soft brown sugar

175 g unsalted butter

125 ml golden syrup

I often make these chewy bars with my four godchildren. They love the whole process – the counting (weighing out the ingredients turns into a little maths lesson), the cooking and, most of all, eating the finished results. You can swap the cranberries for dried cherries, chopped fresh dates or any dried fruit you have to hand.

1 Preheat the oven to 170°C (Gas Mark 3). Grease a shallow 30 cm × 20 cm baking tin and line with baking paper (leave a little overhanging the two long sides to help remove the slice from the tin).

2 Sift the flour and salt into a large bowl. Stir in the oats, coconut, seeds and cranberries, then mix through the sugar.

3 Melt the butter and golden syrup in a small saucepan over low heat. Remove from the heat and leave to cool for 5 minutes, then pour into the dry ingredients. Mix with a large metal spoon.

4 Press the mixture into the tin and bake for 25-30 minutes or until golden (it may be a little soft when touched but will firm when cool). Leave to cool in the tin, then turn out and cut into squares. Store the bars in an airtight container for up to 7 days.

MUESLI SLICE

PREPARATION TIME: 15 MINUTES

COOKING TIME: 25 MINUTES

MAKES 12

300 g rolled oats (porridge oats)

100 g sultanas

4 tablespoons pumpkin seeds

50 g raw almonds, coarsely chopped

finely grated zest of 1 orange

pinch of salt

125 g unsalted butter, diced

3 tablespoons golden syrup

175 g soft brown sugar

75 ml fruit juice (apple or pear juice)

Dried fruit, brown sugar and golden syrup make this slice slightly chewy and also help it keep well. Just the thing for lunchboxes or an afternoon snack.

1 Preheat the oven to 180°C (Gas Mark 4). Grease a shallow 30 cm × 20 cm baking tin and line with baking paper (leave a little overhanging the two long sides to help remove the slice from the tin).

2 Combine the oats, sultanas, seeds, almonds, orange zest and salt in a large bowl.

3 Place the butter, golden syrup, sugar and fruit juice in a large saucepan and bring to the boil over low heat. Remove from the heat and leave to cool for 5 minutes, then pour into the dry ingredients. Mix with a large metal spoon.

4 Press the mixture into the tin and bake for 20 minutes or until golden. Leave to cool in the tin, then turn out and cut into squares. Store in an airtight container for up to 7 days.

SILVANA'S ALMOND AND BLACKBERRY TRAY BAKE

PREPARATION TIME: 15 MINUTES

COOKING TIME: 55 MINUTES

MAKES 16-24

250 g self-raising flour

pinch of salt

50 g ground almonds

200 g unsalted butter, diced

280 g caster sugar

50 g desiccated coconut

2 free-range eggs

400 g blackberries, fresh or frozen

This is based on a recipe created by my friend, British food writer and television cook Silvana Franco. It's so simple to make - one mixture whizzed in the food processor forms the base and topping. If you want to vary the fruit, try chopped pineapple, mango, plum or raspberries instead.

1 Preheat the oven to 180°C (Gas Mark 4). Grease a shallow 20 cm x 30 cm baking tin and line with baking paper (leave a little overhanging the two long sides to help remove the slice from the tin).

2 Place the flour, salt, ground almonds, butter and sugar in a food processor and whizz just until the butter is evenly distributed and it starts to clump together (alternatively, you can rub in the butter by hand). Remove 85 g of the mix and place in a bowl, then stir in the coconut and set aside.

3 Add the eggs to the remaining mixture in the food processor and whizz quickly (or mix with a wooden spoon). It doesn't need to be very smooth.

4 Spread this mixture over the base of the tin, then scatter with half the blackberries. Sprinkle with the reserved coconut mixture and bake for 40 minutes. Dot the remaining berries over the surface and cook for a further 15 minutes or until firm to the touch.

5 Cool in the tin, then turn out and cut into slices or squares. Store in the fridge for up to 2 days.

ORANGE AND ALMOND SLICE

PREPARATION TIME: 20 MINUTES

COOKING TIME: 40 MINUTES

MAKES 20

150 g unsalted butter, melted

350 g soft brown sugar

finely grated zest of 1 orange

pinch of salt

2 large free-range eggs, lightly beaten

150 g self-raising flour

150 g blanched almonds,
roughly chopped

ALMOND TOPPING

100 g unsalted butter, diced

100 g caster sugar

125 ml double cream

2 tablespoons plain flour

pinch of salt

finely grated zest of 1 orange

100 g flaked almonds

I first made this delicious slice about 20 years ago when I worked as a cook in the UK at a rather grand private country house. The Queen Mother (and about forty other dignitaries) were coming for tea and I needed to prepare a selection of cakes and bakes that could be made ahead of time. This was the perfect solution as it can easily be baked a day ahead. Sadly HM didn't try the slice, but I still have the (now very faded) fax from Clarence House with instructions for making cucumber sandwiches.

1 Preheat the oven to 180°C (Gas Mark 4). Grease a 30 cm × 20 cm baking tin (at least 2.5 cm deep) and line with baking paper (leave a little overhanging the two long sides to help remove the slice from the tin).

2 For the base, combine the butter, sugar, orange zest and salt in a large bowl and stir in the egg. Sift over the flour and add the almonds. Mix gently until combined.

3 Spoon the mixture into the tin and bake for 20 minutes or until golden and firm to the touch. Allow to cool.

4 To make the topping, melt the butter in a small saucepan over low heat. Remove from the heat and stir in the sugar, cream, flour, salt and orange zest. Return the pan to the heat and bring the mixture to the boil, then cook, stirring well, for 1-2 minutes or until slightly thickened. Remove from the heat and stir in the almonds.

5 Spread the topping mixture over the cooled base and return to the oven for another 15 minutes or until golden. Cool in the tin, then turn out and cut into slices. Store in an airtight container for up to 5 days.

LEMON SLICE

PREPARATION TIME: 20 MINUTES,
PLUS REFRIGERATION TIME

COOKING TIME: 40 MINUTES

MAKES 20

350 g plain flour

pinch of salt

200 g unsalted butter, diced and chilled

125 g icing sugar, sifted

1 free-range egg yolk

1-2 tablespoons cold water

LEMON TOPPING

4 free-range eggs

500 ml double cream

275 g caster sugar

110 g plain flour

finely grated zest and juice of 3 lemons

icing sugar, for dusting

This is a lovely indulgence, featuring a delicious, lemony custard topping sitting on a sweet pastry base.

1 Sift the flour and salt into a large bowl. Rub the butter into the flour with your fingertips until it resembles coarse breadcrumbs. Stir in the icing sugar. Add the egg yolk and 1 tablespoon cold water and mix together wth a large wooden spoon until it clumps together. Add a little extra cold water if needed so the base just comes together. Gently gather the base into a flat disc shape, then wrap in plastic film and chill for 30 minutes.

2 Preheat the oven to 180°C (Gas Mark 4). Grease a 30 cm × 20 cm baking tin (at least 2.5 cm deep) and line with baking paper (leave a little overhanging the two long sides to help remove the slice from the tin).

3 Roll out the dough between two sheets of baking paper until large enough to fit the tin. Line the tin with the dough, then bake for about 15 minutes or until golden and dry to the touch.

4 Meanwhile, to make the topping, beat the eggs, cream and sugar together with hand-held electric beaters until pale and well combined. Sift over the flour. Add the lemon zest and juice and continue to beat until light and well mixed.

5 Remove the base from the oven and immediately pour on the topping. Return to the oven and bake for a further 20-25 minutes or until set. Remove and cool completely in the tin. To serve, dust with a little icing sugar and cut into squares. Store in the fridge for up to 4 days.

BANANA, DATE AND LEMON SLICE

PREPARATION TIME: 20 MINUTES

COOKING TIME: 35 MINUTES

MAKES 20

100 g fresh dates, pitted and chopped

1 tablespoon golden syrup

100 g unsalted butter, diced and softened at room temperature

175 g demerara or raw sugar

150 g self-raising flour

150 g plain flour

½ teaspoon mixed spice

pinch of salt

1 large ripe banana, mashed with a fork

LEMON ICING

300 g icing sugar

30 g unsalted butter, softened at room temperature

juice of ½ lemon

1–2 tablespoons boiling water

Dates, bananas and golden syrup make this lovely and moist. The non-iced slice can be baked ahead of time, if liked. Allow it to cool completely, then cover with plastic film and freeze for up to a month. When you're ready to eat it, let it thaw at room temperature, then spread with the icing and serve.

1 Preheat the oven to 180°C (Gas Mark 4). Grease a 30 cm × 20 cm baking tin (at least 2.5 cm deep) and line with baking paper (leave a little overhanging the two long sides to help remove the slice from the tin).

2 Combine the dates, golden syrup and 3 tablespoons water in a small saucepan and bring to the boil. Reduce the heat and simmer for 2–3 minutes, then set aside to cool.

3 Place the butter and sugar in a bowl and beat with hand-held electric beaters until well mixed. Sift over the flours, mixed spice and salt and gently stir in with a wooden spoon. Add the date mixture and mashed banana and mix until combined.

4 Spoon the mixture into the tin and bake for 30 minutes or until firm to the touch. Cool in the tin for 10 minutes, then transfer to a wire rack to cool completely.

5 To make the icing, sift the icing sugar into a bowl. Add the butter and lemon juice and mix with a wooden spoon. Add enough boiling water to make a spreadable icing.

6 Spread the icing over the cooled base and cut into fingers to serve. Store in an airtight container for up to 7 days.

SIMPLE SPICED BANANA SLICE

PREPARATION TIME: 20 MINUTES

COOKING TIME: 25 MINUTES

MAKES 12-15

185 g unsalted butter, diced and softened at room temperature

185 g caster sugar

1 teaspoon vanilla extract

3 free-range eggs, lightly beaten

200 g self-raising flour, sifted

pinch of salt

½ teaspoon ground cinnamon

½ teaspoon ground allspice

2 very ripe bananas, mashed with a fork

150 g pecans, roughly chopped

icing sugar, for dusting

Here, one of my favourite banana cakes is cooked in a brownie tin to make a deliciously simple slice. Look for over-ripe bananas for the best flavour.

1 Preheat the oven to 180°C (Gas Mark 4). Grease a shallow 30 cm × 20 cm baking tin and line with baking paper (leave a little overhanging the two long sides to help remove the slice from the tin).

2 Place the butter, sugar and vanilla in an electric mixer and mix on medium speed for 7-8 minutes or until pale and fluffy. Transfer the beaten egg to a jug. Reduce the speed of the mixer and, with the motor running, add the egg to the mixture, followed by an occasional spoonful of flour. Reduce the speed and gradually mix in the remaining flour, salt, cinnamon and allspice. Fold in the banana and pecans with a large metal spoon until combined.

3 Spoon the mixture into the tin and smooth the top. Bake for about 25 minutes or until golden, risen and firm to the touch. Cool completely in the tin, then turn out and cut into squares. Dust with icing sugar and serve. Store in an airtight container for up to 5 days.

CHEWY PECAN SQUARES

PREPARATION TIME: 15 MINUTES

COOKING TIME: 30 MINUTES

MAKES 15-18

185 g unsalted butter, melted

450 g soft brown sugar

2 teaspoons vanilla extract

pinch of salt

3 large free-range eggs, lightly beaten

175 g plain flour

1 teaspoon baking powder

200 g pecans, roughly chopped

COFFEE ICING

100 g unsalted butter, diced and softened at room temperature

200 g icing sugar

2 teaspoons instant coffee powder

1 tablespoon boiling water

The combination of brown sugar and coarsely chopped pecans gives this slice a wonderfully chewy texture. It can be made without the coffee icing - in fact, I have made it without for many years and only recently added the icing - but it really does give it a fabulous finish.

1 Preheat the oven to 180°C (Gas Mark 4). Grease a shallow 30 cm × 20 cm baking tin and line with baking paper (leave a little overhanging the two long sides to help remove the slice from the tin).

2 Combine the butter, sugar, vanilla and salt in a large bowl and stir in the egg. Sift over the flour and baking powder and add the pecans. Mix gently until combined.

3 Spoon the pecan mixture into the tin and bake for 25-30 minutes or until golden and a skewer inserted in the centre comes out clean. Remove and cool completely in the tin.

4 To make the coffee icing, place the butter in an electric mixer and beat until soft and pale. Sift in the icing sugar and beat until smooth and creamy. Dissolve the coffee powder in the boiling water, then mix it into the icing. When cool, spread over the top of the slice.

5 Cut into squares or rectangles to serve. Store in an airtight container for up to 5 days.

PANFORTE

PREPARATION TIME: 25 MINUTES

COOKING TIME: 40 MINUTES

SERVES ABOUT 20

100 g shelled hazelnuts

100 g blanched almonds

200 g candied orange and lemon peel, coarsely chopped

100 g dried figs, finely chopped

finely grated zest of 1 lemon

1 teaspoon ground cinnamon

¼ teaspoon ground coriander

¼ teaspoon ground cloves

¼ teaspoon grated nutmeg

pinch of salt and white pepper

1 tablespoon cocoa

70 g plain flour

150 g caster sugar

4 tablespoons runny honey

50 g unsalted butter

icing sugar, for dusting

Panforte is a dense, flat Italian fruit slice that comes from Siena and is made for the Christmas celebrations. This version is a rich, textured cake filled with nuts, dried figs, candied peel, cocoa and spices, held together with a boiled syrup made from sugar and honey. Serve it in very thin slices.

1 Preheat the oven to 150°C (Gas Mark 2). Line a 23 cm springform tin with baking paper or rice paper and grease the paper with a little butter.

2 Place the hazelnuts and almonds on a baking tray and lightly toast them in the oven for a few minutes or until golden. Set aside to cool.

3 Combine the nuts, peel, figs, lemon zest, spices, salt and pepper in a large ceramic bowl. Sift in the cocoa and flour and mix well.

4 Gently heat the sugar, honey and butter in a heavy-based saucepan. Stir initially to dissolve the sugar and then do not mix again. Bring the syrup to the boil and keep cooking until it reaches 120°C on a sugar thermometer (or when a little of it dropped into cold water forms a soft ball when moulded between your finger and thumb).

5 Pour the syrup onto the nut mixture and stir quickly to blend – you must work fast as it will become stiff. Spoon the mixture into the tin and smooth the top. Bake for 30-35 minutes (no more) - it will harden as it cools.

6 Cool in the tin until it is firm, then remove the sides of the tin. Dust heavily with icing sugar before slicing and serving. Wrap in plastic film and store in a cool dark place for up to 1 month.

MARMALADE SQUARES

PREPARATION TIME: 20 MINUTES

COOKING TIME: 40 MINUTES

MAKES 24

350 g plain flour

pinch of salt

200 g unsalted butter, chilled and diced

150 g muscovado sugar

MARMALADE FILLING

1 rounded teaspoon bicarbonate of soda

1 large free-range egg, lightly beaten

120 ml double cream

50 g pecans, coarsely chopped

50 g mixed candied peel

100 g orange marmalade

2 tablespoons orange juice

Muscovado sugar is dark and moist and gives a lovely flavour to the base of this slice. It is often available in health-food shops or delicatessens, but if you can't find it, use regular dark brown sugar instead.

1 Preheat the oven to 180°C (Gas Mark 4). Grease a shallow 30 cm × 20 cm baking tin and line with baking paper (leave a little overhanging the two long sides to help remove the slice from the tin).

2 Sift the flour and salt into a large bowl. Rub the butter into the flour with your fingertips until it resembles coarse breadcrumbs. Add the sugar and mix until it clumps together.

3 Spread half this mixture into the base of the tin, pressing down firmly. Bake for 10-15 minutes or until light brown. Remove and set aside to cool.

4 To make the filling, tip the remaining base mixture into a large bowl and stir through the bicarbonate of soda. Mix in the egg, cream, nuts, mixed peel and half the marmalade. Pour over the cooled base and bake for 20-25 minutes or until just firm and golden brown.

5 Meanwhile, warm the orange juice and remaining marmalade in a small saucepan. Brush over the top of the warm slice, then leave to cool in the tin. Cut into squares and serve. Store in an airtight container for up to 5 days.

CRUNCHY-TOPPED LEMON SLAB

PREPARATION TIME: 20 MINUTES

COOKING TIME: 30 MINUTES

MAKES 12

250 g unsalted butter, diced and softened at room temperature

1 tablespoon finely grated lemon zest

250 g caster sugar

4 free-range eggs, lightly beaten

275 g self-raising flour, sifted

1 teaspoon baking powder

pinch of salt

100 ml buttermilk (or regular milk soured with a squeeze of lemon)

juice of 1 lemon

LEMON TOPPING

125 g granulated sugar

juice of 1 lemon

This simple slice has a delicious crunchy topping made by quickly combining granulated sugar and lemon juice and pouring this over the top of the slice while still hot.

1 Preheat the oven to 180°C (Gas Mark 4). Grease a shallow 30 cm × 20 cm baking tin and line the base and sides with baking paper, extending the paper 5 cm above the tin.

2 Place the butter, lemon zest, sugar, egg, flour, baking powder, salt, buttermilk and lemon juice in a large bowl and beat with a wooden spoon or hand-held electric beaters for 1-2 minutes or until just combined. It's important not to beat the batter too much – just long enough to make it smooth.

3 Spoon the batter into the tin, smooth the top and bake on the middle shelf of the oven for about 30 minutes. The slice is cooked when it is risen and golden and has slightly shrunk from the sides. Cool in the tin for 5 minutes.

4 To make the topping, combine the sugar and lemon juice (don't let the sugar dissolve). Quickly spoon it over the top of the slice, then set aside to cool. Cut into squares and serve. Store in an airtight container for up to 5 days.

MITZIE WILSON'S NUTTY TRAY BAKE

PREPARATION TIME: 25 MINUTES

COOKING TIME: 35 MINUTES

MAKES 15

50 g dark chocolate,
broken into pieces

250 g plain flour

pinch of salt

100 g soft brown sugar

120 g unsalted butter, melted

NUT TOPPING

125 g dark brown sugar

75 g unsalted butter

2 tablespoons golden syrup

1 tablespoon double cream

300 g mixed nuts, toasted (see above)

This recipe is from British food writer and friend Mitzie Wilson, whose recipes are always simple and delicious. Try a mixture of cashews, walnuts, macadamias and pistachios - you can toast the nuts by tossing them in a frying pan over medium-high heat until golden.

1 Preheat the oven to 180°C (Gas Mark 4). Grease a shallow 30 cm × 20 cm baking tin and line with baking paper (leave a little overhanging the two long sides to help remove the slice from the tin).

2 Place the chocolate in a heatproof bowl set over a saucepan of barely simmering water (make sure the bowl doesn't touch the water) until melted.

3 Sift the flour and salt into a bowl, add the sugar and then pour in the melted butter and chocolate. Mix well, then press evenly into the base of the tin. Bake for 15-20 minutes, then leave to cool slightly.

4 Meanwhile, to make the topping, combine the sugar, butter and golden syrup in a medium saucepan over medium heat. Stir often to dissolve the sugar but don't let the mixture boil. Add the cream and mix well, then stir in the nuts until they are coated with the sauce. Spread evenly in the tin and bake for 10 minutes. Cool completely, then cut into slices to serve. Store in an airtight container for up to 5 days.

SULTANA FLAPJACKS

PREPARATION TIME: 20 MINUTES

COOKING TIME: 35 MINUTES

MAKES 15

400 g rolled oats (porridge oats)

300 g soft brown sugar

120 g sultanas

250 g unsalted butter

120 ml golden syrup

I first tasted flapjacks during a visit to the north of England. I had always thought of flapjacks as another name for pancakes, but this is perhaps more of an American thing. Here, they are a sweet, chewy slice full of golden syrup and oats. The addition of sultanas is my variant. Make sure that the tin is well lined with baking paper as the wonderful stickiness of flapjacks can make them stick to the tin when cold.

1 Preheat the oven to 170°C (Gas Mark 4). Grease a shallow 30 cm × 20 cm baking tin and line with baking paper (leave a little overhanging the two long sides to help remove the slice from the tin).

2 Combine the oats, sugar and sultanas in a large bowl. Melt the butter and golden syrup in a saucepan over low heat, then pour onto the dry ingredients. Mix with a large metal spoon until combined.

3 Spoon the mixture into the tin, pressing lightly to even the top. Bake for 25–30 minutes or until golden (it will still be a bit wet in the centre, but will firm up when cool).

4 Leave to cool in the tin, then turn out and cut into squares. Store in an airtight container for up to 7 days.

CITRUS AND HAZELNUT SQUARES

80 g unsalted butter, diced and softened at room temperature

60 g caster sugar

140 g plain flour

pinch of salt

40 g hazelnuts, toasted (see above) and chopped

icing sugar, for dusting

CITRUS FILLING

2 large free-range eggs

185 g caster sugar

2 tablespoons plain flour

finely grated zest of ½ orange

finely grated zest of 1 lemon

½ teaspoon baking powder

In this recipe, a hazelnut-flavoured pastry is topped with a thin citrus topping. If you can't find ready-toasted hazelnuts, you can easily toast them yourself by tossing them in a frying pan over medium-high heat for a few minutes until golden.

1 Preheat the oven to 180°C (Gas Mark 4). Grease a shallow 20 cm square baking tin and line with baking paper (leave a little overhanging two sides to help remove the slice from the tin).

2 Place the butter and sugar in a bowl and sift over the flour and salt. Add half the hazelnuts, then beat with a wooden spoon until the mixture is combined and slightly crumbly. Press the mixture into the base of the tin and bake for 10–12 minutes or until golden.

3 Meanwhile, to make the filling, place all the ingredients in a bowl and beat with hand-held electric beaters until frothy. Pour the mixture over the hot base, then sprinkle the remaining hazelnuts over the top. Bake for another 20 minutes or until golden around the edges and just set in the centre.

4 Remove and cool completely in the tin. To serve, cut into squares and dust with icing sugar. Store in an airtight container in the fridge for up to 5 days.

JANE CURRAN'S CARROT AND COCONUT BARS

PREPARATION TIME: 15 MINUTES

COOKING TIME: 40 MINUTES

MAKES 12

250 g self-raising flour

pinch of salt

2 teaspoons ground cinnamon

300 g raw or demerera sugar

100 g desiccated coconut

100 g sultanas

75 g walnuts, roughly chopped

1 large carrot, grated

2 free-range eggs, lightly beaten

½ teaspoon vanilla extract

120 g unsalted butter, melted

100 ml vegetable oil

icing sugar, for dusting

Jane Curran is a brilliant baker and generous friend who is very happy to share her recipes. This one is a beauty - lots of flavour for very little work. It is perfect as it is, needing only a dusting of icing sugar to serve.

1 Preheat the oven to 180°C (Gas Mark 4). Grease a shallow 30 cm x 20 cm baking tin and line with baking paper (leave a little overhanging the two long sides to help remove the slice from the tin).

2 Sift the flour, salt and cinnamon into a large bowl. Stir in the sugar, coconut, sultanas, walnuts and carrot, then make a well in the centre.

3 In a separate bowl, mix together the egg, vanilla, butter and oil. Pour into the well in the flour mixture and stir until just combined.

4 Pour the batter into the tin and smooth the top. Bake for 35-40 minutes or until golden brown and firm to the touch. Cool in the tin for about 10 minutes, then turn out onto a wire rack to cool completely. Cut into bars and serve with a dusting of icing sugar. Store in an airtight container for up to 5 days.

RASPBERRY AND LEMON CURD SLICE

PREPARATION TIME: 10 MINUTES

COOKING TIME: 40 MINUTES

SERVES 12

185 g unsalted butter, diced and softened at room temperature

185 g caster sugar

3 free-range eggs, lightly beaten

finely grated zest of 1 lemon

185 g self-raising flour, sifted

pinch of salt

125 g lemon curd

150 g raspberries, fresh or frozen

1 tablespoon granulated sugar

A simple lemon cake is transformed by placing dollops of lemon curd over the surface and topping with raspberries. The lemon curd shouldn't be spread out evenly – the point of the dollops is to give little bursts of lemon flavour when eaten.

1 Preheat the oven to 180°C (Gas Mark 4). Grease and line the base of a 22 cm square cake tin.

2 Put the butter, caster sugar, egg, lemon zest, flour and salt in a large bowl and beat with a wooden spoon or hand-held electric beaters until just combined. It's important not to beat the batter too much – just long enough to make it smooth.

3 Spoon the batter into the tin and smooth the top. Dollop heaped teaspoons of lemon curd over the batter and then scatter with the raspberries, pressing them down lightly. Sprinkle with the granulated sugar.

4 Bake for 35-40 minutes or until risen and golden. A skewer inserted in the centre should come out clean. Cool in the tin for about 10 minutes, then lift out (using the overhanging paper) onto a wire rack to cool completely. Cut into bars and serve. Store in an airtight container in the fridge for up to 5 days.

ICED PUMPKIN SLICE

PREPARATION TIME: 25 MINUTES

COOKING TIME: 40 MINUTES

MAKES 20

150 g peeled, seeded pumpkin, cut into 2 cm chunks

125 g unsalted butter, diced and softened at room temperature

250 g soft brown sugar

1 teaspoon vanilla extract

2 large free-range eggs, lightly beaten

125 g self-raising flour, sifted

125 g plain flour, sifted

pinch of salt

finely grated zest of ½ lemon

½ teaspoon ground ginger

125 ml buttermilk (or regular milk soured with a squeeze of lemon juice)

CREAM-CHEESE TOPPING

175 g cream cheese, softened at room temperature

450 g icing sugar, sifted

125 g unsalted butter, diced and softened at room temperature

¼ teaspoon ground nutmeg

Using pumpkin in baking is not as strange as it seems (just think of pumpkin scones or pumpkin pie) – it adds flavour, moisture and a lovely rich colour. In this more-ish slice, its natural sweetness combines beautifully with ginger, lemon and vanilla.

1 Steam the pumpkin over a saucepan of boiling water for 15 minutes or until soft when pierced with a knife. Drain well, then mash with a potato masher or purée with a stick blender. Allow to cool.

2 Preheat the oven to 180°C (Gas Mark 4). Grease a shallow 30 cm × 20 cm baking tin and line with baking paper (leave a little overhanging the two long sides to help remove the slice from the tin).

3 Place the butter, sugar and vanilla in an electric mixer and mix on medium speed for 7-8 minutes or until pale and fluffy. Transfer the beaten egg to a jug. Reduce the speed of the mixer and, with the motor running, gradually add the egg to the mixture, followed by an occasional spoonful of flour. Reduce the speed and gradually mix in the remaining flour, salt, lemon zest and ginger. Using a large metal spoon, fold in the buttermilk and pumpkin purée until combined.

4 Spoon the batter into the tin and smooth the top. Bake for 25 minutes or until golden, risen and firm to the touch. Cool in the tin for about 10 minutes, then turn out onto a wire rack to cool completely.

5 To make the topping, place all the ingredients in a bowl and beat until smooth. Spread over the cooled cake, then cut into squares to serve. Store in an airtight container in the fridge for up to 5 days.

CHOC MARSHMALLOW SQUARES

PREPARATION TIME: 25 MINUTES,
PLUS REFRIGERATION TIME

COOKING TIME: 30 MINUTES

MAKES 16

250 g plain flour

pinch of salt

180 g unsalted butter, chilled and diced

60 g caster sugar

1 free-range egg yolk

1–2 tablespoons milk or water

MARSHMALLOW FILLING

300 g marshmallows

2 tablespoons double cream

100 g unsalted pistachio kernels,
roughly chopped

75 g glacé cherries, roughly chopped

CHOCOLATE TOPPING

60 g unsalted butter

250 g dark chocolate,
broken into pieces

This delicious slice is simpler to make than it looks. Shop-bought marshmallows are the secret ingredient – they melt easily and, when combined with nuts and cherries, provide a delicious filling.

1 Grease a shallow 30 cm × 20 cm baking tin and line with baking paper (leave a little overhanging the two long sides to help remove the slice from the tin).

2 Sift the flour and salt into a large bowl. Rub the butter into the flour using your fingertips until it resembles coarse breadcrumbs. Sift in the sugar and stir through. Add the egg yolk and milk or water and mix with a large metal spoon until it clumps together and forms a thick dough (it should look like shortbread). Press evenly into the tin – not too firmly, but there should be no holes. Prick well with a fork and chill for 30 minutes.

3 Preheat the oven to 180°C (Gas Mark 4). Bake the base for 20 minutes, then remove and leave to cool.

4 To make the filling, combine the marshmallows and cream in a small heavy-based saucepan and place over low heat until melted but not smooth. Remove the pan from the heat and stir in the pistachios and glacé cherries. Spread the mixture over the base and leave to cool at room temperature.

5 For the topping, melt the butter and chocolate in a heatproof bowl set over a saucepan of barely simmering water, stirring occasionally (make sure the bowl doesn't touch the water). Spread over the marshmallow filling and leave to set at room temperature. Cut into squares to serve. Store in an airtight container in the fridge for up to 5 days.

CHOCOLATE SLICE WITH MACAROON TOPPING

PREPARATION TIME: 20 MINUTES

COOKING TIME: 45 MINUTES

MAKES 16

125 g unsalted butter, diced and softened at room temperature

150 g plain flour

pinch of salt

3 tablespoons cocoa

60 g icing sugar

1 free-range egg, lightly beaten

1 tablespoon milk

1 teaspoon vanilla extract

160 g raspberry jam

150 g white chocolate chips

MACAROON TOPPING

4 large free-range egg whites

150 g ground almonds

150 g caster sugar

3 tablespoons flaked almonds

This is the recipe I turn to when I want something rich and indulgent. The chocolate base is covered with raspberry jam and white chocolate chips, then topped with an almond macaroon. You could also make it with apricot jam, instead of raspberry jam, as almonds and apricots are very good friends.

1 Preheat the oven to 170°C (Gas Mark 3). Grease a shallow 20 cm square baking tin and line with baking paper (leave a little overhanging on two sides to help remove the slice from the tin).

2 Put the butter in a large bowl and sift over the flour, salt, cocoa and icing sugar. Add the egg, milk and vanilla and beat with hand-held electric beaters until combined.

3 Spoon the batter into the tin and smooth the top. Bake for 15-20 minutes or until firm. Set aside to cool for about 5 minutes, and then spread with the jam and top with the chocolate chips.

4 Increase the oven temperature to 180°C (Gas Mark 4).

5 To make the topping, beat the egg whites with a whisk or hand-held electric beaters until fluffy and well mixed (they shouldn't form peaks). Whisk in the ground almonds and sugar until combined. Pour the mixture over the base, then sprinkle with the flaked almonds and bake for a further 25 minutes or until the topping is golden and has puffed up a little. Cool in the tin, then cut into pieces to serve. Store in an airtight container for up to 3 days.

ONE-BOWL BLUEBERRY AND PINE NUT SQUARES

200 g plain flour

pinch of salt

200 g rolled oats (porridge oats)

250 g unsalted butter, diced

175 g soft brown sugar

finely grated zest of ½ orange

100 g pine nuts

250 g blueberries, fresh or frozen

2 tablespoons demerara or raw sugar

Any recipe that only uses one bowl is perfect for me. This mixture makes both the base and topping, which are sandwiched together with fresh blueberries. What could be easier?

1 Preheat the oven to 180°C (Gas Mark 4). Grease a shallow 30 cm × 20 cm baking tin and line with baking paper (leave a little overhanging the two long sides to help remove the slice from the tin).

2 Sift the flour and salt into a large bowl. Add the butter and oats and rub the butter into the dry ingredients with your fingertips until they start to clump together. Add the sugar, orange zest and pine nuts and mix with your fingers until combined.

3 Transfer about two-thirds of the mixture to the tin and press down lightly, making sure it covers the base (take care not to press it too firmly). Scatter the blueberries evenly over the top. Cover with the remaining oat mixture, pressing down lightly, then finish with a sprinkling of demerara or raw sugar.

4 Bake for 25-35 minutes or until golden and cooked through. Remove from the oven and cut into rectangles while still warm, then leave to cool in the tin. Store in an airtight container for up to 5 days.

CHEWY GINGER SLICE

PREPARATION TIME: 15 MINUTES

COOKING TIME: 30 MINUTES

MAKES 16

125 g unsalted butter

3 tablespoons golden syrup

280 g plain flour

2 teaspoons baking powder

pinch of salt

1 teaspoon ground ginger

1 teaspoon ground cinnamon

pinch of ground cloves

300 g soft brown sugar

2 free-range eggs

1 teaspoon vanilla extract

icing sugar, for dusting

This one-bowl mixture is gently spiced and wonderfully chewy, thanks to the golden syrup and brown sugar. I prefer to serve this slice simply dusted with icing sugar, but you could also cover it with a simple buttercream icing (see page 313), if desired.

1 Preheat the oven to 180°C (Gas Mark 4). Grease a shallow 30 cm × 20 cm baking tin and line with baking paper (leave a little overhanging the two long sides to help remove the slice from the tin).

2 Melt the butter and golden syrup in a small heavy-based saucepan.

3 Sift the flour, baking powder, salt and spices into a large bowl and stir in the sugar. Gradually beat in the eggs and vanilla, then pour in the butter mixture and mix until combined.

4 Spoon the batter into the tin and bake for 20-25 minutes or until firm to the touch. Cool in the tin for 10 minutes, then turn out onto a wire rack to cool completely (the centre may sink slightly). Dust with icing sugar, then cut into rectangles to serve. Store in an airtight container for up to 5 days.

BISCUITS
AND
COOKIES

TIPS

1 When trying a new biscuit recipe, it is helpful to bake a test biscuit to see how much it spreads. If it spreads too much, try chilling the dough or adding a little more flour to the mixture.

2 Refrigerator biscuits spread very little. Chill the dough thoroughly before slicing and cut with a nice sharp knife so you don't squash the dough, causing mis-shapen biscuits. It often helps to dip the knife in hot water and wipe dry.

3 Biscuits and cookies that are dropped from a spoon onto the baking tray should be uniform in size and thickness. Chilling the dough before dropping or placing on the tray helps to keep spreading to a minimum.

4 For biscuit doughs that are rolled out and cut, I recommend working in small portions of dough rather than rolling out the whole batch at once. Keep the remainder in the fridge until ready to roll (always chill dough if it is too soft to roll and cut). Once the biscuits are cut and placed on a baking tray lined with baking paper, it is a good idea to chill them for 10-15 minutes before baking.

5 To prevent sticking when rolling and to keep surfaces clean, I always roll out the dough on a sheet of baking paper.

6 Be sure to bake your biscuits or cookies on a tray without sides or with very low sides. If your baking trays have deep sides, turn them upside down and bake the cookies on the bottom. There should be at least 5 cm of space around all sides of the baking sheet to allow for proper heat circulation.

7 If a recipe gives an approximate baking time, such as 12-15 minutes, check the biscuits or cookies at the earlier time to avoid overbaking.

8 After baking, leave the biscuits on the baking tray for 5 minutes (to firm them) before placing them in a single layer on a wire rack to cool. If you stack them on top of each other they will soften and stick together.

9 Before baking another batch of biscuits or cookies, cool and clean your baking tray - hot baking trays will melt biscuit dough, causing it to spread. You should be able to reuse the baking paper.

10 Biscuits and cookies should be thoroughly cooled before being stored. Crisp and soft varieties should never be stored in the same container, otherwise the crisp varieties will quickly soften.

11 Most uncooked biscuit dough can be frozen: wrap it in plastic film and freeze for up to 3 months.

SIMPLE BUTTER BISCUITS

**PREPARATION TIME: 20 MINUTES,
PLUS REFRIGERATION TIME**

COOKING TIME: 15 MINUTES

MAKES 25-30

250 g unsalted butter, diced and
softened at room temperature

125 g icing sugar, sifted

½ teaspoon vanilla extract

1 large free-range egg yolk

375 g plain flour

pinch of salt

**Simple butter biscuits are crisp and less crumbly than
a shortbread, and here is a recipe that does the job of
many. You can roll out the dough and cut it into different
shapes, or make a variety of flavours with a few simple
additions – drizzles of chocolate or icing (see page 317),
crunchy almonds, aromatic spices or lemon zest are
all good. The dough will keep in the fridge for up to four
days. Another way to use it is to roll the dough into a
log about 5 cm in diameter, wrap it in plastic film and
store in the fridge or freezer. When required, slice off
thin rounds and bake them.**

1 Place the butter and icing sugar in a bowl and beat with
hand-held electric beaters until pale and fluffy. Add the
vanilla and egg yolk and beat until combined. Sift in the
flour and salt and mix until smooth. Gather the dough and
gently press into a ball shape. Flatten slightly into a disc,
then wrap in plastic film and refrigerate for 1 hour.

2 Preheat the oven to 180°C (Gas Mark 4). Line two baking
trays with baking paper.

3 Cut the dough in half and roll out each portion on
a lightly floured surface or between two sheets of baking
paper to a thickness of 4-5 mm. Cut into desired shapes,
then place on the trays, leaving room for spreading, and
bake for 10-15 minutes or until pale and dry. Swap the trays
around halfway through baking. Cool on the trays for
5 minutes, then transfer to a wire rack to cool completely.
Store in an airtight container for up to 1 week.

ALMOND CRESCENTS
*Reduce the amount of flour to 325 g and add 50 g ground
almonds. Roll walnut-sized pieces of the chilled dough into
small sausages and then shape into crescents. Bake until
light golden. While still warm, drop each biscuit into a bowl
of caster sugar and toss lightly to coat, then transfer to
a wire rack to cool completely.*

THUMB-PRINT COOKIES
*Roll the dough into balls about 2.5 cm in diameter. Place on
lined trays and press down with your thumb or index finger
to make a small well in the centre. Fill each indent with a
small amount of jam (raspberry or peach are both good),
making sure it keeps within the well. Bake for 15 minutes or
until golden, then transfer to a wire rack to cool completely.*

CLASSIC SCOTTISH SHORTBREAD

PREPARATION TIME: 20 MINUTES,
PLUS REFRIGERATION TIME

COOKING TIME: 30 MINUTES

MAKES 20-25

250 g unsalted butter, diced and
softened at room temperature

125 g caster sugar

300 g plain flour, sifted

75 g rice flour, sifted

pinch of salt

sugar, for dusting (optional)

I usually work the flour into the butter by hand, using a wooden spoon, but you could also use an electric mixer on low speed, beating slowly until combined. The dough can be stored in the fridge for up to 24 hours but, when removed, may be quite crumbly and hard to roll. If this happens, simply knead portions of the dough until it warms slightly.

1 Beat the butter in a bowl with a wooden spoon until soft and smooth. Add the sugar, flours and salt and work the mixture with the spoon until blended. Turn out the dough onto a floured surface and knead lightly to form a firm dough. Wrap in plastic film and refrigerate for 20 minutes.

2 Preheat the oven to 150°C (Gas Mark 2). Line two baking trays with baking paper.

3 Cut the dough in half and roll out each portion between two sheets of baking paper to a thickness of 5-7 mm. Cut into shapes, then place on the trays and bake for 25-30 minutes or until pale and dry. Swap the trays around halfway through baking. Cool on the trays for 5 minutes before transferring to a wire rack to cool completely. Dust lightly with sugar, if you like. Store in an airtight container for up to 1 week.

BROWN-SUGAR SHORTBREAD

PREPARATION TIME: 20 MINUTES,
PLUS REFRIGERATION TIME

COOKING TIME: 30 MINUTES

MAKES 20-25

250 g unsalted butter, diced and
softened at room temperature

125 g soft brown sugar

375 g plain flour, sifted

1 teaspoon ground cinnamon

pinch of salt

finely grated zest of ½ orange

Using brown sugar gives this shortbread a lovely light caramel colour and flavour, which complements the cinnamon. Mixed spice or ground cardamom may be used instead.

1 Beat the butter in a bowl with a wooden spoon until soft and smooth. Add the sugar, flour, cinnamon, salt and orange zest and work the mixture with the spoon until blended. Turn out the dough onto a floured surface and knead lightly to form a firm dough. Wrap in plastic film and refrigerate for 30 minutes.

2 Preheat the oven to 150°C (Gas Mark 2). Line two baking trays with baking paper.

3 Cut the dough in half and roll out each portion between two sheets of baking paper to a thickness of 5-7 mm. Cut into shapes, then place on the trays and bake for 25-30 minutes or until pale and dry. Swap the trays around halfway through baking. Cool on the trays for 5 minutes before transferring to a wire rack to cool completely. Store in an airtight container for up to 1 week.

GINGER SHORTBREAD FINGERS

PREPARATION TIME: 20 MINUTES,
PLUS REFRIGERATION TIME

COOKING TIME: 30 MINUTES

MAKES 20-24

250 g unsalted butter,
chilled and diced

125 g caster sugar

350 g plain flour

2 tablespoons rice flour

pinch of salt

125 g crystallised ginger,
roughly chopped

Crystalised ginger make a delicious addition to shortbread. In this simple recipe, the mixture is combined in a food processor and then the ginger is kneaded in. You can also make the mixture in an electric mixer on low speed, or by hand, using a wooden spoon to combine the ingredients.

1 Place the butter, sugar, flours and salt in a large food processor and process until the mixture comes together. Tip out onto a floured surface and knead in the ginger until distributed evenly. Shape the dough into a rectangular block, then cover with plastic film and refrigerate for about 30 minutes.

2 Preheat the oven to 150°C (Gas Mark 2). Line two baking trays with baking paper.

3 Roll out the dough to a thickness of about 1.5 cm and cut into 7 cm long fingers.

4 Place on the trays and bake for 30 minutes or until pale and dry. Swap the trays around halfway through baking. Cool on the trays for 5 minutes before transferring to a wire rack to cool completely. Store in an airtight container for up to 1 week.

CHOCOLATE CHIP COOKIES

COOKING TIME: 10 MINUTES

MAKES ABOUT 30

125 g plain flour

½ teaspoon bicarbonate of soda

pinch of salt

125 g unsalted butter, diced and softened at room temperature

125 g caster sugar

1 teaspoon vanilla extract

1 large free-range egg, lightly beaten

125 g dark chocolate chips

These are classic, American-style chocolate chip or tollhouse cookies. They are crisp when baked, but will slowly soften after a day or two. For extra crunch and flavour, stir in 50 g chopped pecans.

1 Preheat the oven to 180°C (Gas Mark 4). Line two baking trays with baking paper.

2 Sift the flour, bicarbonate of soda and salt into a bowl.

3 Place the butter, sugar and vanilla in a separate bowl and beat with hand-held electric beaters until pale and fluffy. Beat in the egg, a little at a time, alternating with a little of the flour mixture until combined. Fold in the remaining flour, then stir in the chocolate chips.

4 Drop tablespoons of the mixture onto the trays, leaving room for spreading (about 12 per tray). Bake for about 8–10 minutes or until the cookies are firm and coloured. You may need to bake a third tray if any mixture remains. Cool on the trays for a few minutes before transferring to wire racks to cool completely. Store in an airtight container for up to 5 days.

DOUBLE CHOCOLATE CHIP COOKIES

PREPARATION TIME: 20 MINUTES

COOKING TIME: 8 MINUTES

MAKES ABOUT 30

280 g plain flour

½ teaspoon baking powder

40 g cocoa

pinch of salt

250 g unsalted butter, diced and softened at room temperature

185 g caster sugar

150 g soft brown sugar

2 large free-range eggs, lightly beaten

200 g dark chocolate chips

Brown sugar gives these cookies a nice chewy texture and the cocoa boosts the chocolate flavour. They do spread a little so the finished biscuits are quite flat. Take care not to overcook them or they will become too crisp.

1 Preheat the oven to 180°C (Gas Mark 4). Line two baking trays with baking paper.

2 Sift the flour, baking powder, cocoa and salt into a large bowl.

3 Beat the butter and sugars with hand-held electric beaters for 3–4 minutes or until pale and fluffy. Beat in the egg, a little at a time, alternating with a little of the flour until combined. Fold in the remaining flour mixture, then stir in the chocolate chips.

4 Drop tablespoons of the mixture onto the baking trays, leaving about 5 cm between each to allow for spreading. (You may need to bake a third tray if any mixture remains.) Bake for 8 minutes. Leave to cool on the trays for a few minutes before transferring to wire racks to cool completely. Store in an airtight container for up to 5 days.

VANILLA MELTING MOMENTS

250 g unsalted butter, diced and softened at room temperature

85 g icing sugar, sifted, plus extra for dusting

1 teaspoon vanilla extract

260 g plain flour, plus extra for dipping

60 g cornflour

pinch of salt

As the name suggests, these little biscuits literally melt in the mouth, making them very hard to resist. To make lemon melting moments, replace the vanilla with 1 teaspoon finely grated lemon zest. They can also be sandwiched together with a lemon filling made by beating together 60 g softened butter, 100 g sifted icing sugar and 3 teaspoons lemon juice.

1 Preheat the oven to 160°C (Gas Mark 2–3). Line two baking sheets with baking paper.

2 Place the butter, icing sugar and vanilla in a bowl and beat with hand-held electric beaters until pale and fluffy. Sift in the flours and salt and mix until smooth.

3 Place heaped teaspoons of the mixture on the trays, leaving a little room for spreading. Dip a fork in a little extra flour and gently press on the top of each biscuit, flattening it slightly. Bake for 20 minutes or until light golden and firm to the touch. Cool on the trays for 5 minutes before transferring to wire racks to cool completely. Dust with extra icing sugar before serving. Store in an airtight container for up to 5 days.

ANZAC BISCUITS

140 g plain flour

100 g rolled oats (porridge oats)

90 g desiccated coconut

185 g granulated sugar

pinch of salt

3 tablespoons golden syrup

125 g unsalted butter, diced

1 teaspoon bicarbonate of soda

2 tablespoons boiling water

This recipe first appeared in my *Perfect Cookbook*, and I have been making these biscuits for as long as I can remember. What you are looking for is a firm biscuit that is also slightly chewy. This chewiness is achieved with the correct cooking time – they need to be golden, but also slightly soft.

1 Preheat the oven to 180ºC (Gas Mark 4). Line two baking trays with baking paper.

2 Sift the flour into a bowl and stir in the oats, coconut, sugar and salt. Make a well in the centre.

3 Place the golden syrup and butter in a small heavy-based saucepan and stir over low heat until the butter has melted. Dissolve the bicarbonate of soda in the boiling water and add to the butter mixture – it will foam a little. Pour into the well in the dry ingredients and stir with a wooden spoon until combined. Add a little extra water if the mixture is dry.

4 Drop tablespoons of the mixture onto the trays, leaving 3 cm between each to allow for spreading. Bake for about 12-15 minutes or until golden. Cool on the trays for a few minutes before transferring to wire racks to cool completely. Store in an airtight container for up to 2 weeks.

MUM'S CORNFLAKE COOKIES

PREPARATION TIME: 15 MINUTES

COOKING TIME: 15 MINUTES

MAKES ABOUT 24

185 g unsalted butter

140 g self-raising flour

pinch of salt

150 g cornflakes

90 g desiccated coconut

120 g soft brown sugar

150 g sultanas

2 free-range eggs, lightly beaten

I grew up eating these cookies. The tantalising smell as they bake and that first delicious bite evoke such happy memories for me. Simple comfort food at its best.

1 Preheat the oven to 180°C (Gas Mark 4). Line two baking trays with baking paper.

2 Melt the butter in a small saucepan, then set aside to cool slightly.

3 Sift the flour and salt into a large bowl and stir in the cornflakes, coconut, sugar and sultanas. Add the egg and melted butter and mix well.

4 Scoop tablespoons of the mixture into rounds and place on the baking trays, leaving about 5 cm between each to allow for spreading. Bake for 10-12 minutes or until golden brown. Cool on the trays for a few minutes before transferring to wire racks to cool completely. Store in an airtight container for up to 5 days.

GINGERBREAD FOLK

125 g unsalted butter, diced

4 tablespoons golden syrup

175 g soft brown sugar

350 g plain flour

1 teaspoon bicarbonate of soda

2 teaspoons ground ginger

½ teaspoon mixed spice

pinch of salt

1 free-range egg, lightly beaten

You can hang your gingerbread folk from the Christmas tree by making a little hole in the top of each biscuit before baking (I usually use a skewer or toothpick). When the biscuits have cooled, thread a ribbon through each hole. To decorate your biscuits, beat 1 egg white with hand-held electric beaters until foamy. Gradually add 1 teaspoon lemon juice and about 250 g sifted icing sugar, beating until the mixture is thick and smooth. Tint the mixture with a couple of drops of food colouring if liked. Spoon the icing into a piping bag, attach a fine nozzle and pipe faces or decorative shapes onto the gingerbread biscuits.

1 Place the butter, golden syrup and brown sugar in a small heavy-based saucepan over low heat. Cook, stirring, until the butter has melted and the mixture is smooth. Remove from the heat and allow to cool.

2 Sift the flour, bicarbonate of soda, spices and salt into a large bowl and make a well in the centre. Pour in the egg and melted butter mixture and mix well.

3 Turn out onto a lightly floured surface and knead until smooth. Wrap in plastic film and refrigerate for 30 minutes.

4 Preheat the oven to 180°C (Gas Mark 4). Line two baking trays with baking paper.

5 Roll out the dough between two sheets of baking paper to a thickness of 5 mm. Cut out shapes with biscuit cutters and place on the trays. Bake for 10 minutes or until firm and golden brown. Cool on the trays for a few minutes before transferring to wire racks to cool completely. The smaller the biscuit the crunchier it will be – large folk usually are slightly chewy and become chewier the longer they are kept. Store in an airtight container for up to a week.

SESAME AND PECAN THINS

PREPARATION TIME: 25 MINUTES,
PLUS REFRIGERATION TIME

COOKING TIME: 25 MINUTES

MAKES ABOUT 45

250 g unsalted butter, diced and
softened at room temperature

185 g caster sugar

1 teaspoon vanilla extract

250 g plain flour

pinch of salt

80 g sesame seeds

80 g ground pecans or almonds
(see recipe introduction)

75 g dark chocolate

1 teaspoon vegetable oil

I usually grind my own pecans or almonds by pulsing them in a food processor until coarsely ground; they are the right consistency when they look like coarse breadcrumbs.

1 Place the butter, sugar and vanilla in a bowl and beat with hand-held electric beaters until pale and fluffy. Sift in the flour and salt, then fold in the sesame seeds and ground nuts until combined.

2 Turn out the dough onto a floured surface and divide in half. Knead each half for a few minutes, then wrap in plastic film and refrigerate for 1 hour.

3 Preheat the oven to 180°C (Gas Mark 4). Line two baking trays with baking paper.

4 Roll out one portion of dough on a lightly floured surface or between two sheets of baking paper to a thickness of 3–4 mm. Cut into rounds using a 5 cm cookie cutter, then place on the trays and bake for 8–10 minutes or until lightly browned and firm to the touch. Cool on the trays for 5 minutes before transferring to wire racks to cool completely. Repeat with the remaining dough, making sure the trays have returned to room temperature before adding the next batch of dough.

5 Melt the chocolate and oil in a bowl set over a saucepan of barely simmering water, stirring occasionally (make sure the bowl doesn't touch the water). Drizzle over the cooled biscuits and allow to set. Store in an airtight container for up to 1 week.

CHOCOLATE CREAMS

PREPARATION TIME: 30 MINUTES, PLUS REFRIGERATION AND STANDING TIME

COOKING TIME: 20 MINUTES

MAKES ABOUT 25

250 g unsalted butter, diced and softened at room temperature

125 g icing sugar, sifted, plus extra for dusting (optional)

½ teaspoon vanilla extract

1 large free-range egg yolk

375 g plain flour

pinch of salt

CHOCOLATE GANACHE FILLING

150 g dark chocolate, broken into pieces

100 ml double cream

Filled with rich chocolate ganache, these sweet, buttery biscuits are like melting moments for chocoholics.

1 Place the butter and sugar in a bowl and beat with hand-held electric beaters until pale and fluffy. Add the vanilla and egg yolk and beat until combined. Sift in the flour and salt and mix until smooth. Gather the dough and gently press into a ball shape. Flatten slightly into a disc, then wrap in plastic film and refrigerate for 1 hour.

2 Preheat the oven to 180°C (Gas Mark 4). Line two baking trays with baking paper.

3 Cut the dough in half and roll out each half on a lightly floured surface or between two sheets of baking paper to a thickness of 4–5 mm. Cut into rounds using a 5 cm cookie cutter, then place on the trays and bake for 10–15 minutes or until pale and dry. Swap the trays around halfway through baking. Cool on the trays for 5 minutes before transferring to wire racks to cool completely.

4 To make the ganache, melt the chocolate with the cream in a small heavy-based saucepan over low heat, stirring until smooth. Cool to room temperature then place in the fridge for about 10 minutes or until just starting to firm. Beat well with a wooden spoon.

5 Sandwich the ganache between the biscuits and set aside for 2 hours before serving. Dust with icing sugar, if desired. Store in an airtight container for up to a week.

HAZELNUT STARS

PREPARATION TIME: 25 MINUTES,
PLUS REFRIGERATION TIME

COOKING TIME: 20 MINUTES

MAKES ABOUT 40

200 g skinned hazelnuts

250 g unsalted butter, diced and softened at room temperature

120 g icing sugar, sifted, plus extra for dusting

1 teaspoon finely grated lemon zest

1 teaspoon vanilla extract

1 large free-range egg yolk

300 g plain flour

pinch of salt

These pretty little biscuits are deliciously buttery and nutty. For best results, grind the hazelnuts yourself, rather than buying the ready-ground version. Once chilled, the mixture will become quite crumbly – I usually knead it until it warms up and starts to become more pliable.

1 Toast the hazelnuts in a dry frying pan until golden. Cool, then grind to a coarse powder in a food processor, using the pulse button.

2 Place the butter, icing sugar and lemon zest in an electic mixer and beat until pale and fluffy. Add the vanilla and egg yolk and beat until combined. Sift in the flour and salt and tip in the hazelnuts, then mix on low speed until smooth. Gather the dough and gently press into a ball shape. Flatten slightly into a disc, then wrap in plastic film and refrigerate for 1 hour.

3 Preheat the oven to 160°C (Gas Mark 2-3). Line two baking trays with baking paper.

4 Cut the dough into three portions and roll out each portion on a lightly floured surface or between two sheets of baking paper to a thickness of 4 mm. Cut into star shapes using a star-shaped cookie cutter, then place on the trays and bake for 18-20 minutes or until pale, dry and lightly golden. Swap the trays around halfway through baking. Cool on the trays for 5 minutes before transferring to wire racks to cool completely. Dust with icing sugar before serving. Store in an airtight container for up to 5 days.

LIME FLOWER BISCUITS

PREPARATION TIME: 30 MINUTES,
PLUS REFRIGERATION TIME

COOKING TIME: 40 MINUTES

MAKES ABOUT 24

250 g unsalted butter, diced and
softened at room temperature

125 g caster sugar

360 g plain flour, sifted

pinch of salt

finely grated zest of 1 lime

WHITE CHOCOLATE FILLING

200 g white chocolate,
roughly chopped

75 ml pouring cream

finely grated zest of ½ lime

**As the name of these biscuits suggests, I usually
cut the dough with a flower-shaped cookie cutter,
but regular round cutters are also fine.**

1 Beat the butter in a bowl with a wooden spoon until soft
and smooth. Add the sugar, flour, salt and lime zest and
mix until combined. Turn out onto a floured surface and
knead lightly to form a firm dough. Wrap in plastic film and
refrigerate for about 1 hour.

2 Preheat the oven to 150°C (Gas Mark 2). Line two baking
trays with baking paper.

3 Cut the dough in half. Put one half back in the fridge and
roll out the other half between two sheets of baking paper
to a thickness of 4 mm. Cut into shapes using a flower-
shaped cookie cutter, then place on the trays and bake for
15-20 minutes or until pale and dry. Swap the trays around
halfway through baking. Cool on the trays for 5 minutes
before transferring to wire racks to cool completely.

4 Repeat with the remaining portion of dough, cutting
a 1 cm hole in the centre of each, if desired (this is the top
half of the biscuit and the holes let you see the lime filling).
Bake and cool as above.

5 Meanwhile, to make the filling, place the chocolate, cream
and lime zest in a heatproof bowl set over a saucepan of
simmering water (the base of the bowl shouldn't touch the
water). Stir occasionally until melted. Allow to cool, beating
occasionally with a wooden spoon to lighten the mixture.

6 Sandwich the cooled biscuits together with a little of the
filling (using the biscuit with the hole as the top of each).
Store in an airtight container for up to 3 days.

DATE DAINTIES

PREPARATION TIME: 15 MINUTES

COOKING TIME: 10 MINUTES

MAKES 18

220 g plain flour

1 teaspoon cream of tartar

½ teaspoon bicarbonate of soda

pinch of salt

125 g caster sugar

120 g unsalted butter, chilled and diced

2 large free-range eggs, lightly beaten

120 g pitted dates, roughly chopped

12 walnuts, roughly chopped

This recipe came from my grandmother's handwritten cookbook. We suspect most of the book was written at the time of her marriage in about 1930, and it is full of sweet things. My father has fond memories of date dainties during his childhood in the 1940s. They're like a cross between a rock cake and a biscuit, and I think they are well worth reviving.

1 Preheat the oven to 200°C (Gas Mark 6). Line two baking trays with baking paper.

2 Sift the flour, cream of tartar, bicarbonate of soda and salt into a bowl. Stir in the sugar and then rub in the butter with your fingertips. Stir in the egg, then the dates and walnuts and mix well.

3 Place dessertspoons of the mixture on the baking trays and bake for 10 minutes or until firm and golden. Cool on the trays for 5 minutes before transferring to wire racks to cool completely. Store in an airtight container for up to 5 days.

CHEWY OAT AND RAISIN COOKIES

PREPARATION TIME: 20 MINUTES

COOKING TIME: 50 MINUTES

MAKES ABOUT 48

250 g unsalted butter, diced and softened at room temperature

200 g caster sugar

150 g soft brown sugar

finely grated zest of ½ orange

½ teaspoon vanilla extract

2 large free-range eggs

300 g rolled oats (porridge oats)

150 g plain flour

1 teaspoon bicarbonate of soda

1 teaspoon baking powder

pinch of salt

175 g seedless raisins

Packed with the goodness of oats and raisins, these chewy cookies are great for lunchboxes and after-school snacks. Other varieties of dried fruit can also be used - try chopped dried apricot or mango.

1 Preheat the oven to 160°C (Gas Mark 2-3). Line two baking trays with baking paper.

2 Place the butter, sugars, orange zest and vanilla in a large bowl and beat with hand-held electric beaters until pale and fluffy. Add the eggs and beat until combined. Add the rolled oats, then sift in the flour, bicarbonate of soda, baking powder and salt and add the raisins. Mix with a large metal spoon until combined.

3 Drop tablespoons of the mixture onto the trays, leaving room for spreading (about 12 per tray), and bake for about 25 minutes or until the edges are golden. Cool on the trays for 5 minutes before transferring to wire racks to cool completely. Repeat with the remaining dough, making sure the trays have returned to room temperature before adding the next batch of dough. Store in an airtight container for up to 1 week.

ORANGE COOKIES

PREPARATION TIME: 20 MINUTES

COOKING TIME: 20 MINUTES

MAKES 25-30

150 g unsalted butter, diced and softened at room temperature

185 g caster sugar

finely grated zest of 1 orange

125 ml sour cream

1 free-range egg

275 g plain flour, sifted

1 teaspoon baking powder

½ teaspoon bicarbonate of soda

¼ teaspoon salt

juice of ½ orange

These buttery cookies are simple to make, and the sour cream gives an interesting flavour that works beautifully with the freshness of the orange. They are perfect in their simplicity, but can be dusted with icing sugar to serve, if desired.

1 Preheat the oven to 180°C (Gas Mark 4). Line two baking trays with baking paper.

2 Place the butter, sugar and orange zest in a large bowl and beat with hand-held electric beaters until pale and fluffy. Add the remaining ingredients and beat until smooth.

3 Drop tablespoons of the mixture onto the baking trays, leaving room for spreading (about 12 per tray), and bake for 10 minutes or until the edges are golden. Cool on the trays for 5 minutes before transferring to wire racks to cool completely. Repeat with the remaining dough, making sure the trays have returned to room temperature before adding the next batch of dough. Store in an airtight container for up to 5 days.

NIGEL SLATER'S TOASTED HAZELNUT BISCUITS

PREPARATION TIME: 25 MINUTES

COOKING TIME: 30 MINUTES

MAKES 8-10

175 g unsalted butter, diced and softened at room temperature

50 g caster sugar

50 g muscovado or dark brown sugar

60 g skinned hazelnuts

4 tablespoons ground almonds

200 g plain flour

pinch of salt

chopped hazelnuts, extra, for sprinkling

icing sugar, for dusting

These thick, pale and rough-textured cookies are at their best eaten slightly warm on the day of baking. For this reason, the recipe only makes a smallish batch. Nigel takes them out of the oven while they seem a little undercooked so they retain a slightly soft centre until they cool.

1 Preheat the oven to 160°C (Gas Mark 2-3). Lightly grease a baking sheet.

2 Place the butter and sugars in a bowl and beat with hand-held electric beaters until pale and fluffy.

3 Toast the hazelnuts in a dry frying pan until golden and then grind to a coarse powder in a food processor, using the pulse button. Mix them together with the ground almonds.

4 Sift the flour and salt into the butter and sugar mixture. Add the nut mixture and stir until thoroughly combined (if you like, knead the dough gently for a minute or two to mix it fully).

5 Roll generously heaped tablespoons of the mixture into large unruly balls. Place them on the baking tray, leaving room for spreading, and scatter the chopped hazelnuts over the top.

6 Bake for 25 minutes or until the biscuits are barely coloured. The insides should be slightly soft. Cool on the baking tray for 5 minutes, then lift them off with a palette knife. Eat them slightly warm and certainly within 24 hours.

MUESLI COOKIES

PREPARATION TIME: 20 MINUTES

COOKING TIME: 20 MINUTES

MAKES ABOUT 20

125 g unsalted butter

3 tablespoons golden syrup

125 g demerera or raw sugar

175 g untoasted muesli

100 g self-raising flour

pinch of salt

pinch of ground ginger

Muesli comes with so many different flavourings these days that it is easy to vary these cookies. I have made them with all sorts of untoasted varieties and they've all come out beautifully, so feel free to experiment.

1 Preheat the oven to 170°C (Gas Mark 3). Line two baking trays with baking paper.

2 Combine the butter, golden syrup and sugar in a medium saucepan and place over low heat, stirring occasionally, until the butter has melted.

3 Place the muesli in a large bowl, then sift in the flour, salt and ginger and mix to combine. Pour over the butter mixture and mix well with a wooden spoon. Allow to cool slightly.

4 Place heaped teaspoons of the mixture on the trays, leaving about 5 cm between each to allow for spreading. Bake for about 15 minutes or until golden. Cool on the trays for 5 minutes before transferring to wire racks to cool completely. Store in an airtight container for up to 1 week.

FLORENTINES

PREPARATION TIME: 25 MINUTES

COOKING TIME: 30 MINUTES

MAKES ABOUT 36

125 g unsalted butter

4 tablespoons double cream

165 g caster sugar

75 g glacé cherries, chopped

120 g mixed peel

75 g dried cherries, cranberries (craisins) or sultanas

100 g flaked almonds

100 g plain flour, sifted

pinch of salt

25 g pine nuts

150 g dark or white chocolate, chopped

Just about everybody loves a florentine biscuit. Traditionally, they should be slightly darker around the edges, and nice and crisp when cool. Although they are usually drizzled or coated with chocolate, they are also lovely without it.

1 Preheat the oven to 180°C (Gas Mark 4). Line two or three baking trays with baking paper.

2 Place the butter, cream and sugar in a saucepan over low heat and bring to the boil, stirring to dissolve the sugar. Simmer for 2–3 minutes or until thickened slightly.

3 Meanwhile, combine the fruit, almonds, flour, salt and pine nuts in a large bowl. Pour the hot butter mixture over the dry ingredients and mix well with a wooden spoon until combined.

4 Drop scant tablespoons of the mixture onto the baking trays, leaving plenty of room for spreading. Dip a fork in a bowl of cold water (to prevent sticking) and use it to flatten and spread the mounds into 7–8 cm rounds. Depending on the size of your trays, you may need to cook these in batches.

5 Bake for 7–10 minutes or until golden and slightly darker around the edges. Cool on the trays for about 5 minutes before transferring to wire racks to cool completely. Repeat with any remaining dough.

6 Melt the chocolate in a bowl set over a saucepan of barely simmering water, stirring occasionally until smooth (make sure the bowl doesn't touch the water).

7 Drizzle the chocolate over the florentines and leave to set before serving. Store in an airtight container for up to 5 days.

NUT LACE WAFERS

PREPARATION TIME: 20 MINUTES

COOKING TIME: 5 MINUTES

MAKES ABOUT 18

75 g blanched almonds

100 g granulated sugar

4 tablespoons plain flour

pinch of salt

finely grated zest of ½ orange

60 g unsalted butter, diced

1½ tablespoons double cream

½ teaspoon vanilla extract

During baking, these biscuits spread out to form thin, lacy wafers, so make sure you leave plenty of space between each one on the baking tray.

1 Preheat the oven to 190°C (Gas Mark 5). Line two baking trays with baking paper.

2 Place the almonds and sugar in a food processor and process until the almonds are finely chopped. Tip into a bowl and stir in the flour, salt and orange zest.

3 Melt the butter in a small saucepan over low heat. Add to the dry ingredients, along with the cream and vanilla and mix well to combine.

4 Drop teaspoons of the mixture onto the baking trays, leaving about 6 cm between each to allow for spreading, and bake for 5 minutes or until golden and spread. Cool on the trays for 5 minutes before transferring to wire racks to cool completely. Store in an airtight container for up to 5 days.

CHOCOLATE MARYLAND BISCUITS

125 g unsalted butter, diced and softened at room temperature

120 g caster sugar

1 free-range egg, lightly beaten

1 free-range egg yolk

1 teaspoon vanilla extract

175 g self-raising flour

pinch of salt

100 ml milk

100 g dark chocolate chips

These cook to form nice crunchy biscuits filled with chocolate chips. The mixture freezes well so if you don't want to bake the whole batch, freeze any leftover mixture in a plastic bag. To use, thaw completely and then follow the cooking instructions below.

1 Preheat the oven to 170°C (Gas Mark 3). Line two baking trays with baking paper.

2 Place the butter and sugar in a bowl and beat with hand-held electric beaters until pale and fluffy, then beat in the egg, egg yolk and vanilla. Sift in the flour and salt, then fold in with a large metal spoon until combined. Add the milk and half the chocolate chips and mix until combined.

3 Place tablespoons of the mixture on the trays, leaving about 5 cm between each to allow for spreading. Press the remaining chocolate chips into the tops of the dough. Bake for 10–15 minutes or until golden. Cool on the trays for 5 minutes before transferring to wire racks to cool completely. Repeat with the remaining dough. Store in an airtight container for up to 1 week.

COCONUT AND LIME MACAROONS

COOKING TIME: 20 MINUTES

MAKES 15

2 large free-range egg whites

150 g desiccated coconut

100 g caster sugar

20 g unsalted pistachio kernels, roughly chopped

grated zest of 1 lime

These are based on the old-fashioned coconut macaroons that were once found in most cake shops. I've updated them by using pistachios and lime zest.

1 Preheat the oven to 180°C (Gas Mark 4). Line two baking trays with baking paper.

2 Whisk the egg whites in a large clean bowl until it becomes cloudy and full of bubbles - you want the mixture to be frothy, but not stiff. Using a wooden spoon, mix in the coconut, sugar, pistachios and lime zest.

3 Place tablespoons of the mixture on the trays, leaving room as they may spread a little. Bake for 12-15 minutes or until lightly golden and firm to the touch. Let them cool completely on the baking trays. Store in an airtight container for up to 1 week.

GERMAN-STYLE CINNAMON BISCUITS

PREPARATION TIME: 20 MINUTES,
PLUS REFRIGERATION TIME

COOKING TIME: 15 MINUTES

MAKES ABOUT 24

125 g unsalted butter, diced and
softened at room temperature

100 g soft brown sugar

1 teaspoon vanilla extract

1 large free-range egg, lightly beaten

200 g plain flour

½ teaspoon bicarbonate of soda

½ teaspoon mixed spice

pinch of salt

3 tablespoons caster sugar

1 tablespoon ground cinnamon

These biscuits always get an airing around Christmas time (or Christmas in July), as the combination of mixed spice and cinnamon evokes the flavours of traditional European festivities. The biscuits are covered with cinnamon sugar before baking, which gives them a lovely spiced coating when cooked.

1 Preheat the oven to 180ºC (Gas Mark 4). Line two baking trays with baking paper.

2 Place the butter, sugar and vanilla in a large bowl and beat with hand-held electric beaters until pale and fluffy. Add the egg and beat in. Sift in the flour, bicarbonate of soda, mixed spice and salt, then fold in with a large metal spoon until combined. Cover with plastic film and refrigerate for about 1 hour.

3 Combine the caster sugar and cinnamon in a small bowl. Shape the dough into walnut-sized balls and drop into the cinnamon sugar, tossing until well coated. Place on the baking trays, leaving a little room for spreading (about 12 per tray), and bake for 15 minutes or until just set when lightly touched. Cool on the trays for 5 minutes before transferring to wire racks to cool completely. Store in an airtight container for up to 1 week.

VIENNESE BISCUITS

PREPARATION TIME: 25 MINUTES

COOKING TIME: 20 MINUTES

MAKES ABOUT 20

125 g unsalted butter, diced and softened at room temperature

2 tablespoons icing sugar, sifted

1 free-range egg

½ teaspoon vanilla extract

150 g plain flour

pinch of salt

150 g dark chocolate, chopped

Making these buttery vanilla biscuits is one of the best excuses I know to get out the piping bag. Their fine texture means they melt in the mouth, and the dark chocolate coating adds extra richness to this classic Austrian treat.

1 Preheat the oven to 170°C (Gas Mark 3). Line two baking trays with baking paper.

2 Place the butter and icing sugar in a bowl and beat with a wooden spoon until soft and smooth. Beat in the egg and vanilla until combined, then sift in the flour and salt and mix well.

3 Attach a 1 cm plain nozzle to a piping bag and pipe the biscuit dough into fingers or horseshoe shapes on the trays. Bake for 10-15 minutes or until pale and dry. Cool on the trays for 5 minutes before transferring to wire racks to cool completely.

4 Melt the chocolate in a bowl set over a saucepan of barely simmering water, stirring occasionally (make sure the bowl doesn't touch the water). Dip the ends of the cooled biscuits into the chocolate and leave to set. Store in an airtight container for up to 1 week.

GREEK HONEY BISCUITS

75 g plain flour

375 g self-raising flour

1 teaspoon ground cinnamon

½ teaspoon ground cloves

pinch of salt

125 g unsalted butter, chilled and diced

finely grated zest of ½ orange

185 ml light olive oil

125 ml orange juice,
plus extra if needed

2 teaspoons brandy

HONEY SYRUP

250 ml runny honey

125 ml water

2 teaspoons ground cinnamon

50 g walnuts, finely chopped

After tasting these syrupy Greek biscuits one Easter, I was determined to learn how to make them myself. This recipe came from the mother of my long-time neighbour Elena . . . eventually. It took a lot of nagging but my persistence paid off in the end. When the mood takes her, Elena's mother sometimes adds a drop or two of rosewater to the dough.

1 Preheat the oven to 190°C (Gas Mark 5). Line two large baking trays with baking paper.

2 Sift the flours, spices and salt into a large bowl. Rub the butter into the flour mixture with your fingertips until it clumps together and resembles coarse breadcrumbs. Stir in the orange zest, then gradually add the olive oil, orange juice and brandy and mix to a soft dough. If the mixture is dry, add extra orange juice; if it's too soft, add extra flour. Turn out onto a floured surface and knead for 10 minutes.

3 Roll the dough into walnut-sized balls and place on the baking trays. Flatten slightly, then bake for about 15 minutes or until golden. Cool on the trays for 1-2 minutes before dipping in the syrup.

4 Meanwhile, to make the syrup, combine the honey, water and cinnamon in a small saucepan and bring to the boil, then reduce the heat and simmer for 1 minute. Using a slotted spoon or two forks, dip the warm biscuits into the hot syrup for 1 minute, then place on a baking tray lined with baking paper to cool. Sprinkle with finely chopped walnuts. Store in an airtight container for up to 1 week.

COFFEE KISSES

PREPARATION TIME: 30 MINUTES

COOKING TIME: 12 MINUTES

MAKES 15

175 g unsalted butter, diced and
softened at room temperature

75 g caster sugar

200 g plain flour

pinch of salt

3 tablespoons cocoa

2 teaspoons instant coffee powder

1 tablespoon boiling water

COFFEE FILLING

180 g icing sugar, sifted

50 g unsalted butter, softened
at room temperature

2 teaspoons instant coffee powder

1 tablespoon boiling water

**These chocolate and coffee shortbreads sandwiched
together with a coffee-flavoured filling are a real
mid-afternoon pick-me-up. I prefer to use instant
coffee powder dissolved in boiling water here as this
gives a good coffee flavour to these little morsels.**

1 Preheat the oven to 180°C (Gas Mark 4). Line two baking
trays with baking paper.

2 Place the butter and sugar in a large bowl and beat with
hand-held electric beaters until pale and fluffy. Sift in the
flour, salt and cocoa. Dissolve the coffee in the boiling water
and add to the mixture. Mix with a wooden spoon.

3 Attach a large star-shaped nozzle to a piping bag
and pipe the biscuit dough into 30 stars (about 3 cm
across) on the trays, leaving a little space for spreading.
Bake for 10–12 minutes or until just firm. Cool on the trays
for about 5 minutes before transferring to wire racks to
cool completely.

4 To make the filling, beat together the icing sugar and
butter until smooth. Dissolve the coffee in the boiling water,
then beat into the mixture.

5 Sandwich the cooled biscuits together with a little of
the filling. Store in an airtight container for up to 5 days.

CRACKLED CHOCOLATE COOKIES

PREPARATION TIME: 20 MINUTES,
PLUS REFRIGERATION TIME

COOKING TIME: 12 MINUTES

MAKES ABOUT 20

150 g plain flour

60 g cocoa

1 teaspoon baking powder

pinch of salt

200 g caster sugar

60 g unsalted butter, chilled and diced

2 free-range eggs, lightly beaten

1 teaspoon vanilla extract

100 g icing sugar

These delicious fudgy biscuits are so named because they are dipped in icing sugar before going into the oven. During baking, the cookies expand slightly, resulting in a wonderful crackled look.

1 Sift the flour, cocoa, baking powder, salt and sugar into a large bowl. Rub the butter into the flour mixture with your fingertips until it clumps together and resembles coarse breadcrumbs.

2 Whisk together the egg and vanilla together, then add to the flour mixture. Mix with a large metal spoon until combined, then cover with plastic film and refrigerate for 30 minutes.

3 Preheat the oven to 200°C (Gas Mark 6). Line two baking trays with baking paper.

4 Sift the icing sugar into a bowl. Shape the dough into walnut-sized balls and drop into the icing sugar, tossing until well coated. Place on the baking trays, leaving about 5 cm between each to allow for spreading. Bake for 10-12 minutes or until just set when lightly touched. Cool on the trays for 5 minutes before transferring to wire racks to cool completely. The cookies will crack on cooling. Store in an airtight container for up to 5 days.

FRENCH MACAROONS

**PREPARATION TIME: 25 MINUTES,
PLUS STANDING TIME**

COOKING TIME: 18 MINUTES

MAKES ABOUT 20

175 g icing sugar

125 g ground almonds

3 large free-range egg whites

pinch of salt

55 g caster sugar

WHITE CHOCOLATE AND RASPBERRY GANACHE

150 g white chocolate, chopped

75 ml double cream

50 g raspberries, coarsely chopped

French macaroons are looking to knock cupcakes and friands off the top of the teatime treat list. These little beauties are made with almonds and are crisp on the outside, yet light and chewy on the inside. They can be eaten as they are or sandwiched together with chocolate ganache or plain or flavoured buttercream.

1 Preheat the oven to 150°C (Gas Mark 2). Line two baking trays with baking paper.

2 Sift the icing sugar into a bowl. Add the ground almonds.

3 Place the egg whites and salt in a clean, dry bowl and whisk with hand-held electric beaters until they form soft peaks. Gradually beat in the caster sugar until very stiff and shiny. Add any colouring or flavouring at this stage.

4 Add half the almond and sugar mixture to the beaten egg whites and gently fold in with a flexible rubber spatula. Repeat with the remaining almond mixture. When the mixture is just smooth and there are no streaks of egg white, spoon it into a piping bag fitted with a large plain nozzle.

5 Pipe 4 cm circles onto the trays, leaving about 2.5 cm between each one to allow for spreading. Tap the trays a couple of times on the bench top (this helps create the rise), then set aside for about an hour or two (to help give them a nice shine). Bake for 15–18 minutes or until dry and risen slightly. Cool completely on the trays.

6 To make the ganache, melt the chocolate with the cream in a bowl set over a saucepan of barely simmering water, stirring until smooth (make sure the bowl doesn't touch the water). Chill, then beat well with a wooden spoon. Swirl through the chopped raspberries.

7 Sandwich the macaroons together with the ganache filling. Set aside for about 1 hour or until the filling is firm. Store in an airtight container for up to 5 days.

BUTTERCREAM FILLING (FOR FLAVOURED MACAROONS)
Beat 150 g softened unsalted butter until pale and fluffy, then sift over 100 g icing sugar and beat until combined. Add flavouring and/or colouring if desired. Spread a bit of buttercream on the inside of the macaroons, then sandwich them together.

CHOCOLATE MACAROONS

PREPARATION TIME: 25 MINUTES,
PLUS STANDING TIME

COOKING TIME: 18 MINUTES

MAKES ABOUT 20

125 g icing sugar

3 tablespoons cocoa

100 g ground almonds

3 free-range egg whites

pinch of salt

3 tablespoons caster sugar

CHOCOLATE GANACHE FILLING

150 g dark chocolate, chopped
into small pieces

100 ml double cream

These rich and slightly chewy treats are a perfect way to use up excess egg whites. I find they work especially well with egg whites that have been refrigerated for 24 hours before using.

1 Preheat the oven to 150°C (Gas Mark 2). Line two baking trays with baking paper.

2 Sift the icing sugar and cocoa into a bowl and mix through the ground almonds.

3 Place the egg whites and salt in a clean, dry bowl and whisk with hand-held electric beaters until they form soft peaks. Gradually beat in the caster sugar until very stiff and shiny.

4 Add half the almond mixture to the beaten egg whites and gently fold in with a flexible rubber spatula. Repeat with the remaining almond mixture. When the mixture is just smooth and there are no streaks of egg white, spoon it into a piping bag fitted with a large plain nozzle.

5 Pipe 4 cm circles onto the trays, leaving about 2.5 cm between each one to allow for spreading. Tap the trays a couple of times on the bench top (this helps create the rise), then set aside for about an hour or two (to help give them a nice shine). Bake for 15-18 minutes or until dry and risen slightly. Cool completely on the trays.

6 To make the ganache, melt the chocolate with the cream in a bowl set over a saucepan of barely simmering water, stirring until smooth (make sure the bowl doesn't touch the water). Chill, then beat well with a wooden spoon.

7 Sandwich the macaroons together with the chocolate ganache filling. Set aside for 2 hours or until the filling is firm. Store in an airtight container for up to 5 days.

CHOCOLATE AND HAZELNUT MERINGUES

PREPARATION TIME: 20 MINUTES

COOKING TIME: 20 MINUTES

MAKES ABOUT 25

50 g skinned hazelnuts

2 large free-range egg whites

pinch of salt

100 g icing sugar, plus extra for dusting

1 tablespoon cocoa

These little meringues are crisp on the outside and a little chewy on the inside. I usually drop tablespoons of the mixture on the baking tray for a free-form result, but they can also be piped into neat rounds or into an 'S' shape.

1 Preheat the oven to 150°C (Gas Mark 2). Line two baking trays with baking paper.

2 Toast the hazelnuts in a dry frying pan until golden. Allow to cool, then finely chop.

3 Place the egg whites and salt in a clean, dry bowl and whisk with hand-held electric beaters until they form soft peaks. Gradually beat in the icing sugar until very stiff and shiny.

4 Add the cocoa and chopped nuts and gently fold in with a flexible rubber spatula, being careful not to lose too much volume.

5 Drop tablespoons of the mixture onto the trays, leaving about 2.5 cm between each one to allow for spreading. Bake for 18-20 minutes or until dry to the touch and slightly risen. Cool completely on the trays.

6 Dust with icing sugar before serving. Store in an airtight container for up to 5 days.

PIGNOLI BISCUITS

PREPARATION TIME: 20 MINUTES

COOKING TIME: 20 MINUTES

MAKES 25–30

185 g ground almonds

220 g caster sugar

1 rounded tablespoon plain flour

finely grated zest of 1 lime

2 free-range egg whites

½ teaspoon vanilla extract

4 tablespoons pine nuts

icing sugar, for dusting (optional)

These Italian macaroon-style biscuits are made with egg whites, almonds and pine nuts, giving them a unique flavour and texture. They make a really lovely gift at Christmas time.

1 Preheat the oven to 170ºC (Gas Mark 3). Line two baking trays with baking paper.

2 Combine the almonds, caster sugar, flour and lime zest in a large bowl. Beat the egg whites lightly with a fork until fluffy, then pour into the dry ingredients. Add the vanilla and beat with hand-held electric beaters (or in an electric mixer) for 3 minutes or until thick and smooth.

3 Place heaped teaspoons of the mixture on the baking trays and sprinkle the pine nuts over the top. Bake for about 20 minutes or until golden. Cool on the trays for 5 minutes before carefully transferring to wire racks to cool completely. You may need to bake a third tray – remember to make sure the tray is cool before adding any mixture. Dust with icing sugar (if using) and store in an airtight container for up to 1 week.

AMARETTI

**PREPARATION TIME: 25 MINUTES,
PLUS STANDING TIME**

COOKING TIME: 35 MINUTES

MAKES ABOUT 50

3 free-range egg whites

pinch of cream of tartar

180 g caster sugar

2 teaspoons almond essence

180 g ground almonds

1 heaped teaspoon cornflour

125 g icing sugar, sifted

**These innocent little biscuits seem to be very divisive –
you either love or hate the strong almond flavour. I am
definitely a fan, and particularly like the light texture
that comes from the aerated egg whites. To decorate,
sprinkle coffee sugar crystals or raw sugar over the top
before baking, if desired.**

1 Preheat the oven to 150°C (Gas Mark 2). Line three
baking sheets with baking paper.

2 Place the egg whites and cream of tartar in an electric
mixer and whisk until they form soft peaks. With the motor
running, gradually beat in the caster sugar, a tablespoon at
a time, until the mixture is very stiff and shiny. Beat in the
almond essence.

3 Combine the ground almonds, cornflour and icing sugar,
then carefully fold half into the beaten egg whites with
a flexible rubber spatula. Repeat with the remaining almond
mixture. When the mixture is just smooth and there are no
streaks of egg white, spoon the mixture into a piping bag
fitted with a 1 cm plain nozzle.

4 Pipe 2.5 cm circles onto the sheets, leaving about 2.5 cm
between each one to allow for spreading, and bake (in batches
if necessary) for about 35 minutes or until golden brown
and firm. Switch off the oven and leave them for a further
20 minutes with the door ajar. Remove and cool completely
on the trays. Store in an airtight container for up to 1 week.

LOUKIE WERLE'S ESPRESSO BISCUITS

PREPARATION TIME: 25 MINUTES,
PLUS REFRIGERATION TIME

COOKING TIME: 20 MINUTES

MAKES ABOUT 50

300 g plain flour

pinch of salt

200 g unsalted butter, diced and softened at room temperature

150 g caster sugar

2 tablespoons ground espresso coffee beans

3 tablespoons cocoa

1 teaspoon ground cinnamon

Australian food writer and teacher Loukie Werle is one of my favourite cooks, and I have enjoyed cooking many of her Italian recipes over the last few years, including this one. These biscuits are a real treat; they are quickly made in the food processor and the mixture can be rolled into a log, chilled (or frozen) and then sliced and baked when needed.

1 Place all the ingredients in a food processor and whiz until well combined. Turn out onto a lightly floured surface and gently knead into a ball. Cut the dough into quarters and roll each quarter into a log about 4 cm in diameter. Wrap in foil and refrigerate for about 1 hour or until firm.

2 Preheat the oven to 180°C (Gas Mark 4). Line two baking trays with baking paper.

3 Cut the chilled dough into 5 mm thick slices and place about 3 cm apart on the baking trays. Bake for about 20 minutes or until golden, swapping the trays around halfway through baking. Cool on the trays for 5 minutes before transferring to wire racks to cool completely. Store in an airtight container for up to 5 days.

ALMOND TUILES

PREPARATION TIME: 30 MINUTES

COOKING TIME: 40 MINUTES

MAKES ABOUT 30

60 g blanched almonds

120 g caster sugar

2 free-range egg whites

50 g unsalted butter, melted

4 tablespoons plain flour, sifted

½ teaspoon vanilla extract

120 g flaked almonds

These delicate, crisp wafers are best made in small batches so you have time to shape the tuiles around a rolling pin before they cool. If you want to get on with it though, have two baking trays on the go so you don't have to wait for one tray to cool each time.

1 Preheat the oven to 180°C (Gas Mark 6). Line a baking tray with baking paper.

2 Place the blanched almonds and 2 tablespoons of the sugar in a food processor and pulse until finely ground.

3 Whisk the egg whites with a fork until foamy and then gradually whisk in the remaining sugar. Add the melted butter, flour, vanilla and ground almond mixture and fold in with a large metal spoon.

4 Make four tuiles at a time. Drop tablespoons of the mixture well apart on the baking tray. With the back of a spoon, spread the mixture out to form a thin and almost translucent circle about 6 cm in diameter. Sprinkle each with a few of the flaked almonds. Bake for 4–5 minutes or until golden and the edges have browned slightly.

5 Have a rolling pin ready, as this is needed to shape the warm tuiles as soon as they come out of the oven.

6 Remove the tray from the oven. Use a spatula or palette knife to carefully remove each biscuit and drape it over the rolling pin until cooled completely (they will firm as they cool). Transfer to a wire rack. Repeat with remaining mixture, working in batches of four. Store in an airtight container for up to 4 days.

PISTACHIO AND CARDAMOM THINS

PREPARATION TIME: 20 MINUTES,
PLUS REFRIGERATION TIME

COOKING TIME: 10 MINUTES

MAKES ABOUT 45

250 g unsalted butter, diced and
softened at room temperature

200 g caster sugar

2 free-range eggs, lightly beaten

350 g plain flour, sifted

pinch of salt

1 teaspoon baking powder

1 teaspoon ground cardamom

75 g unsalted pistachio kernels,
finely chopped

**This dough is perfect for anyone who wants to bake
a batch of biscuits at a moment's notice. You form it
into a log that can be chilled or frozen, then, when you
want a biscuit you simply slice off as many rounds of
dough as you need and bake them.**

1 Mix all the ingredients together in an electric mixer
on low speed until combined.

2 Divide the mixture in half and shape each half into a log
about 5 cm in diameter. Wrap them in baking paper and
refrigerate until just firm. Remove from the fridge and roll
the log on the bench top a couple of times to refine the log
shape. Rewrap and return to the fridge for at least 3 hours
or until very firm.

3 Preheat the oven to 180°C (Gas Mark 4). Line a large
baking tray with baking paper.

4 Ensure the dough is well chilled, then unwrap it and cut
into thin (3-4 mm) slices. Place on the baking tray and bake
for 8-10 minutes or until firm. Depending on how many
biscuits you want to make, you may have to cook them in
batches. Cool on the tray for 5 minutes before transferring
to wire racks to cool completely. Store in an airtight container
for up to 3 days.

BUTTERSCOTCH AND CINNAMON THINS

PREPARATION TIME: 20 MINUTES,
PLUS REFRIGERATION TIME

COOKING TIME: 15 MINUTES

MAKES ABOUT 60

225 g unsalted butter, diced and
softened at room temperature

50 g caster sugar

100 g dark brown sugar

125 g plain flour, sifted

125 g self-raising flour, sifted

pinch of salt

½ teaspoon ground cinnamon

1 large free-range egg, lightly beaten

finely grated zest of 1 small orange

As with the previous recipe, this biscuit dough can also be rolled into a log and baked when required. Bake a few more than you need – I warn you now, the warm, comforting combination of butterscotch and cinnamon make these incredibly more-ish.

1 Mix all the ingredients together in an electric mixer on low speed until combined.

2 Divide the mixture in half, and shape each half into a rectangle about 5 cm thick. Wrap them in baking paper and refrigerate until just firm. Remove from the fridge and reshape each rectangle by lightly tapping it on the bench top a couple of times to refine the rectangular shape. Rewrap and return to the fridge for at least 2 hours or until very firm.

3 Preheat the oven to 180°C (Gas Mark 4). Line a large baking sheet with baking paper.

4 Ensure the dough is well chilled, then unwrap it and cut into thin (3-4 mm) slices. Place on the baking tray and bake for 10-15 minutes or until golden. Depending on how many biscuits you want to make, you may have to cook them in batches. Cool on the tray for 5 minutes before transferring to wire racks to cool completely. Store in an airtight container for up to 3 days.

POLENTA AND ORANGE REFRIGERATOR BISCUITS

PREPARATION TIME: 20 MINUTES,
PLUS REFRIGERATION TIME

COOKING TIME: 15 MINUTES

MAKES ABOUT 35

250 g unsalted butter, diced and softened at room temperature

185 g caster sugar

1 teaspoon vanilla extract

finely grated zest of 2 oranges

75 g polenta (fine cornmeal)

350 g plain flour, sifted

pinch of salt

I always keep a supply of this dough in the freezer and bake a few biscuits at a time as needed. The polenta adds a slightly grainy texture, giving this wonderfully simple recipe a nice point of difference.

1 Mix all the ingredients together in an electric mixer on low speed until combined.

2 Divide the mixture in half and shape each half into a log about 5 cm in diameter. Wrap them in baking paper and refrigerate until just firm. Remove from the fridge and roll the log on the bench top a couple of times to refine the log shape. Rewrap and return to the fridge for at least 3 hours or until very firm.

3 Preheat the oven to 180°C (Gas Mark 4). Line a large baking tray with baking paper. (Use two trays if you are making a large batch.)

4 Ensure the dough is well chilled, then unwrap it and cut into thin (3-4 mm) slices. Place on the baking tray and bake for 10-15 minutes or until firm. Cool on the tray for 5 minutes before transferring to wire racks to cool completely. Store in an airtight container for up to 3 days.

TARTS

AND

CHEESECAKES

TIPS

1 The most important things to remember when making pastry are to use really chilled butter and to not handle the dough too much.

2 It is also a good idea to chill the dough well before rolling out. Once the pie or tart dishes have been lined with pastry, I will often chill them again before baking so the butter in the dough is nice and cold – this helps the dough keep its shape and crisp nicely, and prevents shrinking.

3 A useful tip is to roll out the pastry on a sheet of baking paper as it stops the pastry sticking to the bench top, and also makes it easier to transfer the pastry to the tin.

4 The pastries in the following recipes are generally made by hand. If you would rather make the pastry by machine, put the flour, salt, sugar (if using) and butter in a food processor and pulse until the mixture resembles coarse breadcrumbs. Add the liquid and pulse until the mixture just clumps together in a ball – it is important not to overwork the dough as this will overwork the gluten and make the pastry tough. Add a little extra liquid if the dough doesn't clump together. Press gently into a ball and flatten slightly. Proceed with the recipe.

5 Any spare pastry can be frozen for up to 2 months. Thaw in the refrigerator before rolling out.

6 Sometimes a recipe will ask for the pastry to be baked before the filling is added – this is called baking blind. Once the tin has been lined with pastry, cover it with a sheet of baking paper, leaving a little paper overhanging the sides of the tin. Fill the tin with baking beads (available in kitchenware shops) or dried chickpeas, beans or rice. The idea is that the weight of the beads or chickpeas will stop the pastry from rising as it cooks. Place the weighted pastry in the oven and cook for 10-15 minutes, then remove the baking paper and weights and return to the oven for 5-10 minutes or until the pastry is pale golden and looks dry. Set aside to cool.

7 When making cheesecakes, I find the ingredients for the filling combine better if the cream cheese has been sitting at room temperature for about an hour beforehand.

8 Once made and cooled at room temperature, chill the cheesecake well before serving.

9 Cheesecakes can be frozen either whole or in portion sizes for up to 2 months. Thaw frozen cheesecake in the refrigerator overnight.

TREACLE TART

PREPARATION TIME: 25 MINUTES,
PLUS REFRIGERATION TIME

COOKING TIME: 30 MINUTES

SERVES 4-6

250 g golden syrup

75 g fresh white breadcrumbs

1 granny smith apple, peeled,
cored and grated

finely grated zest and juice of 1 lemon

custard or vanilla ice-cream, to serve

SWEET SHORTCRUST PASTRY

200 g plain flour

pinch of salt

2 tablespoons caster sugar

100 g unsalted butter,
chilled and diced

3-4 tablespoons cold water

I have updated this old-fashioned favourite by adding a grated apple to the filling; it creates a nice counterbalance to the sweetness of the golden syrup. The best breadcrumbs to use are made freshly from day-old bread.

1 For the pastry, sift the flour, salt and sugar into a large bowl. Using your fingertips, rub the butter into the flour until it resembles coarse breadcrumbs. Using a large fork or flat-bladed knife, stir in enough of the water to make the pastry come together in clumps – it should stick together. If there is still dry flour left in the bowl, you may need to add a little extra water.

2 Gather the dough and gently press into a ball shape (don't knead). Flatten slightly into a disc, then wrap in plastic film and refrigerate for 1 hour before using.

3 Preheat the oven to 190°C (Gas Mark 5) and grease a 20 cm pie dish or tart tin.

4 Turn out the dough onto a lightly floured surface and roll out to a round large enough to line the tin. Line the dish or tin with the pastry, pressing gently against the side and base. Trim the pastry, then chill until needed.

5 Heat the golden syrup in a saucepan over low heat. Remove from the heat and stir in the breadcrumbs, apple and lemon zest and juice.

6 Place the dish or tin on a baking tray and pour the filling into the pastry shell. Bake for about 25 minutes or until the filling is set and golden. Serve warm with custard or ice-cream.

WALNUT AND ORANGE TART

PREPARATION TIME: 25 MINUTES, PLUS REFRIGERATION TIME

COOKING TIME: 50 MINUTES

SERVES 8

185 ml golden syrup

2 large free-range eggs

75 g sugar

250 g walnut halves

40 g unsalted butter, melted

finely grated zest of 1 orange

ORANGE PASTRY

250 g plain flour

pinch of salt

3 tablespoons caster sugar

125 g unsalted butter, chilled and diced

finely grated zest of 1 orange

3-4 tablespoons orange juice

This one's a delight: crisp, orange-flavoured pastry topped with a lovely gooey walnut filling. The tart is best eaten on the day it is baked, and is particularly delicious served just warm.

1 For the pastry, sift the flour, salt and sugar into a large bowl. Using your fingertips, rub the butter into the flour until it resembles coarse breadcrumbs. Stir in the orange zest. Using a large fork or flat-bladed knife, stir in enough of the orange juice to make the pastry come together in clumps - it should stick together. If there is still dry flour left in the bowl, you may need to add a little extra juice.

2 Gather the dough and gently press into a ball shape (don't knead). Flatten slightly into a disc, then wrap in plastic film and refrigerate for 1 hour before using.

3 Preheat the oven to 200°C (Gas Mark 6). Grease a 25 cm tart tin (with a removable base).

4 Turn out the dough onto a lightly floured surface and roll out to a 28 cm round. Line the tin with the pastry, pressing gently against the side and base. Trim the pastry and prick the base a few times with a fork, then place in the freezer for 10 minutes.

5 Line the pastry with baking paper, leaving some overhanging the tin. Half-fill the pastry case with a layer of baking beads, uncooked dried beans or rice and bake for 10-15 minutes until just coloured. Remove the weights and paper and bake the pastry case for a further 6-8 minutes or until dry and lightly coloured. Allow to cool.

6 Meanwhile, warm the golden syrup in a small saucepan over low heat. Lightly whisk the eggs and sugar in a large bowl. Stir in the warm syrup and remaining ingredients and mix well.

7 Reduce the oven temperature to 180°C (Gas Mark 4). Place the tin on a baking tray and pour the filling into the pastry shell (fill almost to the top but make sure the mixture does not overflow). Bake for 25-30 minutes or until the filling is firm to the touch. Cool on a wire rack and serve slightly warm or at room temperature.

FRESH DATE AND COCONUT TART

PREPARATION TIME: 30 MINUTES,
PLUS REFRIGERATION TIME

COOKING TIME: 25 MINUTES

SERVES 8

125 g unsalted butter, diced

250 ml golden syrup

250 ml coconut cream

24 large fresh dates, halved
lengthways and pitted

2 tablespoons dark rum

whipped cream or ice-cream,
to serve (optional)

CARDAMOM PASTRY

250 g plain flour

½ teaspoon ground cardamom

pinch of salt

3 tablespoons caster sugar

125 g unsalted butter, chilled and diced

3–4 tablespoons cold water

The best dates to use for this luscious tart are the large fresh ones, sometimes called Medjool dates. Coconut cream is very similar to coconut milk but contains less water, giving it a thicker, more paste-like consistency that adds a lovely creamy quality to the tart.

1 For the pastry, sift the flour, cardamom, salt and sugar into a large bowl. Using your fingertips, rub the butter into the flour until it resembles coarse breadcrumbs. Using a large fork or flat-bladed knife, stir in enough of the water to make the pastry come together in clumps – it should stick together. If there is still dry flour left in the bowl, you may need to add a little extra water.

2 Gather the dough and gently press into a ball shape (don't knead). Flatten slightly into a disc, then wrap in plastic film and refrigerate for 1 hour before using.

3 Preheat the oven to 200°C (Gas Mark 6) and grease a 25 cm tart tin (with a removable base).

4 Turn out the dough onto a lightly floured surface and roll out to a 28 cm round. Line the tin with the pastry, pressing gently against the side and base. Trim the pastry and prick the base a few times with a fork. Place in the freezer for 10 minutes.

5 Line the pastry with baking paper, leaving some overhanging the tin. Half-fill the pastry case with a layer of baking beads, uncooked dried beans or rice and bake for 10 minutes. Remove the weights and paper and bake the pastry case for a further 6–8 minutes or until dry and lightly coloured. Allow to cool.

6 Meanwhile, melt the butter, golden syrup and coconut cream in a large saucepan. Bring to a gentle simmer, then add the dates and cook for about 2 minutes. Remove the dates from the mixture with a slotted spoon and set aside. Add the rum to the pan, stir well and then remove from the heat.

7 Brush the pastry case with some of the syrup from the saucepan, then arrange the dates in the case. Brush with syrup. Return the tart to the oven and cook for 5 minutes, then remove and brush again with any remaining syrup. Serve at room temperature with whipped cream or ice-cream, if desired.

RASPBERRY AND PINE NUT TART

PREPARATION TIME: 30 MINUTES,
PLUS REFRIGERATION TIME

COOKING TIME: 30 MINUTES

SERVES 4-6

100 g ground almonds

100 g caster sugar

100 g unsalted butter, diced and
softened at room temperature

3 large free-range eggs, lightly beaten

2 tablespoons dark rum or brandy

100 g raspberries, fresh or frozen

3 tablespoons pine nuts

SWEET SHORTCRUST PASTRY

200 g plain flour

pinch of salt

2 tablespoons caster sugar

100 g unsalted butter,
chilled and chopped

3-4 tablespoons cold water

If you find the idea of making pastry a little daunting, you can use ready-prepared shortcrust pastry here, if you like. The almond filling is a French frangipane and is delicious topped with fresh raspberries and pine nuts.

1 For the pastry, sift the flour, salt and sugar into a large bowl. Using your fingertips, rub the butter into the flour until it resembles coarse breadcrumbs. Using a large fork or flat-bladed knife, stir in enough of the water to make the pastry come together in clumps - it should stick together. If there is still dry flour left in the bowl, you may need to add a little extra water.

2 Gather the dough and gently press into a ball shape (don't knead). Flatten slightly into a disc, then wrap in plastic film and refrigerate for an hour before using.

3 Preheat the oven to 200°C (Gas Mark 6) and grease a 20 cm fluted tart tin (with a removable base).

4 Turn out the dough onto a lightly floured surface and roll out a round large enough to line the tin. Line the tin with the pastry, pressing gently against the side and base. Trim the pastry and prick the base a few times with a fork. Place in the freezer for 10 minutes.

5 Meanwhile, place the almonds, sugar and butter in a bowl and beat with a wooden spoon until well mixed. Continue to beat, gradually adding the egg and rum or brandy.

6 Place the tart tin on a baking tray and pour the filling into the pastry shell (fill almost to the top but make sure the mixture does not overflow). Sprinkle the raspberries and pine nuts over the top, gently pushing them into the mixture. Bake for 25-30 minutes or until the filling is firm to the touch and the pine nuts are golden. Cool on a wire rack and serve at room temperature.

CHOCOLATE TART

PREPARATION TIME: 30 MINUTES,
PLUS REFRIGERATION TIME

COOKING TIME: 50 MINUTES

SERVES 8

100 g unsalted butter, diced

100 g dark chocolate,
broken into pieces

150 g caster sugar

4 tablespoons plain flour

3 free-range eggs

RICH SHORTCRUST PASTRY

250 g plain flour

pinch of salt

3 tablespoons caster sugar

125 g unsalted butter, chilled and diced

1 large free-range egg

1 free-range egg yolk, beaten

ICING

100 g dark chocolate,
broken into pieces

125 ml milk

1 tablespoon icing sugar, sifted

What could be better for a chocolate lover than a rich chocolate-filled tart topped with chocolate icing? Tempted? Just wait until you taste this gorgeous treat.

1 For the pastry, sift the flour, salt and sugar into a large bowl. Using your fingertips, rub the butter into the flour until it resembles coarse breadcrumbs. Pour in the egg and egg yolk and mix gently with a large fork or flat-bladed knife until the pastry comes together in clumps - it should stick together. If there is still dry flour left in the bowl, you may need to add a little cold water.

2 Gather the dough and gently press into a ball shape (don't knead). Flatten slightly into a disc, then wrap in plastic film and refrigerate for 1 hour before using.

3 Preheat the oven to 200ºC (Gas Mark 6) and grease a 25 cm tart tin (with a removable base).

4 Turn out the dough onto a lightly floured surface and roll out to a 28 cm round. Line the tin with the pastry, pressing gently against the side and base. Trim the pastry, then place in the freezer for 10 minutes.

5 Line the pastry with baking paper, leaving some overhanging the tin. Half-fill the pastry case with baking beads, uncooked dried beans or rice and bake for 10 minutes. Remove the weights and paper and bake the pastry case for a further 6-8 minutes or until dry and lightly coloured. Allow to cool.

6 Meanwhile, melt the butter and chocolate in a bowl set over a saucepan of barely simmering water, stirring occasionally until smooth (make sure the bowl doesn't touch the water). Beat together the sugar, flour and eggs with a wooden spoon, then add the chocolate mixture, stirring until combined.

7 Reduce the oven temperature to 180ºC (Gas Mark 4). Place the tin on a baking tray and pour the filling into the pastry shell (fill almost to the top but make sure the mixture does not overflow). Bake for 20-25 minutes or until the filling is firm to the touch. Remove the side of the tart tin and leave to cool completely on a wire rack.

8 When cool, make the icing. Melt the chocolate and milk in a small saucepan over low heat, then beat in the icing sugar until smooth. Spread thinly over the cooled tart. Serve at room temperature. Store in the fridge for up to 3 days.

NO-PASTRY BLACKBERRY AND LIME TARTS

PREPARATION TIME: 25 MINUTES

COOKING TIME: 25 MINUTES

SERVES 6

180 g unsalted butter

50 g plain flour

pinch of salt

180 g icing sugar, plus extra for dusting

100 g ground almonds

finely grated zest of 2 limes

5 free-range egg whites

200 g blackberries

50 g flaked almonds

cream, custard or ice-cream, to serve

This mixture is similar to that of a friand, giving a lovely almond tart that doesn't need any pastry. You can also bake this in a 23 cm tart tin, if you like – just increase the cooking time to 25-30 minutes. Blackberries are delicious here, but raspberries or blueberries also work really well.

1 Preheat the oven to 190°C (Gas Mark 5). Lightly grease six individual tart or flan tins with removable bases (ideally with a base measurement of about 5 cm).

2 Melt the butter in a small saucepan over low heat and gently cook for 1-2 minutes or until the butter has turned golden (take care not to burn it).

3 Sift the flour, salt and icing sugar into a large bowl and stir in the ground almonds and lime zest. Lightly beat the egg whites with a fork until foamy, then pour into the dry ingredients. Add the warm butter and mix with a wooden spoon until smooth. The mixture will be quite wet; this is fine.

4 Pour or spoon the mixture into the tins to about three-quarters full. Top with the blackberries and sprinkle with the flaked almonds. Bake for 20 minutes or until golden and risen. Allow to cool in the tins for 5 minutes, then remove from the tins and transfer to a wire rack to cool completely.

5 Dust with extra icing sugar and serve with cream, custard or ice-cream. Store in an airtight container for up to 3 days.

BOMBE ALASKA MINCE PIES

PREPARATION TIME: 25 MINUTES

COOKING TIME: 5 MINUTES

SERVES 12

12 homemade or bought mince pies

3–4 tablespoons vanilla ice-cream

3 free-range egg whites

125 g caster sugar

icing sugar, for dusting (optional)

A spoonful of meringue is a simple way to transform ready-made mince pies into something special. I pipe the meringue into cone-shaped witches' hats but you can just spoon it on, if preferred.

1 Preheat the oven to 200ºC (Gas Mark 6).

2 Remove and discard the pastry tops from the mince pies and replace with a small scoop (about 1 heaped teaspoon) of ice-cream. Transfer to a baking tray and place in the freezer while you make the meringue.

3 Place the egg whites in a large clean, dry bowl and whisk with hand-held electric beaters until soft peaks form. Gradually add the caster sugar, a little at a time, whisking well after each addition. Continue to whisk until the mixture is glossy and stiff peaks form.

4 Remove the tray of pies from the freezer and pipe the meringue over the ice-cream, covering the top and forming nice peaks about 6–7 cm high. Bake for 5 minutes or until the meringue is cooked. Dust with icing sugar (if using) and serve immediately.

PEAR AND ALMOND TART

1 sheet ready-rolled puff pastry, thawed

1 tablespoon caster sugar

2 tablespoons ground almonds

finely grated zest of ½ orange

30 g unsalted butter, diced

2 ripe pears, peeled and cored

2 tablespoons runny honey

30 g flaked almonds

icing sugar, for dusting

vanilla ice-cream, to serve

I've been making this old favourite in various forms for many years. I still have the original recipe that inspired me on a now-yellowing cutout from a newspaper.

1 Preheat the oven to 200°C (Gas Mark 6) and line a large baking tray with baking paper. Place the pastry on the baking tray. Using a sharp knife, mark a 2 cm border around the edge of the pastry, scoring (but not cutting all the way through) the pastry. Prick the area inside the border a few times with a fork.

2 Combine the sugar, ground almonds and orange zest and sprinkle over the pastry (keeping within the border). Dot with the diced butter.

3 Slice the pears and arrange decoratively on the pastry sheet (again, keeping within the border). Drizzle with the honey and sprinkle with the flaked almonds. Bake for 20–25 minutes or until the pastry border is golden and risen. Dust with a little icing sugar, cut into four portions and serve warm with ice-cream.

CRISP APPLE TART

PREPARATION TIME: 30 MINUTES

COOKING TIME: 25 MINUTES

SERVES 4

1 sheet ready-rolled puff pastry, thawed if frozen

40 g unsalted butter

40 g caster sugar

1 free-range egg

50 g ground almonds

3–4 small apples

1 tablespoon raw or demerara sugar

2 tablespoons apricot jam

1 tablespoon lemon juice

In any season there is usually at least a couple of varieties of apple available. This constant availability means that apples are often overlooked, which is such a shame. For me, nothing is better than soft, cooked apples, crisp pastry and a little caramel or sugar.

1 Preheat the oven to 200°C (Gas Mark 6) and line a large baking tray with baking paper. Place the pastry on the tray and chill in the fridge while you make the filling.

2 Beat the butter and caster sugar with hand-held electric beaters until soft and fluffy, then beat in the egg and ground almonds to make a smooth cream. Peel, core and halve the apples. Cut each half into thin slices.

3 Remove the pastry from the fridge. Fold over the edges by 1 cm to make a border, then prick the area inside the border a few times with a fork. Spread the almond mixture over the pastry (keeping it within the border). Lay the apple slices in neat rows over the almond mixture, overlapping them a little like fish scales. Sprinkle with the raw or demerara sugar.

4 Bake for about 25 minutes or until the pastry is crisp and the apple is tender and lightly golden.

5 Meanwhile, warm the apricot jam and lemon juice in a small saucepan over low heat. Brush over the cooked tart and serve warm or cold.

TARTE TATIN

PREPARATION TIME: 30 MINUTES,
PLUS REFRIGERATION TIME

COOKING TIME: 50 MINUTES

SERVES 6-8

200 g plain flour

100 g unsalted butter,
chilled and diced

pinch of salt

50 g caster sugar

1 free-range egg yolk

1-2 tablespoons cold water

ice-cream, to serve

APPLE TOPPING

450 g apples (try granny smith,
golden delicious, gala or fuji)

juice of 1 lemon

60 g unsalted butter

120 g caster sugar

The right variety of apple to use for this popular dessert is the one you like best. There are some differences in how the various apples perform during cooking, but the final choice should be based on taste preferences rather than any concept of ideal performance.

1 Sift the flour into a large bowl. Using your fingertips, rub the butter into the flour until it resembles coarse breadcrumbs. Stir in the salt and sugar, then make a well in the centre and add the egg yolk and cold water. Mix with a large metal spoon or flat-bladed knife until it comes together in clumps (add a little extra water if necessary). Gather the dough and gently press into a ball shape (don't knead). Flatten slightly into a disc, then wrap in plastic film and refrigerate for 30 minutes before using.

2 Preheat the oven to 180°C (Gas Mark 4).

3 To prepare the apple topping, peel, core and quarter the apples, then cut the pieces in half again. Toss in the lemon juice.

4 Melt the butter in a large (about 25 cm) heavy-based frying pan with an ovenproof handle. Sprinkle over the sugar and let it bubble for a few minutes, then add the apple. Cook over medium heat, turning the apple regularly, for about 10-15 minutes or until the apple has softened and the buttery syrup is golden brown.

5 Roll out the pastry on a lightly floured surface to a round just larger then the frying pan. Carefully place the pastry over the apple, tucking the edges down the side of the pan to encase the apple mixture. Make three or four slashes in the pastry with a sharp knife.

6 Bake for 25-30 minutes or until the pastry is golden. Let the tart rest for about 5 minutes, then place a plate over the top of the frying pan and invert the tart onto the plate. If any bits of apple stick to the pan, remove them and tuck them back into place. Serve warm with ice-cream.

PASSIONFRUIT-CURD TARTS

PREPARATION TIME: 30 MINUTES,
PLUS REFRIGERATION TIME

COOKING TIME: 45 MINUTES

MAKES 12

250 g plain flour

120 g unsalted butter,
chilled and diced

pinch of salt

2 tablespoons icing sugar, sifted

1 free-range egg yolk

3–4 tablespoons cold water

icing sugar, for dusting

PASSIONFRUIT CURD

12 ripe passionfruit

3 free-range eggs

1 free-range egg yolk

175 g caster sugar

120 g unsalted butter, finely diced

Crumbly pastry and tangy passionfruit is a match made in heaven.

1 Sift the flour into a large bowl. Using your fingertips, rub the butter into the flour until it resembles coarse breadcrumbs. Stir in the salt and icing sugar, then make a well in the centre and stir in the egg yolk and cold water. Mix with a large metal spoon or flat-bladed knife until it comes together in clumps (add a little extra water if necessary). Gather the dough and gently press into a ball shape (don't knead). Flatten slightly into a disc, then wrap in plastic film and refrigerate for 30 minutes before using.

2 To make the passionfruit curd, remove the pulp from the passionfruit, about three fruit at a time, and transfer to a fine-mesh sieve. Using the back of a metal spoon, push as much juice as you can through the sieve into a bowl. Reserve the seeds. Repeat with the remaining fruit. You should have about 150 ml juice.

3 Whisk the eggs and egg yolk with the passionfruit juice in a heatproof bowl. Place the bowl over a saucepan of simmering water (make sure the bowl doesn't touch the water) and whisk until warm. Add the sugar and butter and whisk over the simmering water until all the ingredients are combined.

4 Transfer the mixture to a small saucepan and stir frequently with a wooden spoon over low heat for about 10–15 minutes or until the mixture thickens slightly and coats the back of the spoon. Remove the pan from the heat if the mixture starts to catch on the bottom of the pan, and continue to stir until smooth. Add about 2 tablespoons of the reserved seeds to the mixture. Place a round of baking paper directly on the surface and set aside to cool and thicken.

5 Preheat the oven to 200°C (Gas Mark 6) and grease a 12-hole tart tin. Roll out the pastry on a lightly floured surface to a thickness of 3–4 mm. Using a large cup or pastry cutter, cut rounds from the pastry that are slightly bigger than the holes in the prepared tart tin, then press one round into each of the holes. Prick the pastry with a fork and bake oven for 15–20 minutes or until golden. Allow to cool in the tin for 5 minutes, then transfer the tart cases to a wire rack to cool completely.

6 Fill the cooled tart cases with the passionfruit curd. Dust with icing sugar just before serving.

NO-CRUST CHEESECAKE

COOKING TIME: 45 MINUTES

SERVES 8

600 g cream cheese, softened
at room temperature

100 g unsalted butter, diced and
softened at room temperature

125 g caster sugar

1 teaspoon vanilla extract

1 teaspoon finely grated lemon zest

1 tablespoon lemon juice

3 free-range eggs, lightly beaten

300 ml sour cream

**The idea of a crustless cheesecake is a recent
discovery for me. The point of difference is that,
unlike other baked cheesecakes, it's cooked in a bain
marie (or water bath) – mainly because the delicate
cream-cheese mixture doesn't have the protection of
the crumbed base. Make sure the tin is well wrapped in
foil to keep it watertight. This cheesecake is gorgeous
served alone or enjoy it with fresh fruit.**

1 Preheat the oven to 170°C (Gas Mark 3). Grease a 20 cm
springform tin and line the base with baking paper. Wrap
the outside of the tin with a large sheet of foil, making
sure that the tin is waterproof.

2 Place the cream cheese, butter, sugar, vanilla, lemon
zest and lemon juice in a large bowl and beat until just
combined. Gradually beat in the egg and then fold in
the sour cream.

3 Spoon the mixture into the tin, then place the tin
in a deep baking dish. Place the baking dish in the oven
and pour enough boiling water into the dish to come about
halfway up the side of the tin. Bake for about 45 minutes
or until the centre is set (the edges should have just pulled
away from the side of the tin). Turn off the oven, leave the
door ajar and allow the cheesecake to cool in the oven.
When completely cool, chill in the fridge for at least
4 hours before serving.

BLUEBERRY SWIRL CHEESECAKE

PREPARATION TIME: 25 MINUTES,
PLUS REFRIGERATION TIME

COOKING TIME: 50 MINUTES

SERVES 8-10

200 g plain sweet biscuits

80 g unsalted butter, melted

200 g blueberries, fresh or frozen

2 heaped tablespoons icing sugar,
sifted, plus extra for dusting (optional)

juice of ½ lemon

500 g cream cheese, softened
at room temperature

185 g caster sugar

4 free-range eggs

100 ml sour cream

1 teaspoon vanilla extract

1 teaspoon finely grated lemon zest

2 teaspoons lemon juice, extra

This cheesecake is topped with decorative swirls of blueberry puree. However, if you want to cut out a step or two, leave out the blueberry swirl – it's still a great cheesecake without it. You can also use raspberries or blackberries in place of the blueberries, if preferred. If you don't have a food processor, you can crush the biscuits by placing them in a plastic bag and bashing them with a rolling pin. Transfer the crumbs to a bowl and mix through the melted butter.

1 Grease a 23 cm springform tin and line the base with baking paper.

2 Place the biscuits in a food processor and pulse until crushed. Add the butter and process until the mixture comes together. Using your fingertips, press the crumb mixture into the base of the tin. Refrigerate for 30 minutes.

3 Preheat the oven to 170ºC (Gas Mark 3).

4 Purée the blueberries, icing sugar and lemon juice in a food processor or blender and then pass through a fine-mesh sieve. Transfer to a small saucepan and simmer over low heat, stirring occasionally, for about 5 minutes. Set aside to cool.

5 Beat the cream cheese and caster sugar with hand-held electric beaters until creamy and well combined. Add the eggs, sour cream, vanilla, lemon zest and extra lemon juice and beat for 2–3 minutes or until light and fluffy.

6 Spoon the mixture onto the cheesecake base and smooth the top. Drizzle with the blueberry purée and make swirl patterns with the blade of a flat-bladed knife. Bake for 40–45 minutes or until the top is a pale golden colour and the filling is just set in the middle. Leave to cool completely in the tin, then refrigerate for 6-12 hours before serving. Dust with icing sugar, if desired.

CLASSIC NEW YORK CHEESECAKE

250 g plain sweet biscuits

¼ teaspoon ground ginger

pinch of salt

100 g unsalted butter, melted

750 g cream cheese, softened
at room temperature

250 g caster sugar

2 tablespoons plain flour

4 free-range egg yolks

125 ml sour cream

2 teaspoons vanilla extract

1 teaspoon finely grated lemon zest

2 teaspoons lemon juice

icing sugar, for dusting

Cheesecakes come in many forms but I love this classic baked version, flavoured simply with lemon and vanilla. In search of the perfect recipe, I have been reading through my old notebooks and rediscovering a few old favourites, like this one. The cheesecake needs to be chilled well before serving so if you can, make it the day before you want to serve it. This also works with Italian amaretti (almond-flavoured biscuits) for the base, but you can use any simple sweet biscuit you like.

1 Grease a 23 cm springform tin and line the base with baking paper.

2 Place the biscuits, ginger and salt in a food processor and pulse until crushed. Add the butter and process until the mixture comes together. Using your fingertips, press the crumb mixture into the base of the tin and two-thirds of the way up the side. Refrigerate for 30 minutes.

3 Preheat the oven to 160°C (Gas Mark 2-3).

4 Place the cream cheese, sugar and flour in an electric mixer and beat until creamy and well combined. Add the egg yolks one at a time, beating after each addition, and then beat in the sour cream, vanilla, lemon zest and juice. Beat for 2-3 minutes or until the mixture is light and fluffy.

5 Spoon the mixture onto the cheesecake base and smooth the top. Bake for 35-40 minutes or until pale golden and just set in the middle. Cool completely in the tin, then refrigerate for 6-12 hours before serving. To serve, dust with icing sugar, then cut the cheesecake into slices.

MASCARPONE CHEESECAKE

PREPARATION TIME: 20 MINUTES,
PLUS REFRIGERATION TIME

COOKING TIME: 35 MINUTES

SERVES 8

175 g plain sweet biscuits

75 g unsalted butter, melted

400 g mascarpone, at room temperature

finely grated zest of 3 lemons

juice of 1 lemon

125 g caster sugar

2 free-range eggs, separated

2 tablespoons cornflour

In this simple cheesecake, mascarpone makes a good substitute for cream cheese, and the lemon zest and juice cut through the richness, giving a good balanced flavour.

1 Grease a 20 cm springform tin and line the base with baking paper.

2 Place the biscuits in a food processor and pulse until crushed. Add the butter and process until the mixture comes together. Using your fingertips, press the crumb mixture into the base of the tin. Refrigerate for 30 minutes.

3 Preheat the oven to 180°C (Gas Mark 4).

4 Place the mascarpone, lemon zest, lemon juice, sugar, egg yolks and cornflour in a large bowl and beat with hand-held electric beaters until creamy and well combined. In a clean bowl with clean beaters, whisk the egg whites until they form soft peaks. Carefully fold the egg whites into the mascarpone mixture with a large metal spoon.

5 Spoon the mixture onto the cheesecake base and smooth the top. Bake for about 35 minutes or until firm to the touch. Cool completely in the tin, then refrigerate for 3-4 hours before serving.

BASICS

ICINGS AND FILLINGS

BASIC BUTTERCREAM ICING

150 g unsalted butter, diced and softened at room temperature

1 teaspoon vanilla extract

300 g icing sugar, sifted

1–2 tablespoons milk

This classic icing is easy to make and perfect for decorating most cakes. You can vary it by adding flavouring and colour. When you need to add colouring, I recommend using colour paste, which is more intense; if you use liquid colouring, you may need to add more icing sugar. This mixture will make enough to cover a medium cake or 12 small cakes. It can easily be doubled to give you enough for filling for the cake, if needed.

Using an electric mixer or hand-held electric beaters, beat together the butter and vanilla. Add the icing sugar in three batches, beating well between additions. Beat in the milk, and continue beating until smooth. Add extra liquid if the icing is too stiff. Stir in food colouring paste (if using) until well combined.

For lemon buttercream: *replace the vanilla and milk with freshly squeezed lemon juice.*

For coffee buttercream: *replace the vanilla and milk with 2 tablespoons instant coffee powder that has been dissolved in 1 tablespoon boiling water.*

For chocolate buttercream: *replace the vanilla with 60 g melted dark chocolate (see page 91), adding enough milk to give a spreadable consistency.*

LEMON CREAM-CHEESE ICING

125 g cream cheese, softened at room temperature

60 g unsalted butter, diced and softened at room temperature

350 g icing sugar, sifted

2 tablespoons lemon juice

A light lemony flavour cuts through the richness of this classic cream-cheese icing. This is perfect for carrot, banana and other dense cakes and muffins. Decorate with lemon zest, if desired. This mixture will make enough to cover a medium cake or 12 small cakes.

Place the cream cheese and butter in a bowl and beat with hand-held electric beaters or a wooden spoon until combined. Beat in about one third of the icing sugar and then the lemon juice. Gradually beat in the remaining icing sugar until the mixture reaches a spreadable consistency.

ROYAL ICING

2 large free-range egg whites

2 teaspoons lemon juice

about 350 g icing sugar, sifted

This simple royal icing recipe produces a hard white icing that can be used to decorate biscuits, cookies, cakes, and gingerbread folk or houses. Although it is traditionally used without the addition of food colouring, you can add whatever colour you like. This makes enough to decorate 20 gingerbread folk or a medium-sized gingerbread house. It may also be used to ice a medium cake or 12 small cakes.

Using an electric mixer or hand-held electric beaters, beat together the egg whites and lemon juice until fluffy. Gradually add the icing sugar and beat on low speed until combined and smooth. The icing hardens when exposed to air so if you are not using it immediately, transfer it to an airtight container. Cover with plastic film when not in use.

MARZIPAN AND WHITE ICING

3 tablespoons apricot jam

1 tablespoon cold water

500 g ready-made marzipan

icing sugar, for dusting

500 g white icing (often called sugar paste)

The classic way to ice a fruit cake for Christmas, weddings or celebrations is to cover it with marzipan and then white icing. The quantities given are enough to cover a 23 cm round cake. Don't worry if your cake is slightly domed (this is quite normal), but if it is very peaked, just trim off a small amount from the top.

To cover in marzipan, warm the apricot jam and cold water, then pass through a fine-mesh sieve so the mixture is smooth. Place the cake on a board slightly larger than the cake and brush with the warm jam. Roll out the marzipan on a surface dusted with icing sugar to a size that is large enough to cover the cake. Lift the marzipan over the cake and ease to fit smoothly over the top and around the sides. Trim off any excess. Wrap in plastic film and leave overnight.

Remove the plastic film and lightly brush the marzipan with water. On a surface dusted with icing sugar, roll out the white icing to a size that's large enough to cover the marzipan-covered cake. Lift the icing over the cake and smooth it down the side. Trim off the excess icing around the base. Dust your palms with icing sugar and gently 'polish' the surface of the icing with the heal of your hand, to smooth out any creases and uneven areas. If desired, roll out the remaining white icing to a thickness of about 5 mm and cut into pretty shapes. Use to decorate the cake.

FLUFFY WHITE ICING

200 g caster sugar

75 ml water

¼ teaspoon cream of tartar

2 free-range egg whites

1 teaspoon vanilla extract

This icing sets a little like meringue. I use it mainly for covering chocolate cakes and fruit cakes. Once spread on the cake it, it can be smoothed with a flat-bladed knife, or shaped into peaks (a bit like a meringue). This quantity will cover a medium cake or 12 small cakes.

Place the sugar, water and cream of tartar in a small saucepan and bring to the boil, stirring to dissolve the sugar. Using an electric mixer, beat the egg whites and vanilla until they reach soft peaks. With the motor running, gradually pour in the hot sugar syrup, beating constantly for 6-7 minutes or until stiff peaks form. Use straight away.

LEMON OR ORANGE GLAZE

250 g icing sugar

2 tablespoons lemon or orange juice

Perfect for butter cakes, this simple citrus icing is more of a soft runny glaze. Make sure the juice is freshly squeezed. There is enough here to cover a medium cake or 12 small cakes.

Sift the icing sugar into a bowl. Add the juice and beat with a wooden spoon until smooth, adding extra juice if needed to achieve a spreadable consistency.

DARK CHOCOLATE GLAZE

150 g dark chocolate, broken into pieces

150 ml double cream

This gives a nice, shiny glaze that's perfect for pouring over a medium cake or 12 small cakes.

Place the chocolate and cream in a heatproof bowl set over a saucepan of barely simmering water (make sure the bowl doesn't touch the water). Stir until the chocolate is melted and the mixture is smooth and combined. Allow to cool slightly to thicken, then pour over the cake or cakes. The glaze will harden on cooling.

DARK CHOCOLATE GANACHE

250 g dark chocolate,
broken into pieces

200 ml double cream

Dark chocolate ganache has loads of uses: pour it over a medium cake or 12 small cakes, or chill it slightly and beat until fluffy to use as a filling or icing. You can also add 1 tablespoon brandy or flavoured liqueur, if desired.

Place the chocolate in a heatproof bowl. Heat the cream in a small saucepan over medium heat, bringing it just to the boil. Pour it over the chocolate and stir occasionally until the chocolate is melted and the mixture is smooth. Allow the ganache to cool slightly before pouring over the cake or cakes. Start at the centre of the cake and work outward. For a fluffy frosting or chocolate filling, allow the ganache to cool until thick, then beat with a wooden spoon or whisk until light and fluffy. Spread over the cake or cakes.

WHITE CHOCOLATE GANACHE

250 g white chocolate,
broken into pieces

100 ml double cream

This can be used as a topping or as a filling. There's enough for one medium cake or 12 small cakes.

Place the chocolate and cream in a heatproof bowl set over a saucepan of barely simmering water (make sure the bowl doesn't touch the water). Stir until the chocolate is melted and the mixture is smooth and combined. Allow to cool slightly to thicken, then beat with a wooden spoon or whisk until light and fluffy. The mixture will thicken to a spreading consistency as it cools.

CHOCOLATE FUDGE ICING

75 g unsalted butter

2 tablespoons milk

2 tablespooons cocoa

300 g icing sugar, sifted

This is lighter than a regular buttercream and is just the thing for icing a simple chocolate or coffee cake or chocolate cupcakes. It sets, but not too firmly. This makes enough to cover a medium cake or 12 cupcakes.

Place the butter, milk and cocoa in a small saucepan and heat gently over low heat until the butter has melted, mixing well to combine. Take it off the heat and allow to cool for 10 minutes. Add the icing sugar in three batches, beating with a wooden spoon between additions until smooth.

SIMPLE ICING FOR DRIZZLING

150 g icing sugar

1-2 tablespoons warm water
or lemon juice

food colouring (optional)

**This simple icing is great for drizzling over butter
biscuits or plain cakes or slices. It makes enough to
drizzle over 25-30 biscuits.**

Sift the icing sugar into a bowl, add the water or lemon
juice and food colouring (if using) and beat with a wooden
spoon until combined. Add extra water if needed to achieve
a drizzling consistency.

MASCARPONE AND LEMON FILLING

250 g mascarpone,
at room temperature

120 g lemon curd

**This creamy, lemony filling is ideal for a classic
Victoria sponge cake (see page 18) or lemon sponge.
This quantity makes enough to fill a medium cake.**

Lightly beat the mascarpone and then fold through the
lemon curd until combined.

MASCARPONE AND COFFEE FILLING

1 tablespoon instant coffee powder

1 tablespoon boiling water

250 g mascarpone,
at room temperature

2 tablespoons icing sugar, sifted

1 heaped tablespoon golden syrup

**Use this to fill coffee or chocolate cakes, or sponges
made with nuts. There is enough here to fill a medium
sponge cake.**

Dissolve the coffee powder in the boiling water. Place
in a bowl with the remaining ingredients and beat until
smooth and combined.

PASSIONFRUIT AND MASCARPONE FILLING

250 g mascarpone,
at room temperature

2 tablespoons icing sugar, sifted

pulp of 2-3 passionfruit, drained
through a fine-mesh sieve,
plus extra if needed

**This rich passionfruit-flavoured cream is perfect for
filling sponge cakes. This quantity will fill a medium
sponge cake.**

Beat together all the ingredients in a bowl until smooth
and combined. Add a little extra passionfruit, if desired.

TIPS ON FLOUR

Flour is basically ground wheat and is an essential ingredient in baking. Wheat flour contains gluten which gives texture and shape to baked goods.

Store flour in an airtight container in a cool, dry place. During summer I store opened packets in a sealed plastic container in the fridge to avoid the fatty acids in the grain starting to oxidise and become rancid. Once open, a packet of flour should be used within a year.

WHEAT FLOURS

Plain flour is made from soft wheat varieties and gives the baked product a tender texture. Plain flour has a lower protein and lower gluten content, and is used for making cakes, biscuits, pastry, scones and muffins because these should be less chewy than pizza bases and breads. It is available as white or unbleached.

Self-raising flour is low-gluten white or wholemeal flour with an added raising agent (usually baking powder). To make your own, add 2½ teaspoons and a pinch of salt to every 500 g plain flour.

Wholemeal flour contains all of the wheat grain. It is used as a matter of personal preference in various baked products, including cakes, biscuits, slices, scones and muffins.

Strong white or bread flour is made from wheat with a higher gluten and protein content and is used mainly for bread making where you want a good chewiness. It is processed to remove all the bran and wheatgerm, and has a high capacity to retain water.

NON-WHEAT FLOURS

Gluten-free flour: most gluten-free flours are a non-wheat blend of milled rice, potato, tapioca, maize or buckwheat flours. Variations occur between brands and most of these can be substituted for plain or self-raising flour in cake recipes.

Cornflour is ground from corn (also known as maize) into a fine white flour. When used in baking it gives a soft texture to a finished cake. It is one of the secret ingredients for a chewy-centred pavlova and is mostly used for thickening recipes and sauces. It is often added to gluten-free mixes. However, if this is an issue for you, check the label as some types of cornflour are milled from wheat and are labelled wheaten cornflour.

Rice flour is made from ground uncooked rice and is available as either fine or coarsely ground. It is often used in shortbread recipes to add a slightly coarse texture. It is gluten free.

Semolina flour is ground from hard durum wheat. This coarsely textured, pale-yellow flour is used in baking, puddings, bread and biscuits.

Polenta (or cornmeal) is ground corn (also called maize), available in fine or coarsely ground varieties. It is usually the finer version that is used in baking. Polenta is gluten free.

Tapioca flour is made from the ground root of the cassava plant. It is a light, soft, fine white flour that adds chewiness to baked goods. It is gluten free.

TIPS ON SUGAR

It is essential to add some type of sweetener to most baked goods, to add flavour, tenderness and a bit of 'browning'. This usually comes in the form of sugar, but may also come from honey, golden syrup, maple syrup, treacle or molasses.

Working top to bottom from the image at left, the main varieties are outlined below.

Muscovado sugar is a very dark brown sugar that is used mostly in fruit cakes or where you want biscuits to be soft and chewy. It has a good caramel flavour and a high proportion of molasses. As with all brown sugars, once opened it should be stored in an airtight jar or container. If the sugar dries out, add an apple quarter or slice of bread to the jar for a few days to help it to soften.

Demerara or raw sugar is firm sugar with large crystals. It is more refined than muscovado sugar. It is usually used for sprinkling on the top of cakes, pies, biscuits or muffins before baking as it adds a nice crunchiness when cooked.

Brown sugar is a moist, lightly caramel-flavoured sugar that contains less molasses than muscovado or darker sugars. It is available in dark or light varieties. It is mainly used for cakes, biscuits and some muffins. Store as for muscovado sugar.

Caster sugar is the best choice for cake making - its small grains are easy to combine with other ingredients, ensuring that your cake has a good texture. It is also used in meringues as it dissolves and mixes easily with beaten egg whites. To make vanilla sugar, add 1-2 split vanilla beans to a jar of caster sugar and leave for a couple of weeks for the flavour to develop.

Granulated sugar (or simple white sugar) is the most common variety. In Australia it is made from sugarcane (often in Europe and the United States it is made from sugar beet, a root vegetable).

Icing sugar is a very fine powdery sugar used mostly for icings and dusting cakes and biscuits. It is often used in sweet pastries as it helps create a hard crust. It is available in two forms: 'pure icing sugar' and 'icing sugar mixture'. Icing sugar mixture has a little cornflour added which helps to make a soft icing and also prevents lumps. All references to icing sugar in my recipes are for pure icing sugar. Always sift icing sugar before using so it incorporates more easily.

Golden or unrefined caster sugar is an unrefined small-grained sugar that has a lovely golden colour and a light caramel flavour. It can be used in place of caster sugar - just remember that it will add a slight a golden colour so don't use it if you are making white meringues.

TIPS ON CHOCOLATE

Considered by many to be the food of the gods, chocolate comes in a variety of types and products. When cooking with chocolate I tend to use a good-quality brand as it makes a big difference to the finished result. For most baking recipes, such as brownies and cakes, I use a dark chocolate with about 50% cocoa solids; for truffles, ganache or desserts I look for a higher percentage. For tips on how to melt chocolate, see page 91.

Here's a quick rundown on the types of cooking chocolate available (clockwise from top of image).

Drinking chocolate: usually a mixture of cocoa powder and sugar, this is combined with hot milk to make hot chocolate. Good-quality drinking chocolate can also contain grated dark chocolate.

White chocolate: technically this is not really chocolate as it doesn't contain any cocoa solids – just cocoa butter, milk and sugar.

Cocoa powder: this is what is left when all the cocoa butter has been extracted from the roasted and ground cocoa beans. It is unsweetened and quite bitter, but adds a good chocolate flavour when used in baking.

Chocolate chips: these are usually available in dark, milk or white chocolate. They are perfect for cookies, cupcakes and muffins as they tend to be lower in fat than eating chocolate, which means they don't melt as quickly and so magically stay whole during baking.

Milk chocolate contains similar ingredients to dark chocolate but with added milk (and usually sugar). It has mild creamy sweet flavour.

Chocolate shavings: these are commercially produced curls or shavings of chocolate used for decoration. They come in milk chocolate and marbled varieties.

Plain or dark chocolate is generally used for cooking. It may contain anything from 30% to 75% cocoa solids (check the label). The higher the percentage of cocoa solids, the richer the depth of flavour and the less sugar it contains.

Chocolate sprinkles are essentially chocolate-flavoured 'hundreds-and-thousands' that are used for decorating cupcakes, biscuits, cookies and cakes.

Couverture chocolate (not pictured) is used mainly for chocolate confectionery and dessert-making in professional kitchens; it has a high percentage of cocoa butter that gives it a glossy appearance. It is quite expensive and mostly used by professionals.

TIPS ON EQUIPMENT

CHOOSING THE BEST CAKE TINS

● The best tins for baking are sturdy, heavy-gauge tins, preferably with a removable base, making it easier to remove the cake. Springform tins are less heavy duty and are useful for making and removing fragile cakes. Cheap tins can warp in the oven and also cause the outside of the cake to cook more quickly as they do not conduct heat as well as a sturdier tin.

● Good-quality cake tins are not cheap but it really is worth choosing the best you can afford. I prefer silver tins to the dark ones as I find the dark-coloured tins tend to cook more quickly because the darkness absorbs rather than reflects the heat.

● Non-stick tins are easier to clean, but it is always important to grease and line the tin as recommended in the recipe, rather than relying on their non-stick qualities.

● I have tested some of the silicon cake moulds with success; these should be placed on a metal baking tray when cooking to make them easier to remove from the oven. Generally, they should be greased and floured before use to prevent sticking.

● It is important to use the specified size of tin - both the correct diameter and depth are crucial. If the tin is overfilled then it will probably spill over as it cooks, and if the tin is too large then you will probably end up with a flat and overcooked cake.

● The measurements in the recipes for loaf tins are for the base of the tin.

● I always have a large heavy-duty baking tray on hand as I make it a rule to place all cake tins on the tray before transferring them to the oven. This makes it much easier to remove them after baking and also protects the floor of the oven if any of the mixture spills over during cooking.

OTHER EQUIPMENT

Don't be put off by all the equipment that's available. Sure, a hand-held beater and some electrical equipment will make light work of beating, but many of the recipes can be made with just a mixing bowl and a wooden spoon. Space is limited for me so every piece of equipment has to earn its keep. The items in the list below genuinely make my life in the kitchen easier.

Baking beads: even though dried beans or rice will do a reasonable job, a proper set of ceramic baking beads is really useful for blind-baking pastry.

Cutters: I have far too many biscuit and cookie cutters and love all the various shapes and sizes. Aside from enjoying the way they look, they are essential when making butter biscuits to give a uniform shape and size.

Electric mixers: I have both an electric bench-top mixer and hand-held electric beaters and use them often.

Food processor: this is one piece of equipment that I will always make space for. I use it for making breadcrumbs, puréeing, combining ingredients, chopping nuts, fruit and vegetables and, sometimes, for making pastry.

Glass measuring jugs: both large (1 litre) and small (250 ml) jugs will easily earn their keep. The Pyrex ones are great as they are also heatproof.

Graters: I have worn out a few graters in my time as I am constantly grating parmesan, cheddar, citrus zest and chocolate. I have both a small fine grater and larger one with holes of various sizes to suit all jobs.

Knives: a large flat-bladed knife is useful for combining scone dough and pastry, and a good set of sharp kitchen knives is necessary for chopping and slicing.

Mixing bowls: I love my grandmother's old white ceramic mixing bowl with its very useful pouring spout. Similar bowls with both a spout and a good thick rim for heavy-duty beating are available in cookware shops. Any good ceramic mixing bowls in a variety of sizes will suffice.

Oven thermometer: a small thermometer that sits on the shelf of the oven is useful as the temperature of ovens can vary dramatically.

Pastry brush: an essential piece of equipment. I have some that I use for brushing oil or butter, and some for brushing egg washes or sweet things like jam.

Piping bag and nozzles: these are invaluable for decorating cakes and biscuits, and for piping meringues, macaroons and whipped cream. I have a roll of disposable piping bags, which are useful, and also a few medium and large nozzles.

Rolling pin: the larger and heavier the better.

Saucepans: make sure you have a nice small heavy-based saucepan for melting butter.

Scales: for accuracy I prefer to weigh ingredients like flour rather than use cup measurements, and for this I use reliable battery-operated digital scales.

Sieves: you will need a large fine-mesh sieve for flour and a small fine-mesh sieve for dusting icing sugar and cocoa.

Skewers: I use bamboo skewers to test whether a cake is ready.

Spatula: made from flexible rubber, this is useful for running around the inside edge of a tin to help remove the cake, as well as a basic piece of equipment for icing cakes and folding.

Spoons: measuring spoons for both teaspoons and tablespoons are vital. I also have lots of large metal spoons, which are perfect for folding in ingredients, and wooden spoons of various sizes for mixing and beating.

Whisks: balloon whisks in various sizes are useful for whisking egg whites and cream.

Wire racks: a couple of sturdy wire racks (one round and one rectangular) are essential pieces of baking equipment.

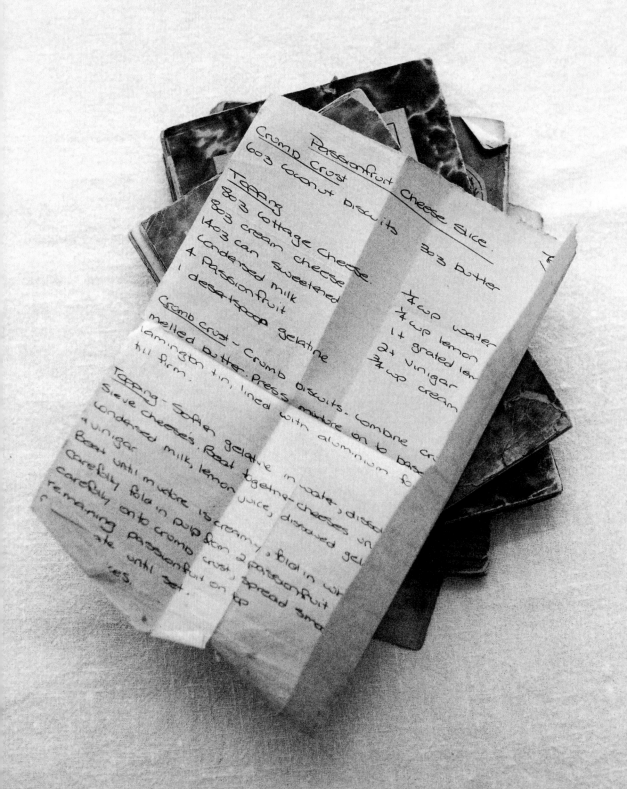

Passionfruit Cheese Slice.

Crumb Crust
6oz coconut biscuits   3oz butter

Topping
8oz cottage cheese
8oz cream cheese
14oz can sweetened
condensed milk
4 passionfruit
1 dessertspoon gelatine

¼ cup water
¼ cup lemon
1 t grated lem
2 t viniger
¾ cup cream

Crumb Crust - Crumb biscuits. Combine cr____
melted butter. Press mixture on to base___
lamington tin, lined with aluminium fo___
til firm.

Topping - Soften gelatine in water, disse___
sieve cheese's. Beat together cheeses un___
condensed milk, lemon juice, dissolved gel___
+ viniger
Beat until mixture is creamy, fold in wh___
carefully fold in pulp from 2 passionfruit___
carefully on to crumb crust, spread sma___
remaining passionfruit on top
____te until set.
___es.

ACKNOWLEDGEMENTS

This book has taken nearly three years of writing, testing and baking. Thank you to the many great cooks and friends who, through this process, have shared their experience and knowledge with me.

Thanks especially to Mitzie Wilson, Jane Curran, Nigel Slater, Katie Stewart, Jill Dupleix and Anna del Conte for sharing their recipes.

To Julie Gibbs, for her support and for having the confidence to do another book with me.

Thanks also to my long-suffering editor Rachel Carter for her expertise, patience, advice and, above all, her good sense of humour.

Also to Evi Oetomo and the design team at Penguin Books (Australia).

To Nato Welton, for his photographic skill and creativity.

And not forgetting my own family, especially my mother, who was the one many years ago who taught me how to make a prize-winning sponge.

INDEX

LANTERN

Published by the Penguin Group
Penguin Group (Australia)
250 Camberwell Road, Camberwell, Victoria 3124, Australia
(a division of Pearson Australia Group Pty Ltd)
Penguin Group (USA) Inc.
375 Hudson Street, New York, New York 10014, USA
Penguin Group (Canada)
90 Eglinton Avenue East, Suite 700, Toronto, Canada ON M4P 2Y3
(a division of Pearson Penguin Canada Inc.)
Penguin Books Ltd
80 Strand, London WC2R ORL, England
Penguin Ireland
25 St Stephen's Green, Dublin 2, Ireland
(a division of Penguin Books Ltd)
Penguin Books India Pvt Ltd
11 Community Centre, Panchsheel Park, New Delhi – 110 017, India
Penguin Group (NZ)
67 Apollo Drive, Rosedale, North Shore 0632, New Zealand
(a division of Pearson New Zealand Ltd)
Penguin Books (South Africa) (Pty) Ltd
24 Sturdee Avenue, Rosebank, Johannesburg 2196, South Africa

Penguin Books Ltd, Registered Offices: 80 Strand, London, WC2R ORL, England

First published by Penguin Group (Australia), 2012

1 3 5 7 9 10 8 6 4 2

Text copyright © David Herbert 2012
Photographs copyright © Nato Welton 2012

The moral right of the author has been asserted

Design by Evi O. © Penguin Group (Australia)
Photography by Nato Welton
Typeset in Interstate by Post Pre-press Group, Brisbane, Queensland
Colour reproduction by Splitting Image, Clayton, Victoria
Printed and bound by South China Printing Co Ltd

National Library of Australia
Cataloguing-in-Publication data:

Herbert, David.

David Herbert's best-ever baking recipes / David Herbert ;
photography by Nato Welton.

9781921382130 (hbk.)

Includes index.
Baking.
Welton, Nato.

641.815